Listening in Language Learning

APPLIED LINGUISTICS AND LANGUAGE STUDY

General Editor
Professor Christopher N. Candlin, Macquarie University

Error Analysis
*Perspectives on second
language acquisition*
JACK C. RICHARDS (ED.)

Stylistics and the Teaching of
Literature
HENRY WIDDOWSON

Listening to Spoken English
Second Edition
GILLIAN BROWN

Language Tests at School
A pragmatic approach
JOHN W. OLLER JNR

Contrastive Analysis
CARL JAMES

Language and Communication
JACK C. RICHARDS AND
RICHARD W. SCHMIDT (EDS)

Learning to Write: First Language/
Second Language
AVIVA FREEDMAN, IAN PRINGLE
AND JANICE YALDEN (EDS)

Strategies in Interlanguage
Communication
CLAUS FAERCH AND
GABRIELE KASPER (EDS)

Reading in a Foreign Language
J. CHARLES ALDERSON AND
A.H. URQUHART (EDS)

Discourse and Learning
PHILIP RILEY (ED.)

An Introduction to Discourse
Analysis
New edition
MALCOLM COULTHARD

Computers in English Language
Teaching and Research
GEOFFREY LEECH AND
CHRISTOPHER N. CANDLIN (EDS)

Bilingualism in Education
*Aspects of theory, research
and practice*
JIM CUMMINS AND
MERRILL SWAIN

Second Language Grammar:
Learning and Teaching
WILLIAM E. RUTHERFORD

The Classroom and the Language
Learner
*Ethnography and second-language
classroom research*
LEO VAN LIER

Vocabulary and Language Teaching
RONALD CARTER AND
MICHAEL McCARTHY (EDS)

Observation in the Language
Classroom
Second Edition
DICK ALLWRIGHT

Listening in Language Learning
MICHAEL ROST

Listening in Language Learning

Michael Rost

Longman

London and New York

Longman Group UK Limited,
Longman House, Burnt Mill, Harlow,
Essex CM20 2JE, England
and Associated Companies throughout the world

Published in the United States of America
by Longman Inc., New York

First published 1990

British Library Cataloguing in Publication Data

Rost, Michael
  Listening in language learning.—(Applied linguistics
  and language study).
  1. Applied linguistics
  I. Title   II. Series
  418

ISBN 0-582-01650-9

Library of Congress Cataloging-in-Publication Data

Rost, Michael.
  Listening in language learning/Michael Rost.
    p.   cm.   (Applied linguistics and language study)
  Includes bibliographical references.
  ISBN 0-582-01650-9
  1. Language and languages -- Study and teaching. 2. Listening.
  I. Title.   II. Series.
  P53.R64   1990
  418'.007--dc20   89-38727 CIP

Produced by Longman Singapore Publishers (Pte) Ltd.
Printed in Singapore

Contents

to Masahiro Oki

Acknowledgements

This project could not have been completed without the assistance and support of many colleagues and friends.

I wish to thank first Christopher Candlin, for offering me the challenge to undertake this project and for providing the sustained guidance I needed to finish it. I also have benefited from commentary on earlier outlines and drafts from several colleagues: Steven Ross, Kevin Gregg, Charlene Sato, John Clark, Tony Lynch, Craig Chaudron, John Oller, Charles Alderson, Teresa Pica, Raoul Cervantes, Stephen Gaies, Lisa Rost, and Andy Blasky. I am very appreciative of suggestions for improvement of an earlier version of the manuscript given by several members of the TESOL program at Temple University, particularly Yoshie Hashido, Laura Mayer, Rick Heimbach, Marie Suzuki, Chika Inoue, Mike Brown, David Peaty, Tamara Swenson, and Jack Yohay. Special thanks to Keiko Kimura for helping with many details in the preparation of the manuscript. And finally, my appreciation to Longman for their support throughout the project.

I also wish to acknowledge the numerous authors whose work has provided an inspirational boost in the planning and development of this manuscript, particularly: Professors Dan Sperber and Deirdre Wilson (in reference to ideas about information theory and relevance theory presented in Chapter 1), Elisabeth Couper-Kuhlen, John Clark and David Brazil (in reference to ideas about auditory decoding in Chapter 2), Christopher Candlin and Clive Perdue (concerning analysis of interactive performance outlined in Chapter 4), Craig Chaudron (concerning questions of assessment presented in Chapter 7), and Gillian Brown, David Nunan, and Michael H. Long (concerning issues of listening tasks and syllabus design discussed in Chapter 8).

The Publishers are grateful to the following for permission to reproduce copyright material:

The University of Illinois Press for an adaptation of a diagram from Shannon, C. and Weaver, W. (1949) *The mathematical theory of communication*. Croom Helm Ltd for an adaptation of a diagram from McGregory, G. (1986) 'Listening outside the participation framework', in McGregor, G. and White, R.S. (eds.) *The art of listening*. Longman Group UK Ltd for an adaptation of a diagram from Dechert, H. (1983) 'How a story is done in a second language', in Faerch, K. and Kasper, G. (eds.) *Strategies in interlanguage communication*. Also for extracts from Rost, M. *Strategies in Listening* (published by Lingual House, 1976). English Language Research, University of Birmingham for an adaptation of a diagram from Brazil, D. (1985) *The communicative value of intonation in English*. An adaptation of a diagram reproduced by permission of the American Anthropological Association from *American Anthropologist* 73:5, 1971 (not for further reproduction). Ablex Publishing Corporation for an adaptation of a diagram from Kay, P. (1987) 'Three properties of the ideal reader', in Freedle, R. and Duran, R. (eds.) *Cognitive and linguistic analysis of test performance*. Also for an adaptation of a diagram from Gerot, L. (1987) 'Integrative work: an exploration in what makes reading comprehension test questions easy or difficult', in Hedley and Barrata (eds.) *Contexts of Reading*. Oxford University Press for an adaptation of a diagram from Anderson, A. and Lynch, T. (1988) *Listening*. Also for a diagram from Fried-Booth, D. (1987) *Project Work*. Cambridge University Press for an adaptation of a diagram from Brown, Gillian and Yule, G. (1983) *Teaching the spoken language*. A.G. Harper for extracts from The Harper Academic Listening Test Booklet (1984). Anderson, A., Brown, G., Lynch, A. and Shadbolt, N. for extracts from Listening Comprehension Project JHH/190/1 for the Scottish Education Department. American council on the teaching of foreign languages (ACTFL) for extracts from the ACTFL Proficiency Guidelines. Indiana University Press for an adaptation of a diagram from Chafe, W. (1977) 'The recall and verbalization of past experienced', in Cole, R. (ed.) *Current issues in linguistic theory*. The North West Regional Examining Board for extracts from the examination paper English as a Second Language, 1983.

We have been unable to trace the copyright holders in the following material: A Proficiency Scale produced by the United States Information Service. Two examination papers produced by the Educational Testing Service (Princeton, N.J., 1983). A table from Legutke, M. (1983) *Project work in the communicative classroom at an elementary level of language learning* (Institut für die Didaktik der Englishchen Sprache und Literatur, Justus-Liebig-Universitat, Giessen). An adaptation of a diagram from Chaudron, C. (1985) 'A method for examining the input/intake distinction', in Gass and Madden (eds.) *Input in Second Language Acquisition* (Newbury House: Rowley, MA.). We would welcome any information which would help us to do so.

General Editor's Preface

Applied Linguistics has benefitted over the last ten years or so by much illuminating discussiion arising from the exegesis of a number of sets of dichotomies or complementarities. One thinks of 'use' and 'usage', 'product' and 'process', 'testing' and 'evaluation', among many others. One such set is of particular relevance to this major new contribution by Michael Rost to the *Applied Linguistics and Language Study Series*, and it is one whose currency has not yet received adequate appraisal in the applied linguistic literature, namely that of the relationship between *hearing* and *listening*, and its associated set, that of *intelligibility* and *interpretability*.

The complementarity is of importance, not only for the subject matter of *Listening in Language Learning*, for which as Michael Rost cogently and expressively argues it is crucial, but for the formulation and conduct of Applied Linguistics research and practice in general. For what the sets of terms do is to compel a connection, a dialogue between the formal and the functional aspects of language as communication, and in two principal dimensions. Firstly, to link code with context, demonstrating that although both parties to an interaction have access through their perception and their competence to the code, they come to this access through the constraints and circumstances of their own contexts, both those that they inherit as speaking and hearing members of a culture and a society, and those imposed through the immediate environment of the particular interaction in question, more or less conducive to accessing the code. Access is, of course, not equivalent among participants any more than knowledge of the code is isomorphic. To achieve some approximation, to enable some code-sharing, requires negotiation of knowledge and experience and this leads us to the second principal dimension of significance. The dialogue between the terms raises in our minds the relationship between what is traditionally termed *comprehension* and what we might want to call '*comprehending*', that is a shift in focus from the products of understanding to the process of achievement. It is here that we can connect the related set of *intelligibility* and *interpretability* alluded to above, the one concerned with perception and decoding and the other with inference and understanding, and, in consequence, show how strategy is central to an understanding of what Listening in language learning implies.

Pursuing the exploration further, it is not difficult to see how we are thus led from an immediate concern with Listening to the broader meaning of communicative competence for applied linguists, namely that connection between an integrated sociolinguistic concept of form and functiona nd psycholinguistic processes of interpretation and expression, in short to the connection between communicative and cognitive strategy which is at the heart of language learning.

Returning to Michael Rosts's theme, we can see how such a general applied linguistic relevance imposes strenuous demands on the author. Like in so many other applied contexts, significance has to be achieved through appraisal of varying and wide-ranging sources. Exploring Listening as an interactive process requires appreciation of linguistic research (and not only the narrowly speaker-oriented focus of articulatory phonetics but the acoustic and psychoacoustic canon of research into speech perception, as Chapter Two amply evidences), as well as a grasp of current research into the pragmatics of speaker-hearer meaning negotiation, as in Michael Rost's Chapter Three, and links to be made between that and the discourse analytical procedures inherent in the discussions of interactional and transactional discourse of Chapters Four and Five.

And what of the practitioner? Relevance for him or her, after all, has to be achieved in the viability of research to the practicalities of instruction, whether in first and second language contexts or in the equally relevant worlds of speech and hearing impairment of professional-client interaction, or of voice-activated computerised information systems. Chapters Six and Seven with their developmental and assessment focus tackle these issues of consumer relevance and, as we might expect from the best applied linguistic research, throw up challenges to theory, thus ensuring that bidirectionality which is its characteristic.

It would be inappropriate, however, to read this book as if it were a compendium of relevant gobbets of information, like some kaleidoscope of brilliants to be shaken into any pattern which personally satisfies any reader or consumer. Rost has an argument to pursue, and in a nutshell it is this: decoding relies not only on personal perception but on listener inference born out of speaker-listener cooperation in discourse, where both parties, whether co-present or not, share responsibility for success or failure in meaning-making. Of course, extra-personal context, as noise, has a part to play in impeding achievement, as does the unrecordable 'noise' of incomplete code competence, varying schemata and social psychological attitude, but ultimately, successful listening has to be learned through cooperative endeavour.

Translating this thesis into action is not, however, initially a practical question. The problem lies first in the world of metaphor, and a world which is not only within the province of applied linguistics. It has to do with the characterisation of process. As Rost amply demonstrates, an approach to the analysis of listening competence as a set of sequenced stages, through which the competent listener must pass, not only has little justification in empirical research, it has profoundly disabling implications in pedagogic practice, whether in language teaching and learning or any other instructional context. It suggests a syllabus of units, a taxonomy of 'skills' through which learners can be induced via graded and (arbitrarily) simplified tasks towards mastery. Now, of course, such a model will find (and has found) ready responses in curriculum planning and syllabus design (one recalls some of the worst excesses of product-based ESP analysis), and particularly so in the assessing of listening ability, and Michael Rost addresses these consequences in his Chapters Seven and, especially, in Eight on *Listening in the Language Curriculum*.

His proposals for 'learning to listen', concentrating on a skills hierarchy based on salience (itself determined by listening *purpose*) offer an alternative to unconnected listening exercises separated from contexts of understanding. What he suggests is analysis beginning from listening problems, moments of misunderstanding if you like, and then linked through an appraisal of appropriate listening (and speaking) strategies to a formulation of relevant pedagogic tasks. Such a problem-based analysis is revealing in a number of respects. Not only does it suggest what are general listening problems for the non-native speaker (or, in principle, any potentially 'listening-disadvantaged' participant) dealing with unmodulated native speaker talk, but more usefully than this, speculates on the variably conducive effects of speaker style, discourse genre and listening context on this process. Here, Michael Rost's wealth of reference is of inestimable advantage to the reader. Drawing on research in first and second language acquisition, cognitive science and artificial intelligence, as well as language pathology and educational research more generally, he builds up a rich picture of the listening world which convinces not only by its range but by the appositeness of its choice of example.

It would be inappropriate in the applied linguistics of today not to comment on the judicious and demanding discussion points and tasks that he selects for each of this Chapters. For it is through these opportunities for reader exploration that the action research characteristic of our field can be initiated and carried out. We are helped in this by the rich multicultural and multilingual illustration and example throughout the book and directed through them to those salient points of inquiry Michael Rost identifies for us.

Professor Christopher N Candlin
Macquarie University,
Sydney, Australia
January 1990

1 Introduction: Listening in verbal communication

1.0 Comprehension or interpretation?

One of the most important concepts associated with verbal interaction is that of understanding. To what extent can we say that the interlocutors in any interaction understand each other? To what extent do they 'comprehend' through the words that an interlocutor uses and to what extent do they 'interpret' ideas that are related to the words that an interlocutor uses? Is understanding a mental phenomenon recoverable through probing the mind of the hearer or is it a social phenomenon recoverable through examination of subsequent behaviour by the listener? These are fundamental questions underlying linguistic inquiry in general, and are clearly of concern for applied linguists and language teachers. Without a realistic view of understanding in verbal interaction, it is difficult to uncover a sensible paradigm for conducting research and impossible to arrive at a coherent pedagogy for developing understanding.

The purpose of this chapter is to provide an introductory discussion of the role of listening in verbal communication. In doing this, I will review essential contributions to applied linguistics from other disciplines, contributions which have an impact on how we view listening. After the construction of a preliminary model of verbal understanding that will be developed in subsequent chapters, an outline will be given of some of the historical issues concerning listening in language teaching in order to set the stage for later chapters that deal with listening in a language curriculum.

1.1 Information-processing and inferencing-based approaches

To explore the issue of understanding in verbal interaction it is necessary to outline the nature of content in language and the nature of roles of the interlocutors. Practically speaking, before we look at how people understand language (or more precisely, how they understand events in which language is used), we need to know what it is that is understood, who is responsible for creating this understandable content, and who is responsible for understanding it.

Most of us will have some ready answers for these questions, or at least some useful metaphors to describe the process of understanding in verbal communication. Let us take a closer look at some of the definitions of language understanding that we commonly use. Many of the metaphors we casually use to think about verbal communication allocate distinct roles to a speaker and a listener. For instance, we often speak of communication as the sending and receiving of information, with our image of one person 'catching' this information that another person somehow 'sends'. Or we often refer to communication as a travelling-thoughts process, with one party 'picking up signals' we transmit. Although these metaphors account for both content and roles of interlocutors, the actual procedures they imply are of course impossible to carry out. Thoughts and messages obviously do not possess the physical properties necessary to travel, nor do people literally follow, pick up, or catch things in the communication process.

Many of these transfer-of-information metaphors are rooted in the rationalist tradition in philosophy, the philosophy which gave rise to **information processing theory**. In the rationalist tradition, words were seen as having meaning:

> To make Words serviceable to the end of Communication, it is necessary that they excite, in the Hearer, exactly the same Idea they stand for in the mind of the Speaker. Without this [People] fill one another's Heads with noise and sounds; but convey not thereby their Thoughts, and lay not before one another their Ideas, which is the end of Discourse and Language.
>
> (John Locke, 1689)

This rationalist view of communication was encapsulated in the popular information-processing metaphors of the 1940s (e.g. Shannon and Weaver, 1949), which viewed communication as a process which attempted to conserve the speaker's meaning — 'the message' — throughout a transmission process. The role of the receiver was to reconstruct the speaker's message as encoded in the signal (Figure 1.1).

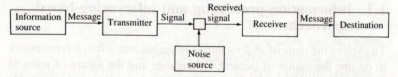

FIGURE 1.1 An information processing model (from Shannon and Weaver, 1949)

Although this basic model was subsequently modified to include listener feedback and noise distortion (e.g. Schramm, 1954; DeFleur, 1966; Dance, 1967), the fundamental information-processing paradigm remains: communication is seen as a potentially perfect encoding—decoding process, in which speaker and hearer approach an isomorphic match of meanings.

Within the transmission metaphor emerge some rather rigid views of what the receiver (the listener) does. Perhaps the most deeply ingrained set of metaphors are those which view listening as an outcome which can be measured quantitatively in relation to what language has been spoken. It is not uncommon to hear people say — particularly second language learners — that they have understood, say, 50 per cent of what a speaker said.[1] The notion of quantity of understanding is apparently based on the belief that a speaker's message can be comprehended: a successful listener can actually enumerate structural units of some sort in what a speaker says and derive meaning directly from those units.

The information-processing model is useful as a hypothesis since it suggests answers to three questions:

(1) What is the content of verbal communication?
    (*Answer:* information.)
(2) Where does this content (i.e. the information) reside?
    (*Answer:* in the words the speaker uses.)
(3) How is understanding of the content achieved?
    (*Answer:* by the listener comprehending the words the speaker uses.)

Although these are critically important questions in applied linguistics, the answers provided by the information-processing metaphor are at best overly simplistic and at worst possibly misleading. The information-processing model overstates the role of the denotative function of language, and distorts the role of the listener in the act of understanding. For these reasons the model must be re-examined.

The view of understanding that I wish to develop in this book is based on the growing theme in cognitive science that people construct rather than receive knowledge, and that understanding in verbal communication is a construction process. I will view verbal communication in terms of **relevance theory** (Sperber and Wilson, 1982, 1986) which holds that communication is fundamentally a collaborative process involving **ostension** (production of signals by a speaker) and **inference** (contextualizing those signals by a hearer).

Ostension, as an act by one interlocutor which is physically perceivable by another, provides two layers of information. First, there is the information which has been pointed out; second, there is the information that the first layer of information has been pointed out. For example, if you and I are sitting together in a room and I know that you like snow and I know that it is just beginning to snow outside and I open the curtains so that you can see the snow falling for yourself, I have performed an ostensive act of communication by opening the curtain.

In terms of relevance theory, for you to understand this act of ostension, you have to understand not only the first layer of information (that it is snowing now) but the second layer of information as well (that I wanted you to see it now). The first layer might be termed the 'locution' and the second layer might be roughly termed the 'illocution'. I, the actor, had some intent in providing this locution to you.

Understanding the ostensive act is an inferential process of finding a relevant link between the two layers of information. It is vital to note here that the relevant link that you find to make sense of the communicative act need not be the only relevant link you could find, nor need it be the link that I had hoped you would find. You can achieve an acceptable understanding without knowing exactly what I had intended.

This placement of responsibility for interpretation on the hearer is a direct departure from the information-processing view of understanding. Relevance theory places responsibility for constructing an acceptable understanding (finding a relevant link) on the listener. This view suggests that understanding involves both decoding processes (in the example so far, you would need to be able to recognize the snow) and inferential processes based on the speaker's actions, which may be both verbal and non-verbal.

When speech is involved in ostensive acts, as it is in verbal communication, the interlocutors use inferential processes in the same way. If, for example, instead of opening the curtains for you to see the snow, I come in from another room and say, 'Hey, it's snowing', the inferencing you must do to understand my ostensive act (here, my saying, 'Hey, it's snowing') is the same, although the decoding process is different. You still must find a relevant link between the first layer of information (my claim that it's snowing) and the second layer of information — that I pointed this out to you now.

An important aspect of relevance theory, and a fundamental departure from the information-processing view of communication, is that successful ostensive-inferential communication cannot be guaranteed. There is no procedure for ensuring mutually acceptable and unambiguous understanding between interlocutors, even when the interlocutors can be said to have mastered the language system involved. Verbal communication is inherently ambiguous in that language has a **connotative function** in addition to a **denotative function**. While speakers of a language may elect to use particular language forms in an attempt to refer to unique objects or entities, they cannot control the connotative functions of language for the listener. The connotative function of language is to orient the listener within a knowledge domain, and not to point out uniquely identifiable entities.

A stereotyped example of this is when a person from a northern country who is visiting a Pacific island tries to describe snow to a child. No matter how accurate the description of snow by the Northerner, the sense that the listener derives is constructed within the listener's own knowledge domain, rather than being simply transferred by the language the speaker uses. This is not to say that the two interlocutors cannot communicate successfully; indeed they can. However, as with speakers from the same language community, they must accept approximative constructions of meaning from the people with whom they are talking.

An obvious implication of using relevance theory is that the role of the hearer constrains the inferences that can be drawn from a speaker's act. In any discourse setting, participants will have varying listener roles. We can view these roles on a continuum of **collaborative discourse:** participant, addressee, audience member, overhearer, judge (Figure 1.2).

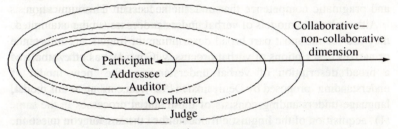

Participant — a person who is being spoken to directly and who has speaking rights equal to others involved in the discourse (e.g. a conversation between two friends on a topic of mutual interest and shared background)

Addressee — a person in a discourse who is being spoken to directly and who has limited rights to respond (e.g. a student in a traditional classroom in which the teacher is lecturing)

Auditor — a person in a discourse who is a member of an audience that is being addressed directly and who has very limited rights to respond and is not expected to respond (e.g. a bus driver announcing the name of the next bus stop to the passengers (audience) on the bus)

Overhearer — a person who is not being addressed, but who is within earshot of the speaker, and who has no rights or expectations to respond (e.g. hearing the conversation of a bank teller and the customer who is in front of you as you stand in line waiting)

FIGURE 1.2 A schematic representation of listener roles in discourse (based on McGregor, 1986)

The roles not only carry differing expectations for collaboration in the discourse; they also to some extent define the strength of inferences that can be drawn.

With a role towards the centre of the discourse, the listener is expected to participate actively in the construction of the discourse, to switch readily to a contributor's role. At the centre, reciprocal rights constrain the attention of the interlocutors. At the same time, however, by the listeners being in a central role the relevant links they can make concerning the speaker's actions are stronger since **speech acts** are directed personally toward them.

This model of understanding will be developed further in Chapter 3 and examples of listener inferencing are provided in Chapter 4 (listening in collaborative discourse) and in Chapter 5 (listening in non-collaborative, i.e. primarily transactional, discourse).

1.2 Frameworks for defining listening

Relevance theory offers a useful backdrop for a discussion of listening in language education, but we also need a model of the use of the linguistic and pragmatic competence that underlie successful communication.

Although some models of verbal understanding have been attempted, they are for the most part broad descriptions of linguistic competence or narrow descriptions of verbal processes. Consider, as an example of a broad description of verbal understanding, the 'new model of understanding' proposed by Demyankov (1983). According to this model, language understanding consists of these stages:

(1) acquisition of the linguistic framework of the language in question;
(2) construction and verification of hypothetical interpretations of what is heard;
(3) discernment of the speaker's intentions;
(4) assimilation of the spoken message;
(5) coordination of the speaker's and listener's motivation for participation in the conversation;
(6) discernment of the tone of the message.

At first glance, it is difficult to criticize this model as a model of understanding because it has included so many aspects of listening ability. It is also very modern-sounding in its introducing a number of seductive constructs such as hypothesis verification, interpretation of speaker intention, integration of information, discernment of tone, speaker— listener coordination.

However, it is clear that a stage-like model does not capture the essence of real-time language understanding. For example, people do not have to 'acquire a linguistic framework of the language in question' before they attempt to use linguistic knowledge to understand what they hear. Nor, as will be demonstrated in later chapters, do listeners need to 'discern a speaker's intention or tone' in order to arrive at a plausible understanding of an utterance. Thus, while a stage model may appear to account for a range of causes for non-understanding or misunderstanding, it does not adequately characterize everyday instances of language understanding.

What such a stage model essentially overlooks is that people listen for a purpose and it is this purpose that drives the understanding process. This purpose is rarely the 'ideal' one of wanting to 'comprehend' the precise sense and implications that a speaker intended. This kind of modelling of the understanding process as logically autonomous and sequentially discrete stages does not demonstrate how a listener makes sense of spoken language in everyday use.

Narrower models have been proposed to account for heuristic processes in 'real time', but these models too suffer from an idealizing of sequences. The well-known work of Clark and Clark (1977) has served as the basis for psychological descriptions of verbal understanding:

(1) [Hearers] take in the raw speech and retain a phonological
    representation of it in 'working memory'.
(2) They immediately attempt to organize the phonological
    representation into constituents, identifying their content and
    function.
(3) As they identify each constituent, they use it to construct underlying
    propositions, building continually onto a hierarchical representation
    of propositions.
(4) Once they have identified the propositions for a constituent, they
    retain them in working memory and at some point purge memory
    of the phonological representation. In doing this, they forget the
    exact wording and retain the meaning.
    (from Clark and Clark, 1977, p. 49)

The advantage of this model is that it is empirically based. The model attempts to account for (experimental) observations of perception and memory; it presents logical explanations of what must happen psychologically, given the limitations of human memory, in order for verbal communication to occur. The disadvantage of the model, at least in a discussion of the role of listening in language learning, is that it suggests that the hearer is a 'language processor' who performs actions in a fixed order, independently of contextual constraints.

Any model of how people come to understand instances of spoken language will have to take into account the definable features of the events and the participants where language is used. This is to say that language understanding occurs in an **interactive context**, even when one layer of the communication is essentially **transactional**.

1.3 Characterizations of listening

While information theory and responses to information theory may form the basis of our current view of listening in applied linguistics, several academic fields have contributed considerable insight to the details of listening. This section reviews selected contributions from reading education, first-language speech education, first-language acquisition, language pathology, and artificial intelligence.

1.3.1 Reading education

One indirect influence on our understanding of listening in language education is the sustained attention given to first- and second-language reading in the past twenty years. As a result of considerable reading research (see Hedley and Barratta, 1985 for a review of first-language research; and Alderson and Urquhart, 1984, for a review of second-language research), a dynamic view of the reader as an active participant in the creation of meaning has developed.

Through the work of educators in classrooms (e.g. Nix, 1983), researchers of psycholinguistic processes (e.g. Alderson, 1984; Krashen, 1988), and researchers of the reader−text interactive process (e.g. Harri-Augstein and Thomas, 1984; Langer, 1984; Glison, 1988; Carrell, 1988), educators have generated interactionist views about how a person must use knowledge of the world outside the text to construct meaning.

A central theme in much of this recent research is the notion of **cognitive skills** and **meta-cognitive skills**, those skills text users employ to create plausible expectations about the text and to sense the type of inferences they need to understand the text. Although reading and listening involve different linguistic decoding skills (i.e. visual vs. aural), the cognitive strategies that underlie effective reading will have much in common with those that underlie effective listening.

Much of the current research in first-language (L1) and second-language (L2) reading draws a distinction between two types of information that contribute to a reader's understanding of sentences which are part of a larger text. The first is information that is given in the sentence itself. The second is information which the reader has derived from interpreting the succeeding parts of the text.

The reader utilizes new information (from the immediate text), given information (recalled from prior text), and inferable information (implied

Processing levels

Schema (an underlying structure that links parts of the text)
  Script (a sequence of events or discrete parts of the text)
    Concept (a mental representation of the current segment of text)
      Formula (a paragraph or other visual unit)
        Phrase/sentence
          Word/lexical item
            Letter
              Graphic feature

FIGURE 1.3   The interaction of top-down and bottom-up processing (based on Dechert, 1983)

by the links between 'new' and 'given' information). Comprehension processes are geared toward continuously updating representations of the text with incoming information (Carpenter and Just, 1977; Marslen-Wilson and Tyler, 1981). The reader is free to fixate upon various sections of the text for longer or shorter periods of time, with reading speed depending on the reader's ability to utilize abstract 'top-down' information (about the overall structure of the text) to interpret incoming 'bottom-up' information (letters and words) (Johnson-Laird, 1984). See Figure 1.3.

Psycholinguistic studies of reading have indirectly shown key differences between reading and listening. One obvious difference is that a reader, unlike a listener, is typically capable of considerable control over the input: the reader can recognize multiple visual signals simultaneously (see McClelland, 1987 for a discussion of the connectionist view), and can dwell upon parts of the text, skip over others, and backtrack.[2] Current views of reading account for interactive processing at different levels of text.

1.3.1.1 Reading and listening
The notion of listening is often paralleled to reading, in which there are texts with which readers interact. However, in addition to the obvious differences in processing mode, the ways that the information in written or spoken texts is 'packaged' are different.

Spoken texts contain features such as variations in pronunciation (i.e. pronunciation of the same phonemes by the same speaker in different linguistic contexts as well as dialectal variations between speakers), irregular pauses, false starts, hesitations, self-revisions, and backtrackings. These features do have correlates in drafts of written texts (e.g. irregular and illegible scrawls, lines crossed out, arrows inserted), but most early written drafts are not made available to readers. Listeners, however, have access to the composer's (that is, the speaker's) on-line planning and editing processes and must somehow make sense of the appearance of planning and editing signals in the discourse.

Listener strategies for making sense of speech must include ways of recognizing unit boundaries and editing heard speech to conform to these boundaries. Whereas trained readers of English are attuned to left-to-right visual orientations and word divisions as well as to sentence and paragraph punctuation, listeners must utilize temporal pause boundaries, rhythmic groupings, tone placements, and intonation rises and falls to segment speech. The auditory recognition skills involved in listening decoding are clearly different from the visual recognition skills needed for reading. (Some of the **decoding concepts** that listeners must utilize are outlined in Chapter 2.)

Grammatical and lexical parsing skills needed for reading and listening would appear to be quite similar since written English texts and spoken English texts are derived from the same linguistic rules. However, even a cursory examination of a descriptive grammar of everyday spoken and written English shows this to be misleading. Cohesion devices (e.g. for co-reference and substitution) that speakers and writers commonly use are quite different. In spoken discourse, for example, speakers need not explicitly verbalize topics as they must usually do in writing. Further, in spontaneously spoken texts there are typically many more grammatical (i.e. non-lexical) words to create a **dynamic message:** the message must be interpreted as it is spoken in order to understand it. On the other hand, in writing there is typically a higher density of lexical words and a greater proportion of nominalized words to create a **synoptic message:** the message must be interpreted without strict time constraints in order to unravel the embedded structures (Halliday, 1986). Embedding devices allow the writer to pack more information into 'idea units' than would be possible in real-time speech composing. Since temporal constraints differ, the procedural knowledge needed for understanding written and spoken language will differ, even though the underlying 'linguistic competence' for written and spoken modes is the same.

1.3.2 First-language speech education

Educators in 'language arts' have long realized the important role of listening in development of general communication skills and thinking skills, but not until the 1970s did listening begin to receive systematic treatment in first-language school curricula.

Studies such as the Scottish Education Department (SED) project (Brown *et al.*, 1985), which will be cited several times in this book, demonstrated that experience in the listener's role in collaborative activities promotes a sensitivity to the demands of the speaker's role; speakers who have first been in the listener's role tend to be more explicit and more concerned with audience comprehension. The findings of the SED project are consistent with those of other investigations of reciprocal teaching as a comprehension-fostering activity (e.g. Palincsar and Brown, 1984).

First-language speech education in the 1970s began to focus on the role of the listener in speech events in order to demonstrate to learners how a listener's purpose influences listener behaviour. Galvin (1985) identifies categories of listening, with general corresponding purposes.

Type of listening	General purpose
transactional listening	learning new information
interactional listening	recognizing personal component of message
critical listening	evaluating reasoning and evidence
recreational listening	appreciating random or integrated aspects of event

Galvin proposes, as other first-language educators have done, that students need to select an appropriate role, distance, and purpose to guide them as they listen. The purpose helps the listener select appropriate strategies for seeking specific clarification, for noting down certain details, for scanning for the intent of the speaker. Listening is viewed then, not only as a linguistic skill, but as a cognitive and social skill involving **non-linguistic judgements** by the listener.

The role of the listener orientation in formal listening settings such as lectures has also begun to receive attention. Hodgson (1984) interviewed students as they viewed video tapes of themselves in lectures and asked them to describe what they were thinking. In analysing the interviews, Hodgson notes that learners tend to adopt a single orientation throughout a lecture, and that this orientation is influenced by the way the learners see their 'role' in the course. Learners with an 'intrinsic' orientation to the informational content of the lecture, who are motivated by a desire to understand the material in its own right, tend to be more curious about the reasons for which a lecturer raises a certain point. They actually appear to behave in a less consistent way than learners with an 'extrinsic' orientation to the task of 'listening and being sure to note down whatever the lecturer indicates is important', learners who react to the 'potential extrinsic demands' of the lecturer.

Hodgson's study makes transparent the fact that the listener brings an orientation to a listening event. One implication is that training in 'listening skills' alone, without regard to pre-listening orientation, may indeed be ineffective.

1.3.3 First-language acquisition research

Listening development promotes what Klein (1987) calls the 'accessibility dimension' of language acquisition. In spontaneous language acquisition, language development occurs only when 'linguistic input' is set against information about the world: who is speaking to whom, where the speakers are, and so on. Eventually, through observing how the linguistic input influences the speakers' and listeners' reactions to each other in specific contexts, the learner begins to establish relationships between identifiable segments of the input and particular pieces of parallel pragmatic information.

Descriptions of developmental sequences in first-language acquisition have done much to clarify the nature of this input that a learner (a child) receives. There is now considerable evidence (e.g. Cross, 1978; Ellis and Wells, 1980; Fivush and Fromhoff, 1988) to suggest that the way parents talk to their children influences how rapidly they acquire the language. The key features of such input appear to be interactional rather than formal. That is, it is the parents' choices of **discourse procedures** (e.g. commands vs. questions) and **devices for sustaining interaction** (e.g. requests for clarification) that provide the framework for language data made available to the child.

As such, language data have come to be characterized as containing both **linguistic** and **interactional signals**. (See Wells, 1982; Schieffelin and Ochs, 1986; Trevarthan, 1977, for reviews.) Based on the newly integrated descriptions of what linguistic and interactional cues the child has access to, we can now look at conversations between children and their caretakers not only in terms of the utterances that are directed to the child, but also in terms of interactive turns in an activity. We see the child's role more accurately as a participant in a collaborative activity than as a mere recipient of input.

The development of L1 listening ability is related in part to learning to achieve contrastive understandings in connected discourse. Bridges *et al.* (1982) have proposed that the acquisition of listening ability in an L1 involves moving from reference-based comprehension to adult-like understanding of how contrasts are made. They note that, under normal circumstances, most children need only identify appropriate references in order for successful communication to take place, especially in a situation in which all the references are visible to both the speaker and listener. Once a listener has successfully found the referents of a speaker's comments, the two of them will have managed to establish jointly a **base meaning** so the conversation can continue. Children's queries of the situation in front of them rarely, if ever, need to go beyond ascertaining which objects, events, or people are being referred to. As soon as the proper references have been identified, the relationship between them goes without saying, since (in most contexts of adult–child interaction) it can be readily discovered from the situation itself. It is not until the child is put in a comprehension test situation that it becomes apparent that in interpreting speech the child does not yet follow the conventional (adult) way of extracting meaning from grammatically contrastive sentence pairs (such as 'The dog is biting the boy' and 'The boy is biting the dog') . It seems that the child's use of such linguistically based contrastive rules is not yet fully developed, for the child regards the tangible facts of the situation as primary (in terms of informativeness) and linguistic forms as secondary.

Bridges *et al.* suggest that means of understanding cannot be directly inferred from a demonstration or display of understanding. Where a child appears to understand utterances in the same way that adults do (that is, through an evaluation of the consistency of verbal and non-verbal cues), the child may be finding **salience** in non-linguistic cues alone (that is, real-world knowledge about the things and people in the immediate environment). Likewise, where children do not appear to understand utterances in the same way that adults do, this does not mean that they are unable to use their own strategies to derive some meaning from what they hear, meaning which will be relevant to them. A key difference then between a child-like understanding and an adult-like understanding will be in the priority the hearer gives to linguistic and non-linguistic contrastive cues.

Studies of first-language acquisition suggest that children acquire **pragmatic principles** for participation and interpretation. Cultural anthropologists have long been interested in characterizing how cultures transmit these pragamatic principles. Goodenough (1957), specifically, proposed that a description of a culture should properly specify what it is that a stranger to a society would have to know in order to perform appropriately any role in any scene staged by the society. One central example of **cultural transmission** is learning how to respond in social rituals. The notion of understanding in a social event suggests that understanding includes knowing what constitutes an appropriate response.

In the following example, we can see how a child might come to learn through induction what responses are appropriate in certain types of interaction. It is an example of teasing and illustrates how an adult caretaker demonstrates to a child an appropriate listener response.

Maria (M, 27 months) is having her hair braided by her Aunt Amalia (A), while her uncle Carlos (C) looks on.

C: [wrinkling his nose at M and shaking his head]
      Fea, fea! (*Ugly, ugly*)
A: 'No es cierto,' dile. 'Soy bonita.'
      (*Tell him 'That's not right. I'm pretty.'*)
M: Soy bonito (*I'm pretty.*)
C: [imitating M's speech] 'No nonito . . . no estas bonita? (*no, no? you're
      not pretty?*)
A: 'Si,' dile, 'soy bonita' (*Yes, tell him 'I'm pretty.'*)
C: Estas fea. (*You look ugly*)
M: Bonita. (*Pretty*)
(from Eisenberg, 1986, p. 188)

Expected speed of response, as well as acceptable type of cooperative response, is also apparently learned during L1 acquisition. To an extent, cooperative verbal skills are also directly teachable — or at least they are believed to be so — as the following examples show.

Adult: [looking at story book, pointing to a character] Kore wa dare desu
           ka? (*Who is this?*)
Child: [no response]
Mother: Nani! Dame ja nai, kotaenaide, dare desu ka to yuu n deshoo. Hai
           to. Hisako to dobutsuen. (*What? You can't do that, just not answer.
           Now come on, who is it? Say, 'It's Hisako at the zoo.'*)
(from Clancy 1986, p. 221)

P: Yotchan, shobojidosha misete. (*Show me your fire engine.*)
Child: [no response]
Mother: Shobojidosha da tte (*She said, 'fire engine'.*)
Child: [no response]
Mother: Sa, hayaku, P-san misete tte yutteiru yo. Isoganakucha.
           Isoganakucha. A, a! (*Come on, hurry, P said to show it to her. You
           have to hurry. Oh!*)
(from Clancy 1986, p. 221)

Acquiring a first language entails gradual development of the ability to maintain **coherent dialogue**. McTear (1985) shows how children learn to participate in conversations of increasingly complex patterns. Most fundamental is the I−R−F (initiation−response−follow-up) pattern in which reference is in the early stages mainly exophoric, and gradually comes to include reference to items that can be recovered from context ('that', 'that one', 'it'). Eventually, conjunctions are used to link turns ('and', 'and then', 'but'), etc.

McTear notes also that children go through a sort of **response development** in their L1. The progression appears to be somewhat as follows:

(1) no verbal response;
(2) inappropriate or irrelevant response;
(3) minimal predicted response;
(4) response plus additional content;
(5) [other appropriate response].

The following is an example of a later stage of child discourse development: response and initiation for further talk (note that both speakers are children).

H: Do you like his big brother?
S: No his br— that is his friend and he lives in a different house see?
H: He lives in the same house . . . that wee boy lives in the same house and the big boy lives in the same house
S: No see the one with sort of curly hair and black hair well he lives in a different house
H: He doesn't
   (from McTear 1985, pp.156—57)

McTear's evidence suggests that the understanding of requests (as displayed in listener response) involves interpersonal as well as linguistic development. In developing their comprehension ability, children become aware of the conditions underlying successful (felicitous) production and comprehension of action requests rather than simply comprehending the language. We can extend this notion in proposing that development of language understanding involves increased understanding of the conditions that prompted the speaker to use certain language.

A/request action » B/action + acknowledge » A/acknowledge action

A/request action » B/refuse » A/withdraw or change topic

A/request action » B/refuse and justification » A/accept justification

A/request action » B/refuse and justification » A/reject justification » B/reject rejection of justification

A/request action and justification » B/reject justification + alternative suggestion » A/reject alternative suggestions + rephrase request » B/refuse

A/rephrase request » B/request clarification » A/clarification » B/comply

---

FIGURE 1.4 **Request sequence development** (modified from McTear, 1985)

1.3.4   Second-language acquisition research

Second language acquisition (SLA) research has made great strides in clarifying the important role of understanding spoken input and the function of listener-initiated interaction in language development. Approaches to SLA research fall into several categories of orientation of researchers: sociolinguistic orientation (usually incorporating methods of discourse analysis), psycholinguistic orientation (usually incorporating methods of input—output analysis), neurolinguistic orientation (usually incorporating input—output analysis with careful selection of subjects), and classroom orientation (usually incorporating interaction analysis methods). (Readers are referred to the work of Ellis, 1985; Kellerman and Sharwood-Smith, 1986; Chaudron, 1988; van Lier, 1988; Beebe, 1988; Larsen-Freeman and Long, 1990 for perspectives on the role of SLA research in language teaching and learning.) This section provides an outline of some of the reasoning developed in SLA research that makes a vital contribution to a discussion of listening development.

The most significant SLA research for our discussion is that (from various orientations) which is concerned with three questions: (1) What features of language and what conditions of language use tend to make language more readily understandable? (2) What does a non-native speaker (NNS) do to make the new language understandable? (3) To what extent do cross-linguistic influences help and hinder L2 understanding? Throughout the discussion in this book, reference is made to SLA research which has addressed these questions.

Various studies in SLA research have attempted to show what it is that language learners do when language is directed to them which they do not initially understand (cf. Hatch, 1983; Long, 1980). In a psycholinguistic paradigm, the learner must convert input (what is said) to intake (what is understood), in order to make inferences not only about meaning on the specific occasion of language use, but for hypothesizing about how the target-language system works. This psycholinguistically motivated view of SLA research, while apparently narrower in scope than the socially motivated view of the learner in first-language acquisition, has provided very useful insights into the listening processes of second-language learners (cf. Pica *et al*, 1987; Long and Porter, 1985).

Research methodologies vary within this psycholinguistic paradigm of SLA. Ellis (1985) has identified four complementary approaches. In one approach the researcher collects and analyses selected input and interaction sequences of learners and makes speculations about what these sequences contribute to second-language development (cf. Hatch, 1983; Long, 1983). A second approach extrapolates from studies of the role of input and interaction in first-language acquisition through identifying features of simplified language of caretakers to children. Proponents of this extrapolation approach (e.g. Krashen, 1981) argue that similar features in the input to second-language learners should facilitate language development. A third approach utilizes correlational studies. Proponents of correlational research argue that by demonstrating commonalities between the frequency of occurrence of certain forms in input (specifically grammatical and lexical items) to a learner and the frequency of these same forms in the learner's output, we can estimate the value of certain types of language exposure for language acquisition (e.g. Wagner-Gough, 1975; Snow and Hoefnagel-Hohle, 1982).

A fourth approach emphasizes the role of experimental studies which control for isolable features of input and interaction. Experimental studies are designed to compare outcomes of treatment groups (i.e. groups assigned to settings in which a particular feature is present) to control groups (i.e. groups assigned to comparable settings in which the particular feature is not present). Superior task performances by one group are used as evidence that the particular feature (e.g. linguistic simplifications by the speaker, opportunities for the listeners to interact) assists language comprehension.

The fundamental reasoning underlying a psycholinguistic approach to SLA research is this: if it can be can shown that a specific linguistic or conversational adjustment (by speaker or listener) promotes comprehension, and if it can be shown that in general comprehensible language and interaction promotes language acquisition, then we can deduce that those specific linguistic and conversational adjustments promote language acquisition. This reasoning is the basis for shifting the proposed paradigm for language instruction from a product orientation (acquiring a fixed body of language forms) to a process orientation (acquiring a fluid set of language skills). Product and process orientations to language instruction are discussed in Chapter 8.

1.3.5 Cognitive science

Within cognitive science, there has developed a broad interest in experimental simulations of comprehension of connected discourse, especially by native speakers of a language. An important development of these many text comprehension studies has been the proposal that cognitive **schemata** constrain the production and comprehension of extended discourse.

Flores d'Arcais and Schreuder (1983) note that some notions utilized in text-comprehension models have contributed significantly to a psycholinguistic theory of language understanding. Central notions are:

(1) comprehending language requires processing structures larger than sentences;

(2) comprehending an extended text[3] consists of using knowledge about the world and schemata about what a normal, plausible text should include;

(3) understanding involves filling in gaps, introducing consistencies, and eliminating implausible interpretations, with a steady use of inference to assemble the different elements in the story into a congruent structure.

Other work (particularly Anderson *et al.*, 1977) has demonstrated how readers and hearers utilize schemata to interpret texts. For instance, experimental subjects will often interpret identical passages differently if prior information they have received (such as a suggested title for the passage) induces them to predict the content of the text they see or hear. Readers and hearers utilize pre-organized knowledge, or schemata, as they interpret the text. According to schema theory, familiar knowledge structures are triggered by the recognition of a sequence of related lexical items (such as: *the mat, the escape, being held, the charge, the lock* in the text of Anderson *et al.* (1977) — see Figure 1.5). Items or propositions that cannot be interpreted clearly then assume a **default value** (i.e. the most neutral or most common possibility) in the particular schema that is activated.

Note how titles, as 'prior thematization', can affect text understanding. If you read identical texts with different titles, you can interpret the same text items differently — that is, according to different schemata.

A Prisoner Plans his Escape
Rocky slowly got up from the mat, planning his escape. He hesitated a moment and thought. Things were not going well. What bothered him most was being held, especially since the charge against him had been weak. He considered his present situation. The lock that held him was strong, but he thought he could break it.

A Wrestler in a Tight Corner
Rocky slowly got up from the mat, planning his escape. He hesitated a moment and thought. Things were not going well. What bothered him most was being held, especially since the charge against him had been weak. He considered his present situation. The lock that held him was strong, but he thought he could break it.

(from Anderson *et al.*, 1977, p. 372)

FIGURE 1.5 Effects of titles on text understanding

Schemata are used not only to make interpretations of texts, but also to recall texts. For example, a number of experiments have demonstrated that when readers or hearers summarize a story, they typically distort facts, exclude facts, and add original facts, all in order to align the story with their culturally acquired schematic knowledge (see Figure 1.6).

Experimental work in cognitive science over a period of two decades has helped give shape to a **schema theory** of human cognition. According to Thorndyke and Yekovich (1980), schema theory can be seen to include four key notions:

(1) **Concept abstraction:** schemata are arranged hierarchically with concepts at different degrees of specificity and typicality.

(2) **Instantiation:** a schema is instantiated during interpretation: a 'copy' of the general schema is created, with data from the current 'input' filling variable slots.

(3) **Prediction:** schemata permit reasoning from incomplete information; default values supplied by the general schema may be substituted

---

The following widely-quoted text has been used to show how cultural expectations guide understanding and recall.

The War of the Ghosts
One night two young men from Egulac went down to the river to hunt seals, and while they were there it became foggy and calm. Then they heard war cries, and they thought: 'Maybe this is a war party'. They escaped to the shore and hid behind a log. Now canoes came up, and they heard the noise of paddles, and saw one canoe coming up to them. There were five men in the canoe, and they said:

'What do you think? We wish to take you along. We are going up the river to make war on the people.'

One of the young men said: 'I have no arrows.'

'Arrows are in the canoe,' they said.

'I will not go along. I might be killed. My relatives do not know where I have gone. But you,' he said, turning to the other, 'may go with them.'

So one of the young men went, but the other returned home.

And the warrior went on up the river to a town on the other side of Kalama. The people came down to the water, and they began to fight, and many were killed. But presently the young man heard one of the warriors say, 'Quick, let us go home: that Indian has been hit.' Now he thought: 'Oh, they are ghosts.' . . .

(from Mandler and Johnson, 1977)

FIGURE 1.6 Cultural expectations and text interpretation

in the description (or anticipation) of an event when the explicit information supplied in the description is incomplete (or withheld).
(4) **Induction:** schemata are learned by induction from numerous previous experiences with various exemplars of the generic concept.

Chapters 3 and 4 examine further how pre-organized knowledge, or schemata, influence language understanding.

1.3.6   Language pathology

The study of language pathology, that is, of how normal communicative and linguistic abilities are disrupted, has contributed to our understanding of listening in two ways. First, an examination of language pathology allows us to see language understanding as consisting of partially **separable processes**. It has been noted repeatedly that following certain brain injuries (such as those brought on by a stroke or a localized head wound), one seldom loses all language abilities. Usually, only a subset of language abilities is impaired, while others remain apparently intact. For instance, aphasic patients with 'pure word deafness' have reasonably intact speech production, but have great difficulty understanding speech addressed to them. According to Goldstein (1984), patients with this form of aphasia complain that speech sounds foreign: the patient can hear the words but can extract no meaning from them.[4]

Studies of auditory aphasia (e.g. Beauvois and Derouesne, 1980; Schwartz, 1984) include examinations of pure word deafness, word-meaning deafness (ability to repeat words without knowing what the words mean), auditory phonological aphasia (ability to understand and repeat words learned before the brain injury, but inability to understand or repeat new words), and agrammatic aphasia (inability to utilize syntactic information to understand utterances). Cumulatively, these studies provide evidence that speech-processing problems are often quite specific: a patient will seem perfectly normal with some speech-interpretation problems, but will perform quite poorly with others involving the injured area of the cortex.

The second, and perhaps more useful, way that the study of language pathology contributes to our understanding of listening is in the area of **compensatory strategies**. Patients with aphasic difficulties still make attempts to communicate through the use of compensatory skills. Ellis and Beattie (1986) cite ways in which patients with pure word deafness utilize gestural cues (especially lip movements) and environmental cues to interpret what is said to them. Agrammatics, for instance, attempt to compensate for confusing sentences (e.g. 'The dog bit the child' or 'The child bit the dog') through use of logical probabilities (i.e. 'Since

Physical: may be due to a lack of healthy hearing and speaking apparatus

Social: may be due to restricted intake; may appear as a lack of sensitivity to the social context and rules of conversation

Cognitive: may be due to developmental disruption; may appear as an inability to establish and maintain discourse topics, and to identify and establish discourse referents

Linguistic: may be due to restricted intake; may appear as a lack of linguistic forms to enable cohesive ties between utterances

FIGURE 1.7 Categories of receptive disorders among L1 speakers

dogs bite children more often than children bite dogs, the sentence I just heard must have been "The dog bit the child".') (Schwartz, 1984). What is applicable to the discussion in this book is the fact that compensatory strategies are used by normal listeners as well, even though the source of difficulties is obviously different from that in aphasia. The use of strategies in development of listening skill is examined in Chapters 6 and 8.

Another type of language understanding difficulty is psychologically rooted rather than neurologically based. These are **receptive disorders** that are found among psychologically disturbed patients. Receptive disorders are often classified according to cause (see Figure 1.7). This section reviews some data samples exemplifying types of receptive disorders, again to provide parallels to developmental problems among normal language users.

Following are two conversational extracts involving individuals with receptive disorders.

    Adult: Did you go camping in the woods?
    Child: [shouts] Go camping in the woods?
    Adult: Yeah, did you ever do that?
    Child: Yeah, he ever do that . . .
    Adult: When are you going home?
    Child: Um . . . he IS going home.
    (from McTear 1985, p. 237)

This class of disorder is referred to as **echolalia**: the child repeats or echoes utterances, apparently without attention to the transactional direction of the discourse.

Slowness to develop an interaction is another type of receptive disorder. Below is a conversation extract which suggests that the child is interacting, but not elaborating in an expected way.

    Adult: do you play with P?
    Child: yes I do

```
Adult:  um-hmm
Child:  play with him
Adult:  after school
Child:  yes
Adult:  um-hmm
Child:  I play with him after school
```
(from McTear, 1985, p. 244)

The child restores the remainder of sentences which the adult was attempting to leave ellipted. The child is essentially repeating utterances where new content is expected. With this type of interactive disorder the child tends to stay on a single topic, without realizing the expectation to move on to another. The following example illustrates this.

```
Child:  It's got twenty windows in it
Adult:  Mm
Child:  It has rooms ... it has ... it has a lift ...
Adult:  Um
Child:  In it [2 second pause] has a lift in it [1.2 second pause] lift in it
Adult:  How long did you stay there for?
```
(from McTear, 1985, p. 245)

Inattention to salience is a key feature of many receptive disorders. In the following example, the child, while obviously being cooperative, requires considerable prompting to attend to a topic which is salient to his interlocutor.

```
Adult:  [showing a picture of boy whose clothes are covered with mud]
Child:  This is a boy going to school
Adult:  Umhmmm
Child:  He's going to school
Adult:  Can you notice anything special about him
Child:  He's going to school at nine o'clock ... it's it could be nine o'clock
        when he comes to school
Adult:  Umhmm
Child:  It could be nine o'clock
Adult:  Humhhh
Child:  Or it could be nine thirty
Adult:  Okay
Child:  He could be out of the bus
Adult:  But do you notice anything special about him?
Child:  Yes
Adult:  In this picture ... what
Child:  That's his school bag
Adult:  Uhhun
Child:  His school bag ... that's his blue trousers, I think that's muck in it
Adult:  Yes that's what I was thinking
Child:  That's muck
Adult:  Do you notice he's all mucky
Child:  Yes because he was playing about with football ...
```
(from McTear, 1985, p. 246)

The expected response to the salient detail of the picture takes place only after many turns of prompting.

Another type of communicative disorder relevant to listening is the inability to remedy communicative breakdown. In the extract below, the child apparently does not realize that a communication breakdown is taking place.

Adult: Which race would you like to be in (in an upcoming sports day)?
Child: I would like to be in X [a town several miles away]
Adult: In X?
Child: Yes
Adult: What do you mean?
Child: I mean something
Adult: Is there a sports day in X
Child: There is not, there is a sports day in Y [at his school]
Adult: Then what's X got to do with it?
Child: Nothing
Adult: Then why did you mention it?
Child: Indeed I did mention it
Adult: Why did you mention it?
Child: I don't know
(from McTear, 1985, p. 247)

The examination of communicative disorders in terms of interactional and transactional problems sheds light on the nature of participant intent and ability to respond that successful understanding entails. Examples of interactional and transactional problems in discourse are given in Chapters 3 and 4.

1.3.7   Artificial intelligence

In computer science there have been gradual movements to develop programs to 'understand' spoken language. Some of the problems — though not the mechanical details of their solutions — that computer programmers face are of interest to language education. These problems are in the 'lower level' areas of phonetic identification and grammatical parsing as well as in 'higher level' inferencing of speaker intentions and speaker assumptions. The problems encountered in getting computers to make sense of natural-language sequences are analogous to the problems that humans experience in making sense out of novel sequences of language. By exploring attempts in artificial intelligence (AI) to improve computer capacity to understand natural (human) language, we are able to identify **knowledge application routines** used by people in understanding language.

Programs which are developed to recognize speech have to deal with the following interesting problems, all of which have clear correlates to human problems of 'bottom-up' speech processing (Studdert-Kennedy, 1981):

(1) Accounting for phonetic variance: not all acoustic realizations of a single phoneme (say /t/) are identical.

(2) Segmenting the speech signal into phonetic units: sequential cues to separation of phonemes (say in /traɪ/): not all phonemes are separable.

(3) Normalizing time: the same speaker does not always give equal timing to the same sounds so it is problematic to construct a single recognition pattern (or template) for the program to utilize.

(4) Normalizing talkers: people speak differently, even speakers of the same dialect and accent, so it is difficult to recognize that the different sounds of two speakers correspond to the same phoneme.

(5) Dealing with errors in initial perception: later perceptions often force the hearer (or computer) to revise an earlier interpretation (the 'garden path' problem), so it is important to build up 'possible values' rather than 'absolute values' when decoding speech.

Another class of problems involved in computer understanding of natural language are those related to understanding the intention of a

Program 1

This program will print out the time of day whenever the precise sequence:

/WHAT TIME IS IT?/

is typed in. This program could be regarded as able to 'understand English language' since it responds appropriately to an English question that would be likely to elicit a similar response from any competent user of English. It has access to an operative clock, just as a person might have easy access to a watch.

Program 2

This program will print out the time of day whenever the sequence, or near sequence: /WHAT TIME IS IT?/ is typed in. That is, the program will accept sequences with minor errors (or varations), such as

/WAHT TIEM IT IS?/,

and still give appropriate responses.

This program could be considered able to understand language better than Program 1 since it allows for variations of input, and interprets deviant forms as acceptable. One might argue that by accepting deviant forms, the computer is inferring its interlocutor's (i.e. the typist's) intent.

speaker and ways of responding. These are clearly parallel to human problems of understanding. However, there are important differences. Let us illustrate some basic language-understanding programs in order to clarify the differences between the human and computer processing [Programs 1 – 4]. (See Winograd and Flores, 1987, for a an enlightening essay on this matter.)

It is often asked if computers really understand human language. To respond, we need a coherent view of language. If we accept a Hallidayan view that language is rooted in a social-interpersonal domain, then we

Program 3

This program has a collection of patterns that are matched against input sequences. For each of these there is a corresponding form to be printed out, where that printout will include fragments of the pattern that was entered.

The program finds a pattern that matches the input and gives back the associated response. For example, if it is programmed with the pattern, 'My name is ____' and corresponding response 'Hello, ____, how are you today?', it would respond to the input 'My name is Jean' with 'Hello, Jean, how are you today?'

This program (ELIZA) (Weizenbaum, 1966) has been run with a collection of patterns that simulated a non-directive psychiatrist interviewing a patient. For example, it responded to 'I am . . .' with *'How long have you been . . . ?'*, thus generating both plausible and implausible exchanges, such as:

PERSON AT KEYBOARD: 'I am depressed'
             ELIZA: *'How long have you been depressed?'*
PERSON AT KEYBOARD: 'I am late'
             ELIZA: *'How long have you been late?'*

Given an input string of 'I hope . . .', it responded with *'What would it mean to you if . . .'*, thus allowing for exchanges such as:

PERSON AT KEYBOARD: 'I hope to lose weight'
             ELIZA: *'What would it mean to you if you lost weight?'*

ELIZA could be taken to be understanding language in a human way (the human name of the program helps the user believe this is so!), since its responses suggest it is understanding language in not only a linguistic sense, but also in ideational and interpersonal senses.

Program 4

This program is a collection of 'scripts'; each corresponds to a particular kind of event sequence. For example, it might have a script for what happens when a person goes to a restaurant:

START
(i)   The person enters,
(ii) is seated by a host or hostess,
(iii) orders some food,
(v)   is brought the food by a waiter/waitress,
(vi) eats the food,
(vii) is brought a bill,
(viii) pays it,
(ix) leaves.
END

When an input is given that invokes the title of this 'script', the program, SAM (which stands for Script Applier Mechanism) (Schank and Abelson, 1977) then compares each subsequent input with one of the event patterns in the script and fills in values based on the input.

If the input does not match the next event in line, it skips over that event and compares it to the next one. Once the input is completely 'represented', the program can use its 'general script' and the specific values given from the input to answer simple questions. For example, given the input:

'John went to a restaurant. John ate a hamburger',

it can use its script to answer 'inferential' questions such as:

'What did John order?' and 'Who brought John the hamburger?'

Scripts are such powerful predictors of information that given clear lexical input but faulty syntax (or no syntax at all), script-based understanding programs can still generate plausible inferences about the content. For instance, given the input:

'John restaurant ate went hamburger',

the program can still employ its knowledge of the script to answer the same questions.

can view understanding as entering into a commitment with the speaker within that domain. No matter how cleverly and thoroughly a computer's 'ideational domain' is programmed and no matter how sophisticated its detail in linguistic recognition, the computer has no choice in its response and therefore cannot be said to be entering into a commitment with an interlocutor. Therefore, we can see that computer understanding can emulate expert performance with certain language subsystems but cannot use language in its interpersonal domain. This distinction of understanding as related to language domains will be re-introduced in Chapter 6.

1.4   Teaching listening

This section introduces some of the issues involved in teaching listening in language classrooms. These issues will be treated in greater depth in later chapters, and particularly in Chapter 6 and Chapter 8. This introduction provides a brief historical overview of oral approaches to teaching English, communicative language teaching (with an emphasis on understanding spoken language), and listening-based language learning.

1.4.1   Oral approaches to language teaching

Views of listening in language education have varied with historical developments in linguistic analysis and learner language (interlanguage) analysis. In spite of widespread interest in direct methods for teaching language dating back nearly a hundred years, listening had not received systematic attention in language learning syllabuses until much later. With the advent of oral approaches (especially Fries, 1945, 1961), listening was viewed as a problem of aural recognition of linguistic structures. Exercises to develop listening ability consisted of various types of identification and discrimination, with verbatim reproduction (dictation) a typical test of aural recognition.

As Brown (1987) points out, later variations of aural recognition exercises included recorded situational dialogues and read-aloud written texts — often played or performed repeatedly — followed by comprehension questions on the content. What makes these exercises variations of the more clearly structure-based activities of the oral approach, as Brown notes, is that essentially the spoken text was being made as similar as possible to a written text, where the learner can, if necessary, have repeated access to the text. However, we can observe that, in terms of syllabus design, both the audio-lingual and the situational approaches emphasized learner identification of language 'products', and that the role of listening was merely to reinforce recognition of those products in the syllabus (Nunan, 1988, 1989).

1.4.2   Listening-based language learning

Given the apparent causal relationship between intake of spoken language and language acquisition (that is, understanding language appears to be a necessary condition for acquiring language), some educators have proposed entire pedagogical systems based on initial listening. In the United States in the late 1960s, James Asher developed a classroom methodology, 'Total Physical Response', around the belief that readiness to talk is somehow biologically determined by the rate at which understanding of spoken language has been acquired (Asher, 1969). Asher's method consisted of an instructor providing highly contextualized (and often quite redundant) series of verbal commands, which he claims to be a necessary first step in language acquisition. In the 1970s several of Asher's colleagues, notably Nord (1975), Postovsky (1974), and Winitz and Reeds (1975) developed foreign-language methodologies involving vast amounts of semantic decoding practice with simple selection tasks and language inputs increasing in a grammatical progression. The procedures of the method were not new — the situational approaches of the early and mid-1900s (cf. Palmer, 1921; Hornby, 1950) had emphasized concentration on direct commands — but the focus on listening as the critical element appeared to be a new approach to a language-learning syllabus, at least at the beginning stages of second-language study.

Later, and apparently within the same tradition of finding ready solutions for language pedagogy, Krashen and Terrell (1983) formulated an approach to language teaching on what they considered to be a natural order of language acquisition. Their approach, which generalized some of the early findings in SLA research, emphasized large amounts of learner comprehension of spoken messages in the early stages of foreign-language instruction. Other SLA researchers, acting more cautiously than Krashen, have suggested only guiding principles (rather than sequentially organized methodologies) for organizing exposure and interaction in language classrooms. Ellis (1985), for instance, provides general recommendations for acquisition-oriented classrooms: large amounts of listening (i.e. input directed at the learner), including exposure to a high quantity of directives and exposure to a high quantity of extending utterances (requests for confirmation, paraphrases and expansions).

1.4.3 Communicative language teaching

Overlapping with interest in listening-based learning, though following a different historical route (via the Council of Europe), communicative language teaching (CLT) provided a newly emphasized role for listening skills in language learning. The large-scale development (but by no means world-wide adoption) of communicative language syllabuses during the 1970s encouraged teachers and learners to work with spoken language as a functional mode of communication. As communicative uses of spoken language began to receive renewed emphasis, listening exercises were judged as valuable to the extent that they simulated the 'real-life' listening conditions that actual users of a language operated within (cf. Ur, 1984; Underwood, 1988).

One outgrowth of this realization was that listening texts for classroom use were often lifted directly from 'authentic' L1-use situations. Listeners in language classes were expected to use language selectively to perform tasks which focused on meaning for the most part, rather than on form. The notion that listening inputs needed to model language that the learners were to acquire was abandoned. 'Authentic' language gained acceptability in CLT circles as useful data for classroom work. Tasks which allowed learners access to authentic language samples, even if those tasks were highly constrained, were considered to provide the best listening exercise (Rixon, 1981).

Among the most important developments within CLT was the ideological branching among those who subscribed to differing versions of the approach.

> There is, in a sense, a strong version of the communicative approach and a weak version. The weak version which has become more or less standard practice in the last ten years, stresses the importance of providing learning with opportunities for using their English for communicative purposes, and characteristically, attempts to integrate such activities into a wider programme of language teaching...The strong version of communicative teaching, on the other hand, advances the claim that language is acquired through communication, so that it is not merely a question of activating an existing but inert knowledge of the language, but of stimulating the development of the language system itself. If the former could be described as 'learning to use English', the latter entails 'using English to learn it'. (Howatt 1984, p. 279)

The version of CLT that an instructor adopts will affect the content and methodology of the classroom. In the 'learning to use English' version, the instructor will seek to set up simulations of spoken language-use activities (e.g. role plays, games, information gap exchanges). In the 'using English to learn it' version, the instructor aims to develop learner-directed projects involving interactive use of language, in spoken and written modes. While both versions provide a role for listening activities, the treatment of listening as a skill differs. We will return to this issue in Chapter 8.

1.5 Conclusion: Orientations towards listening

The purpose of this chapter has been to outline the nature of listening in verbal communication and to specify some of the variables that must be considered in developing approaches to listening in language learning.

The reader will have already noted in this introductory chapter the rather wide range of disciplines called on to initiate an inquiry into the nature of listening and the role of listening in verbal communication.

Throughout this book attempts are made to integrate the relevant perspectives these disciplines afford us in discussing listening in language learning. Chapter 2 examines the role of auditory perception in listening; Chapter 3 provides a complementary view of language understanding from a socio-pragmatic perspective. Chapters 4 and 5 examine listener performance in collaborative and non-collaborative discourse settings. Chapters 6,7, and 8 will apply essential aspects of the framework developed in these earlier chapters to issues of development of listening ability in formal educational settings.

1.6   Discussion questions for readers

1.   Metaphors for verbal communication

Provide one or two metaphors that you commonly use, or often hear used, to refer to verbal communication. What do these metaphors imply about the listener's role?

2.   Listener roles

Keep notes (for, say, one 24-hour period) of the situations in which you think of yourself as a listener. When you look back over your notes, attempt to characterize your role in each situation as *participant, addressee, audience member, overhearer, judge*.

Do these role labels for yourself fit easily in all situations you identified? If not, why not?

3.   Ostensive-inferential communication

Recall the earlier discussion of ostensive-inferential communication. In each instance below, (a) identify what the ostensive signal is that you, the listener, have access to. Consider both verbal and non-verbal elements, and (b) state what the two layers of information are (the locutionary and the illocutionary). In cases of ambiguity, what alternate meanings might there be?

• You are sitting on a train. The person next to you turns to you, puts a hand on your arm, and says in a questioning voice, 'You smoke?'
• It's about six o'clock. You open the door to walk into a shop. A person

inside the shop near the door takes a step toward you and says, 'Sorry, it's after six.'

• You pass a colleague in the hall. Your colleague, who is looking through some mail, glances up and says, 'Good morning' as you walk past.

• The telephone in your home rings. You pick it up and before you have a chance to say anything, a voice at the other end says, 'Is Jean there?' (There is no Jean in your household.)

4.   Information in written and spoken language

Look at the following hypothetical example of the same information being communicated in a written mode (A) and in a spoken mode (B).

To what extent is the information given by the speaker or writer likely to be the same? In what way is the information gained by the reader or listener likely to be different?

A. [index card posted on company bulletin board]
Car for sale. 1986 Capri. Low mileage. Best offer. Call Ann (marketing) 341-0988.

B. [in an office building, Ann pokes her head into a colleague's office one morning]

Ann: Bob...
Bob: Hm?
Ann: Good morning. Um, I heard you were looking for a small used car.
Bob: Yeah, I am. That's right.
Ann: Well, I just wanted to let you know . . .
Bob: Mm-hm.
Ann: about one you might be interested in.
Bob: Oh?
Ann: Yes, my Capri. I've decided to sell it.
Bob: Oh, really?
Ann: And if you're interested, I'd be glad to . . .
Bob: Yeah . . . maybe . . . I'd like to a have a look at it . . .

5.   Production features of written and spoken language

By comparing spoken and written versions of the same content, we can often note characteristic differences of writing and speaking. In order to provide comparative samples, write a short response (about 50–100 words) to one of the questions below:

- What is the best thing about the place you are currently living in?
- What is the worst thing about the place you are currently living in?

Read your draft and then rewrite it.

Some time later, record, on audio tape, a spoken answer to the same question you answered in writing. (You can reverse the writing and speaking steps if you like.)

Transcribe your audio recording and compare it with your written response. What features are similar? What features are different? How do you account for the differences?

Notes

1. It is hard to know precisely the percentages of what a person might be referring to in quantifying understanding in this way, but the metaphor persists, particularly among language learners, since it is apparently useful for presenting degrees of satisfaction with one's current state of understanding.
2. These crucial differences should make one cautious in looking for direct implications from reading research to an understanding of listening. Reading research often utilizes measurements of reading time and time of fixation on parts of a text as bases for inferences about attention during reading (e.g. Treisman, 1969; McClelland and Rumelhart, 1981).
3. Narrative texts have been the most widely researched text type in psycholinguistic research of the 1970s and 1980s. I suppose this is because narratives have a fairly universal appeal and structure; narratives also lend themselves to more reliable text analyses than do expository texts.
4. Detailed examination of these patients reveals that they can perceive vowel sounds quite well, but are poor at identifying consonant sounds. When speech is reduced to less than half its natural rate, however, their performance dramatically improves. The apparent explanation for this is that damage to a left-hemisphere system of the brain disrupts the very fine temporal analysis of acoustic signals. Without this system, the word-deaf patient must rely on a coarser right-hemisphere acoustic analysis system which can identify vowels but cannot discriminate between consonants unless the signal is slowed down considerably (Goldstein, 1984).

2 Auditory perception and linguistic processing

2.0 Auditory perception in verbal communication: use of decoding concepts

Understanding spoken language is essentially an inferential process based on a perception of cues rather than a straightforward matching of sound to meaning. The listener must find relevant links between what is heard (and seen) and those aspects of context that might motivate the speaker to make a particular utterance at a particular time. This chapter focuses on the ways in which the listener decodes utterances. It is demonstrated that the intelligibility of what is heard is reciprocally linked with the interpretability of what is heard through cognitive effects as the listener attends to speech. An outline is given of the ways in which the listener utilizes aural cues and linguistic knowledge to identify a logical form (lexical items and syntactic organization) for what is said. (The following chapter focuses on the inferences that listeners can draw once a logical form is recognized.) The processes of lexical recognition and syntactic parsing are discussed and it is shown how cognitive effects can influence this recognition process.

Let us begin by reviewing some principles of speech perception. In nearly all views of speech perception (e.g. Klatt, 1981; Studdert-Kennedy, 1981; Marslen-Wilson and Tyler, 1980) it is taken as given that a listener performs some type of auditory analysis of the speech signal as it is produced by a speaker. It was once widely believed (in the original 'motor-theory of speech perception') that hearers process speech signals by internally modelling the articulatory gestures which speakers would have to use in order to produce them.[1] However, it is now well established that there is not a direct correspondence between the articulatory, acoustic, and auditory dimensions of spoken language. Further, not everything that is present in the acoustic signal can be perceived by the hearer in real time. Thus, while sounds can be distinguished through their differences in length (time), pitch, loudness, and quality, not all of these differences can be calculated when one hears, as in normal speech, up to 25 individual sounds per second (Liberman *et al.*, 1967).

To compensate for this perceptual limitation, other kinds of linguistic and extra-linguistic information can be used by the hearer to anticipate auditory cues. It is inefficient and unnecessary to use only the 'bottom-up' cues that sound provides in order to make judgements about the significance of sounds that a speaker produces. Rather, it is by virtue of the expectations that listeners have that they need perform only a cursory examination of the acoustic signal. In terms of information processing, listeners perceive language according to the probabilities they have used to generate expectations about it.

Let us outline briefly the acoustic features that are available to the hearer. Some of the temporal features of speech can be identified through time-varying displays of the acoustic signal. Using a cathode ray oscilloscope (CRO), for example, one can visualize the movements of the eardrum in response to pulses of air pressure produced by speech. An oscillograph provides simplified representations of **fundamental frequency** of a sound and **intensity**, the former indicative of **perceived pitch**, and combined, indicative of **loudness**. These two aspects, pitch and loudness, are, as we will see, critical in speech decoding.

The most useful representations of speech are perhaps spectral representations since they combine these two speech concepts. The spectral representation of a burst of speech (i.e. from a spectrogram) displays the distribution of energy (air molecule movements caused by voice projection) in the frequency domain of the speech signal as it reaches different peaks over time. We might say that these two dimensions correspond roughly to the **quality of the sound** that is produced. Taken together, the physical variations in **length**, **frequency**, and **loudness** allow listeners to distinguish new sounds.

These three dimensions of sound are to some extent redundant in the acoustic signal. In each dimension (e.g. length) are cues that are recoverable from cues in other dimensions (e.g. frequency). Because of the redundancy, the listener needs to rely only on samples of features in the stream of speech in order to make sense of a speech signal (Marslen-Wilson and Tyler, 1981). In any sampling of the speech signal, hearers utilize **decoding concepts** to construct a full analysis from a partially heard signal. In the following sections in this chapter we will consider three interdependent concepts that listeners can employ: **phonemic sequencing**, **metrical distribution**, and **tone direction** (Figure 2.1). What we will propose is that the listener gives a shape to heard speech by simultaneously employing decoding concepts in each of these domains.

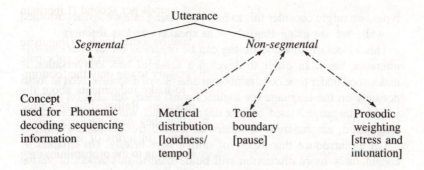

FIGURE 2.1 Phonological information available to a listener

2.1 Time in auditory perception

Before proceeding with a discussion of decoding concepts, let us consider
the type of difficulties that processing speech in real time presents. The
notion of speed often enters discussions of listening ability, as when
second-language learners feel discouraged that they cannot keep up with
the language when it is spoken at its normal speed. Many second-language
learners report that they simply cannot think fast enough to participate
in normal conversations. They feel that if speakers would slow down
or simply say less, that if they just had more time to think about what
they are hearing, they would have much less trouble understanding.

There is of course validity to the idea that time is of the essence in
understanding spoken language. Observation of encoding sequences in
spoken English in spontaneous use has led various investigators —
independently — to the finding that spoken language is produced in spurts,
which we might term 'pause units' (Brown *et al.*, 1980; Brazil, 1983;
Kreckel, 1981). Pause units in conversational English tend to have a mean
length (including hesitations) of about two seconds or approximately six
words each (Chafe, 1980).

We can make some speculations about the nature of temporal
processing based on this simple observation. Some linguists speculate
that each idea unit signifies what psychologist William James had called
a single 'perching of consciousness' or, in everyday terms, a single idea
(Chafe, 1982). If we accept this notion, then when we speak — and listen
— we are accustomed to moving from one idea to the next at the rate
of about one idea every two seconds. Although there is likely to be a
broad range of variation across languages, dialects, speakers and text

types, we might consider this to be a processing rate we are accustomed to while we are using English — as speakers and as listeners.

This aspect of time and timing can be observed on an utterance-by-utterance basis. In order to develop a sense of how conversation is understood under time constraints, our analyses of discourse need to focus not only on the language (or logical forms) used, but also on the way in which language is used, and the degree to which words are abbreviated, lengthened, emphasized, or otherwise altered from expected norms.

Let us introduce this aspect of timing here briefly. (In Chapter 4, considerably more discussion will be devoted to this aspect of verbal communication.) Let us see how timing of speaker turns might affect our sense of a conversation by comparing two presentations of the same extract. In the first version we delete all temporal indications:

[during a telephone conversation between two friends]

N: you'll come about eight right
H: okay
N: anything else to report
H: I'm getting my hair cut tomorrow
N: oh really

In the following extract, we provide three kinds of additional detail:

(1) Temporal indicators:
     : indicates a lengthening of a sound;
     = indicates absence of a pause between the end of one
     speaker's turn and the beginning of the next speaker's turn
     (.) indicates a pause of less than a second
     (.1) indicates .1 seconds, etc.
(2) Verbal and semi-verbal signals which do not add information,
     but do provide performance detail to the conversation
(3) Pronunciation variations in words or phrases:
     /.../ indicates a phonemic change from standard pronunciation;
     _____ underlining indicates segment uttered noticeably louder
     than surrounding syllables

N: anywa::y=
H: =pk! a:nywa:y
     (.3)
N: = you'll come abou:t eight (.) right=
H: = okay
     (.2)
N: anything else to report
     (.3)

H: uh:::m (.4)   Getting my <u>hair</u> cut t/i/ morrow, =
N: =oh, r/i/lly?
(adapted from Button and Casey, 1984, p. 168)

This representational detail more accurately reconstructs the way in which the speakers developed the conversation, and, for our purposes, provides additional cues concerning how the participants themselves might understand the conversation.[2] Preserving details of timing is important in characterizing the processes of decoding.

2.2   Decoding concepts: linear decoding of phonemic segments

Phonemic segments are considered the smallest units of speech that can be reliably produced and identified by speakers and hearers of a language. However, in decoding connected speech, matching sound to individual phonemes is inadequate since individual phonemes are not easily isolable. If, for example, you were to record the word 'bring' on audio tape, you would find it virtually impossible (even with precision equipment) to cut the tape into phonemic segments of /b/ + /r/ + /ɪ/ + / ŋ /, as in Figure 2.2a. As Figure 2.2b suggests, phonemic features overlap and are transmitted in parallel.

If you were to view a spectrogram of the word 'bring', you would also find it quite difficult to identify where the sound formants for /b/ end and the sound formants for /r/ begin or where the vowel /ɪ/ begins and ends. Sounds within the same utterance are coloured by effects of co-articulation with other sounds; this is particularly so for immediately

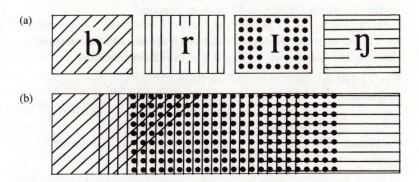

Phonemic information is not transmitted in isolated segments, as suggested in (a), but in parallel, overlapping fashion, as suggested in (b)

FIGURE 2.2   Parallel transmission of phonemic information

juxtaposed sounds (Liberman, 1970). Listeners who anticipate hearing ideal pronunciations of words will have considerable difficulty decoding connected speech since **all phonemes change their perceptual features in different phonetic environments**. As such, any ideal phoneme is an unrealistic standard against which to match heard forms.

This is not to say that the notion of an ideal phoneme is not useful for listeners. Listeners use ideal phonemes as reference templates for interpreting **stable segments** of connected speech (Liberman *et al.*, 1967; Liberman and Mattingly, 1985). However, it must be recognized that reference templates for sound recognition represent abstract averages of the language items used, rather than forms which can be restored during speech decoding.[3]

It is well known that variable realizations of phonemes (e.g. the glottalization of /t/ in *certain*, the flapping of /t/ in *butter*, the unreleased /t/ stop in *plate*) often present problems to L2 listeners who attempt to identify citation forms of the pronunciation of words. One often sees efforts made in conversations with L2 speakers to 'unsimplify' or restore phoneme segments to their ideal state in order to facilitate word recognition. However useful this may be in a given circumstance, the ultimate pedagogic value of these efforts must be questioned.[4]

Restoring a speech signal to template forms may be counterproductive to the development of listening ability since it can be demonstrated that fluent listeners recognize words in connected speech because of the allophonic variations, not in spite of them[5] (Church, 1983, 1987). Awareness of allophonic variation is apparently part of our phonotactic knowledge of a spoken language; as we become familiar with the sound system of a language, we gain a sort of phonologically motivated context sensitivity which enables us to hear variations.

From an articulatory perspective, variable realizations of phonemes are caused by **co-articulation** and **phonological context variability**. (Brown, 1977; Knowles, 1986). These will be manifest as:

free variation (inaudible releases (stops), flapping, intrusions)
assimilation   (specifically, as nasalization, labialization,
                    palatalization, glottalization, voicing, de-voicing,
                    lengthening)
reduction   (centring of vowels, weakening of consonants)
elision   (omission of individual phonemes)

Figure 2.3 displays some examples of common variable realizations. All changes involve the phenomena we have outlined, what may be collectively termed **connected speech rules**. In most cases, one can observe multiple aspects of sound change. (In the figure, however, only one focal point of change is characterized.)

FIGURE 2.3

Phrase	Connected speech rule	IPA transcription
Free variations		
never in the city	flapping of /t/	[sɪɾi]
better give up	unreleased /p/	[gɪvəpˈ]
just the idea of it (Br.)	intrusion of /r/	[aɪdɪɹəvɪt]
Assimilations		
this your handbag	labialization of /n/, elision of /d/	[hæmbæg]
just one bottle	glottalization of /t/ preceding /l/	[baʔł]
grew up in West Berlin	de-voicing of /b/	[wɛspɚlɪn]
not that boy	labialization of /t/ , devoicing of /b/	[ðætˈpɔi]
from the Red Cross	glottalization of /d/	[rɛʔkrɔs]
has a nice shape	palatalization of /s/	[naɪʃeip]
thieves stole most of them	palatalization of /v/	[ðiðstol]
there seems to be a mistake	palatalization of /m/	[sɪnztəbi]
was quite difficult	de-voicing of /d/	[kwaɪːtɪfɪkəlt]
owing to our negligence	palatalization of /ng/	[owɪntu]
didn't you see her	palatalization/co-articulation of /d/,/n/,/t/	[dɪntʃu]
What's this	elision of /t/, co-articulation of /s/ and /th/	[wɔsːɪs]
who asked him	elision of /k/(simplification of cluster)	[æstɪm]
Reductions and elisions		
near where he was found	de-aspiration of /h/	[wɛriwəz]
because of the size	weakening of /k/	[bəkəz]
comfortable chair	centring of /or/, weaking of /r/	[kamftəbl]
going to be a mess	palatalization of /ng/, centering of /oi/	[gʊnəbi]
I'll pay for it	centering of /ai/, elision of /l/	[aːpeɪ]
an unusual dress	de-voicing of /d/ preceding /r/	[ənjuʒəltrɛs]
very good	intervocalic weakening of /g/	[vɛrigud]
after all	weakening of syllable	[æftrɒl]
given to them	elision of /th/	[gɪvɳtuəm]
succeed in imposing	loss of vowel	[səksidɳɪmpozɪŋ]
terrorist attack	elision of segment	[tɛrːɪst]
problem of the environment	elision of segment	[ɛnvairmənt]

2.2.1 Phonological context

Several views of speech perception hold that words are recognized through a temporally-based process of sound-to-word matching. One such model is the 'cohort model'. According to this model words are recognized on the basis of word-initial phonological information (Marslen-Wilson and Tyler, 1981). All words activated on the basis of the word-initial information comprise the cohort. Theoretically, if the word 'coffee' is spoken to a hearer, all words in the hearer's mental lexicon beginning with /k/ are activated, then all beginning with /k-a/, then /k-a-f/, then /k-a-f-i/, as the spoken word is decoded. This activation is said to be an autonomous process in that only acoustic-phonetic information can serve to specify candidates for the word. A particular word is recognized at the point — the critical recognition point — where it is uniquely distinguished from other members of the cohort, that is, form other known words of the language beginning with the same initial sound sequence.

As a complete theory of speech perception, the cohort model is inadequate, but the theory does attempt to explain one decoding concept that listeners can utilize: linear processing. A linear model of real-time perception can be usefully modified through the notions of periodic sampling of the speech signal and recognition weights for individual words. Klatt's (1981) phonological model, called LAFS (Lexical Analysis from Spectra) provides an outline of periodic sampling processes.

Klatt's LAFS model allows for a listener to compute the spectral signal periodically and then compare this input to pre-stored spectral templates in a mental lexicon.[6] An important aspect of this model is that it avoids the need to compute representations for each phonemic segment. In Klatt's view, a competent listener's template for any lexical item could be conditioned by phonotactic knowledge that the item is likely to be uttered in different phonetic environments.

Logogen theory (Morton 1969, 1979; Morton *et al.*, 1985) provides one explanation of how lexical items come to be recognized in speech. Although the theory is not precise about how acoustic-phonetic information is used, it offers insight into the interactive nature of speech decoding and lexical access. The theory proposes that a listener has sensing devices called 'logogens', which represent each word in the listener's mental lexicon. Each logogen (which theoretically corresponds to a neural network) contains all of the information that has been acquired about each given word, such as its referential meaning, its possible syntactic function, and its phonetic structure. A logogen monitors speech for relevant sensory (i.e. auditory or visual/graphic) information and once such information is encountered, the activation level of the logogen is raised. With sufficient activation, the logogen crosses a threshold. At this time, the information about the word that the logogen represents is made available to the listener's 'response system'. Lexical access is then an automatic process once a word has been recognized.

While it is implausible that listeners allot as much attention to isolate word recognition as the theory suggests, it is important to note that the logogen model attempts to account for both context effects and frequency effects. Context effects are those conditions which allow the listener to be primed for quick recognition of lexical items.[7] This priming creates a type of 'spreading activation' during text processing (Collins and Loftus, 1975; Morton, 1969, 1979). When a word is first recognized, activation spreads to neighbouring lexical items or concepts in the mental lexicon (Aitchison, 1987). Anticipation promotes lexical effects, a faster recognition of the neighbouring words in the text.

The concept of word familiarity is handled in this model as well. Words of higher frequency, that is, words of greater familiarity for the listener (e.g. *apple, orange*) have lower activation thresholds than those of lower frequency (e.g. *avocado, kumquat*). Therefore, all else being equal, listeners are more likely to recognize a vague or ambiguous signal as a more frequently encountered item.[8]

2.3 Decoding concepts: hierarchical ordering

In the previous section we characterized how the listener can use **linear cues** in the stream of speech to help form a representation of heard speech. In this section we will characterize how the listener uses **hierarchical cues** to represent the speech signal. What we propose is that by utilizing prosodic cues which extend an entire pause unit, the listener may be able to construct a hierarchy of units in the utterance rather than relying on a linear analysis.

Much of the important prosodic information which enables listeners to identify key lexical items in a string of speech is generally termed **stress**. In English one function of stress in an utterance is to foreground, or make prominent, part of the utterance. Since stress is perceived through a combination of loudness, pause, and pitch movements, it cannot often be placed by purely objective means (Ladd, 1980; see Selkirk, 1984, for a full discussion). Skilled listeners do, however, readily perceive certain items in an utterance as foregrounded, or simply as louder than other parts.

We can visualize stress patterns by utilizing mapping techniques of metrical phonology. Metrical trees and metrical grids can be used to illustrate the perception of weak—strong contrasts in words and relative perception of stress across words in an utterance. Metrical theory posits a hierarchical system of stress contrasts between adjacent syllables in an utterance (Figure 2.4). Each pair of syllables in the utterance represents

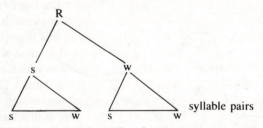

Metrical maps indicate contrasting units of stress in an utterance.

R = root of tree
s = strong
w = weak

FIGURE 2.4 A metrical mapping of an utterance

a stress contrast which is a function of a stress contrast at a higher level in the the encoding of the utterance.

The notion of metrical patterning is useful for understanding speech perception. Indeed, the metrical pattern of an utterance, which is brought about by the interplay of stressed and de-stressed syllables, has been termed the 'grid against which listeners match their perceptions' (Lenneberg, 1967). Any utterance can be mapped onto a metrical tree. By using this type of mental map, a listener can employ the concept of stress hierarchy to make sense of an utterance. The listener can rely more on the stable information in the stressed segments, which is relatively unchanged by phonological context (Grosjean and Gee, 1987). Considering these hierarchically more stable segments first, the listener constructs a **metrical template** of the utterance (Figure 2.5).

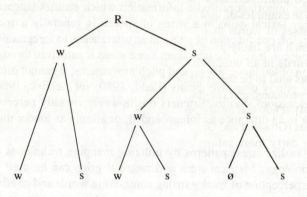

'You'll come about eight'

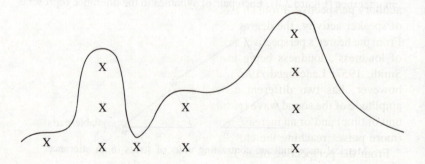

FIGURE 2.5 Two metrical representations of an utterance: a metrical tree and a metrical grid

Listeners who were sure of hearing only the segmental forms for the stressed syllables might still be able to infer the unstressed segments with this type of cognitive template. Activating a metrical template in short-term memory might allow for a delayed decoding of unstressed segments.

Another way of mapping the possible auditory effect of hearing stress contrasts may be represented by a metrical grid. A metrical grid shows the perceived hierarchical distribution of stress over a stretch of speech (Hogg and McCully, 1986). In this auditory representation, the most stressed syllables (assignable to the words *come* and *eight* in Figure 2.5) are perceived as containing stable phonemes which are less likely to undergo allophonic variations. Therefore, theoretically it would be most efficient for a listener to devote greater attention to these stable segments. This strategy entails, metaphorically speaking, identifying stressed lexical items first and unstressed segments later.

If we analyse examples of spoken English, we can begin to generalize about the classes of words that are likely to be stressed in utterances and those which are likely to be unstressed. Stressed items tend to be the **lexical words** in an utterance (nouns, verbs, adjectives, adverbs), clitic segments tend to be the **grammatical words** (articles, auxiliaries, prepositions, pronouns, and conjunctions) (Frederici and Schoenle, 1980; Selkirk, 1984). One survey study of prosodic structure in American speech samples (Grosjean and Gee, 1987) produced a continuum of forms that typically carry more information and therefore more stress.

2.3.1 Functions of stress: attentional signals

Stress can be considered from an articulatory perspective and from an auditory perspective. From an articulatory perspective stress is an aspect of speaker activity, the degree of force with which a sound is uttered. From the hearer's perspective, stress is an auditory sensation, the 'degree of loudness', loudness being the perceptual dimension (Traeger and Smith, 1957; Ladefoged, 1967). The auditory dimension of loudness, however, has two different acoustic correlates: an increase in the amplitude of the sound wave (more energy reaching the hearer's ear per unit of time) and/or an increase in the rate of vibration of the vocal cords (more pulses reaching the ear per unit of time)(Lehiste, 1972).

From the perspective of an English speaker, decisions about where to place stress are made partly on the basis of language conventions and partly on the basis of the speaker's assessment of information status in the current discourse. Certain syllables within multisyllabic words must be given lexical stress; appropriate contrast between syllables is part of the 'correct pronunciation' of a word. Beyond these conventions of English, however, stress can be used to fill communicative functions.

In general, speakers will provide stress on items that are assumed to be 'new' to the listener, or which, while known or given, need to be re-emphasized, or in terms of relevance theory, need to be made 'more manifest'. The speaker will tend to de-stress items that are assumed to be given or recoverable from context. From the listener's perspective, this encoding principle suggests a parallel decoding heuristic: give priority of attention to stressed items. The stressing of new information and the de-stressing of recoverable information is often referred to as the **given– new principle**.

To illustrate the given-new principle, let us look at a hypothetical example of one person questioning another about a past event:

A: Who went with you last night?
B: Mary went with me.
...
A: How did you go?
B: We went by car.
...
A: Did you go in your car?
B: No, we went in her car.

In each of B's responses, we expect the 'new' item to be stressed, while the others are expected to be appropriately de-stressed. For example, it would be unusual to hear:

A: Who went with you?
B: Mary went with me.

It would be unusual to stress 'went' since the questioner is apparently already aware of the fact that they went somewhere.

We expect the speaker to de-stress what is given, unless there is a reason to re-emphasize a given fact or assumption. Indeed, in most conversational usage, the given information can be ellipted entirely:

Who went with you? **Mary**.
How did you go? By **car**.
Did you go in your car? **No**, in **hers**.

The expectation that given information will be de-stressed or ellipted enables the listener to focus upon the new information, as signalled in part by stress placement.

Stressed syllables are generally easy to perceive. Problems of intelligibility arise when unaccented grammatical words in the clitic segments are perceived as part of the lexical words. One strategy that some inexperienced L2 listeners of English underuse is: map the phonetic sequence you hear over an entire stress pattern in order to identify possible words. A listener who can isolate single lexical items, even if grammatical relationships cannot be reliably identified, will in many cases still be able to construct a propositional sense of an utterance. The process of lexis-first decoding is what Schlesinger (1977) calls semantic–syntactic decoding, because the listener perceives the essential lexical cues and rapidly assigns these to case-relational roles as actor, action, object, etc., according to knowledge of the real world, and only resorts to syntactic rules when this heuristic does not work, as in very complex sentence structures.

2.4 Decoding concepts: pitch direction

Speakers raise or lower pitch while speaking through adjustment of laryngeal muscles to increase tension on the vocal cords. In English, pitch shifts can serve two broad purposes. One purpose of pitch differences is segmental: between segments in an utterance, pitch changes can mark new phonemes. The second purpose is suprasegmental: systematic pitch differences that extend over an utterance can also be used by the hearer as a source of information about speaker attitude and intention (Ladd, 1980).

Although intonation can often be used in decoding speech, it is important to note that in no domain of discourse meaning (specifically, in speaker intention) has a strong version of a functional claim been substantiated (Couper-Kuhlen, 1986). This is to say that while the function of intonation in shaping a speaker's meaning is undeniable, the communicative value of intonation by itself is limited. In most cases, intonational cues allow the listener to make only weak inferences about the intended meaning of a speaker. As will be discussed in the next chapter (dealing with listener inferences), intonation may be considered as a class of **gestural cues** which typically co-occur with other cues. It is the violation of expected co-occurrence relations which may signal a special meaning to the listener.

Two of the most consistent suprasegmental functions of intonation are in **signalling status of information** within a sequence of pause units and in **cuing desired responses** from the hearer. It has been noted that a speaker has two intonational choices in this regard: **key** and **termination**. (Brazil, 1985). 'Key' is the choice of pitch in the onset syllable of a tone unit (or pause unit). 'Termination' is the direction of pitch at the end of such a unit (Figure 2.6).

Consider the following contrast of key. In (i) the first pause unit ('I couldn't go') starts with a high key and has a low termination; the second

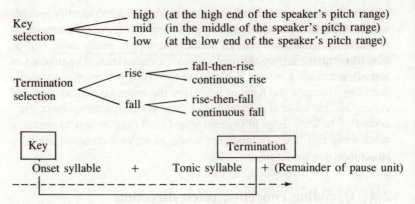

Key and termination provide cues to the information status of an utterance. (based on Brazil, 1985).

FIGURE 2.6 Key and termination

pause unit ('could I?') starts with low key and has high termination. In (ii), the second pause unit has a low termination.

(i) //I COULDn't go// COULD I?//
(second pause unit terminates on a rise (r-tone))

(ii) //I COULDn't go//COULD I?//
(second pause unit terminates on a fall (p-tone))

In nearly all dialects of English, the contrast of low (or mid)-to-high (in the first utterance) and high-to-low (or mid) (in the second utterance) suggests crucial differences in the status of 'I couldn't go', and in the status of 'could I?' The use of a high key suggests, minimally, that the speaker is treating the information to follow as requiring special attention. Termination cues assist listeners in deciding the status of information the speaker intends, although it is important to note that this use of intonation will vary according to the variety of English spoken (Australian vs. American, for example). In American English, for example, terminal rises are most often associated with direct elicits, although this may not be the case for all speakers of English. Compare for example:

(iii) I have to go now (terminal rise)
(iv) I have to go now (terminal fall)

Among American speakers of English (at least), it would be only through this intonational cue that a hearer would interpret the speaker's statement (iii) as an elicit.

In extended sequences, the contrast between pause units with rising termination and those with falling termination can be used to help signal, or reinforce, the status of information as 'new' or 'given'. In the following transcribed utterance, we can predict where rising and falling terminations will occur:

(iv) //when I was in the states//
(v) //we ran into a lot a people//
(vi) //who couldn't speak English//

Pause unit (iv) would most likely end with an 'r' (rising) tone; unit (v) with an 'l' (= level) tone; unit (vi) with an 'p' (falling) tone.

Looking at regularities of terminal tones in spoken discourse, Brazil (1985) proposes that as a rule 'r' tones are associated with given information, information that is already shared by the hearer. To underline this generality, Brazil calls these 'referring tones': they are often used to 'refer to' information already active in the speaker—listener context or to 'remind' the listener of information that should be easily recalled.

Falling intonation, on the other hand, is most often associated with new information. To emphasize this point, Brazil calls falling terminations 'proclaiming tones'. Speakers most often use falling intonation to terminate 'ideas' that are new to the listener. Level tones, in which no clear rise or fall is noted, indicate that the current 'idea' is part of the following information; it will share the same 'given' or 'new' status. By listening for information-status signals, hearers obtain cues for where to focus attention in interpretation. In social conversation, intonation cues also indicate where they can interrupt the speaker and assume a speaking turn (Beattie, 1983).

2.5 Cognitive effects in auditory perception

Recognition of items in speech depends on two kinds of information: representations computed from auditory data (i.e. segmental and metrical cues) and representations computed from context. We use the term 'context' itself to refer to what the listener already knows about the prior discourse.

Tyler and Frauenfelder (1987) draw a distinction between structural and non-structural contexts. **Structural context** results from knowledge of the constraints on the ways that items in language can combine. This type of context operates at levels of phoneme, morpheme, phrase, utterance, and discourse. Rules determining plausible combinations of morphemes in words with suffixes will constitute one type of structural constraint. At each structural level, the system of rules will differ but the function of the constraint for the listener is similar — it allows the listener to make look-ahead and look-behind assessments of language as it is heard. **Non-structural context** results from activation of concepts associated with lexical items used in the text. Non-structural context refers more to a hearer's 'knowledge of the world'. (This aspect of context will be discussed further in Chapter 3.)

2.5.1 Lexical effects

Lexical effects refer to the tendency of listeners to identify heard sounds as interpretable words if any phonological evidence allows them to do so. To illustrate, in one experiment, Ganong (1980) presented subjects with ambiguous phonemes situated along a voicing onset continuum (e.g./k/ ↔ /g/). Even when hearing an isolated word outside of a sentence context (e.g. /k/iss ↔ /g/iss), subjects tended to give more 'word' responses than 'non-word' responses. They tended to identify sounds as English words as long as there was some phonological evidence that a word could be identified (Figure 2.7).

In a similar experiment, Bond and Garnes (1980) presented subjects with three sentence contexts:

(1) *Here's the fishing gear and the (bait).*
(2) *Check the calendar and the (date).*
(3) *Paint the fence and the (gate).*

Fourteen different sound formants were used to constitute the first consonant of the target word (*bait, date, gate*). Listeners were asked

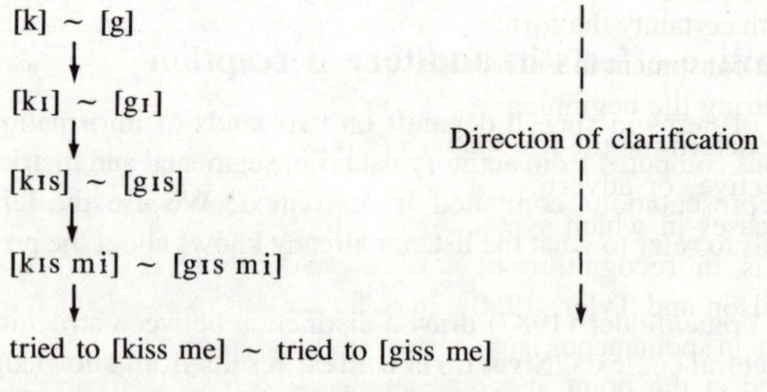

[k] ~ [g]
↓
[kɪ] ~ [gɪ]
↓   Direction of clarification
[kɪs] ~ [gɪs]
↓
[kɪs mi] ~ [gɪs mi]
↓
tried to [kiss me] ~ tried to [giss me]

As the linguistic context expands, the likelihood of word recognition increases.

FIGURE 2.7 An intelligibility matrix

to indicate on prepared answer sheets which of the three words they thought they heard: *bait, date,* or *gate*.

The results show that listeners did report hearing anomalous sentences such as 'Paint the fence and the bait'. However, when the sound formant fell into the appropriate articulatory range, in voiced—voiceless contrast (/b/ vs. /p/, /d/ vs. /t/; /g/ vs. /k/) or when it contained features of the appropriate focus of articulation (labial for /b/, palatal for /d/, velar for /g/), listeners identified the ambiguous stimuli as plausible words.

These results can explained partly in terms of a trace model of lexical access (Ellman and McClelland, 1984). In a trace model, lexical effects operate to modify the analysis of the auditory input. The modification is made on the basis of interaction with other modes of processing. Subjects modify their auditory analysis, or reinterpret their apparent misperception, on the basis of lexical expectations ('fence' goes with 'gate' , etc.). In principle, the lexical level could exert its influence on phonetic decisions after word recognition (e.g. the subject knows 'tate' was said, but realizes the speaker must have wanted to say 'date') or before word recognition (e.g. on hearing, 'Paint the fence and the . . .', the subject knows the next word is going to be 'gate'). Clearly, the contribution of the lexical level to phonetic processing is most valuable to hearers during the process of word recognition.

2.5.2 Syntactic effects

A listener attending to an utterance has information available that constrains the syntactic properties of the upcoming constituent structure. However, data on syntactic processing effects suggest that **syntactic context plays a very limited role in constraining word recognition**. This is not surprising in the case of English since it is only rarely possible to predict with certainty the form class of any given lexical item because each syntactic constituent in English has optional members. In most cases, a listener hearing the beginning of a noun phrase (e.g. 'I gave him the . . .') cannot determine the form class of the next word, which may be a noun, adjective, or adverb.

The only cases in which syntactic constraints do seem to aid word recognition is in recognition of suffixes in polymorphemic words (Marslen-Wilson and Tyler, 1980). In these circumstances (which are relatively rare in spontaneous language use), a polymorphemic word may be recognized at the point at which its stem is recognized since the syntactic context can predict the suffix. For example, having been presented sentence (1) below, the listener will be able to identify the word /justification/ in sentence (2) as soon as the stem /justifi—/ has been heard. (This is done in laboratory settings with 'gating tasks': the listener is presented progressively longer millisecond segments of a word until it can be recognized.)

(1) His action was unjustified.

(2) As far as I'm concerned, there was absolutely no /justifi—/

Although syntactic effects may not be important for decoding specific lexical items, listener familiarity with a speaker's preferred syntactic patterns may influence understanding at a global level. For instance, a speaker's use of long, complex syntactic constructions more characteristic of written style may prevent the listener from using 'normal' syntactic expectations for understanding spoken language.

2.5.3   Schematic effects

Semantic context constraints are those which involve referential associations. Semantic context results from knowledge of the probabilities of certain lexical items occurring in a specific discourse. For example, in a stretch of discourse, when the listener hears 'stock market', the listener may associate this with specific images of stock trading floors, and associate it with similar lexical items, such as *price, commodity, trade*. These associative, or 'schematic', constraints function similarly to structural constraints in that they allow the listener to make more efficient judgements about what has been heard and what might be heard next.

As we discussed earlier, these semantic context effects, which we will term **schematic effects**, allow the listener to be primed for quick recognition of lexical items. Due to priming effects in a spreading activation model (see Section 2.2), when a hearer first recognizes a word, activation spreads to related words or concepts in the mental lexicon. The activation leads to faster recognition of these related words if they are presented in the text.

An important corollary to this observation is that semantic context can

Lexical effect	— tendency to identify known lexical items in a stream of speech, rather than a random series of sounds
Schematic effect	— tendency to hear plausible lexical items, items that are likely to occur in a particular setting or context
Syntactic effect	— tendency to anticipate plausible syntactic continuations for utterances

FIGURE 2.8   Cognitive effects influencing speech perception

also be shown to inhibit correct recognition of words. A variety of studies in psychology laboratories have shown inhibitory effects of biasing of semantic context, for example, through dichotic presentations (in which the listener is presented different inputs in right and left ear) (e.g. Pisoni and Luce, 1987). Other experimental data has shown that extremely low-frequency lexical items will not be recognized at all or are more likely to be misheard (e.g. Bond and Garnes, 1980).

2.6 Parallel analysis

In a complex acoustic environment of many simultaneous (or seemingly simultaneous) auditory signals, perception seems to be strongly affected by heuristic processes that try to parse the input and recover unitary combinations of components. Hearers use their linguistic and pragmatic knowledge as they listen to try to parse what they hear. Quite often, a hearer's efforts at parsing lead to competing organizations for the same auditory stream. The hearer must solve this problem of ambiguity in real time.

Due to limitations of short-term memory, the listener must resolve ambiguity problems quickly, even if this entails an arbitrary decision about the logical form of the heard utterance (Lackner and Garrett, 1972). One view of how listeners deal with ambiguous items is called a parallel analysis. In a parallel analysis the listener computes possible constructions of different combinations of elements until the ambiguity can be resolved. If the ambiguity cannot be resolved as the discourse proceeds, the listener will make the best possible guess and carry forward this representation until it fails and needs to be revised (Johnson-Laird, 1984; Bregman, 1983; Berg, 1987).

2.7 Mishearings

Because of the necessity for a cursory examination of the speech signal and because of the possibilities for noise distortion, as listeners we often mishear the sounds that a speaker actually articulates and therefore do not understand the lexical items that the speaker is using. Moreover, because of time and planning pressures on speakers (i.e. a speaker must plan what to say next and talk at the same time) and because of the tendency of speakers to opt for ease of articulation (often at the expense of intelligibility) and to make performance errors (such as mistiming and mispitching of words), possibilities for mishearings in everyday conversation are numerous.

In this section we will look at some examples of mishearings and see how they result from the cognitive effects we have discussed (lexical effects, schematic effects, syntactic effects). Most mishearings can be identified as occurring at a segmental level. For example, we might hear 'fan'/fæn/ when 'van'/væn/ was said, or we might hear 'nose'/noz/ when 'nodes'/nodz/ was said (see Figure 2.9). Part of the explanation for word mishearing lies in the fact that the number of homophones in connected speech is far greater than a study of word morphology would suggest (Dirven and Oakeshott-Taylor, 1986). For example, in connected speech the following pairs may have the same pronunciation: 'below'—'blow'; 'cress'—'caress'.

Although these mishearings are realized at the level of phonemic features, we cannot attribute the cause of an apparent segmental mishearing simply to confusion between individual phonemes. Hierarchical cues for perception will be involved as well.

Let us look at the context of one reported mishearing to see how combined cognitive effects can influence perception.

[A calling spouse on telephone]
    A: I'm at the Quality Inn near the LA airport.
    B: At the Holiday Inn?
    A: No the Quality Inn ...

In this case, the hearer ostensibly confuses: *quality* for *holiday*, which is due in part (we might assume) to an acoustic (mis)analysis and in part to a (wrong) lexical decision. The acoustic confusion between words can

---

Mishearings that are realized at a segmental level can be categorized in terms of deletions, insertions, and errors.

consonant deletion ('nodes', 'nose') /nodz → noz/

consonant insertion ('braise', 'braids') /breiz → breidz/

consonant transversal ('tin', 'din') /tɪn → dɪn/

vowel transversal (almost always in unstressed words)

('sense', 'since') /sɛns → sɪns/

syllable deletion ('speech science', 'signs');

/spitʃ saɪəns → spitʃ saɪns/

syllable insertion ('greeted', 'created') /gritəd → krieitəd/

metathesis ('science', 'sinus') /saɪəns → saɪnəs/

multiple transversals within words ('foreign cars', 'falling cars') /farən falɪŋ/

FIGURE 2.9 **Mishearings**

be explained in reference to similarities of segments in *quality* and *holiday*. This mishearing would not be corrected by knowledge of stress distribution rules, since the word-stress pattern of *quality* and *holiday* is the same. We should note the possible influence of a schematic effect, namely, that for this listener, *Holiday Inn* may have been heard more frequently in the past and therefore is an expected item.

Some mishearings are realized as multiple feature changes across several words. These are often attributable to cursory mapping of vowel and rhythmic sequences by the listener. For example, we may hear 'Bobby wanted to go' when what was actually said was 'probably won't know'. This kind of mishearing suggests that **prosodic cues** are being used to create a 'template' for decoding. Mishearings in this category may affect only lexical identification and still preserve word boundaries (e.g. 'blow his horn'—'mow his lawn'), but quite often they affect word boundaries as well (Figure 2.10).

We can see that mishearings of this type involve a correct identity of a stressed syllable, but incorrect inferences about the clitic (unstressed) segments. In the examples (Figure 2.10), the hearer constructed a plausible lexical sequence that mapped correctly over what we have called the **rhythmic template** of the utterance.

Mishearings which conform to rhythmic templates suggest that listeners do utilize hierarchical mappings as they decode utterances. The availability of alternate hearings for an utterance (e.g. 'There's a nice team mate' for 'There's some ice tea made') may be a mark of a competent listener. We might suppose that less competent listeners, beginning second-language learners in particular, will be less able to lexicalize a mishearing. Second-language listeners may often experience an absence of lexical effects and will not be able to construct a plausible logical form for an utterance. In the following exchange, for instance, we have a mishearing in which the listener cannot lexicalize the problem:

A: I told him to go (')n find the store.
B: . . . infind? What does 'infind' mean?

(from Bond and Garnes 1980, p. 125)

descriptive	the **script** of
There's so**me ice** tea made	There's a **nice** teammate
go to the car and get the **tuna**	get my car **tun**ed up
to **zero**	his **ear** off
	(from Browman, 1980)

FIGURE 2.10 Mishearings across word boundaries

As examples like this suggest, it is often not clear to L2 listeners whether they are mishearing a known lexical item or encountering a new lexical item.

In conversations between L1 and L2 interlocutors, sequences like the following are not uncommon:

Teacher: [native speaker telling story to an L2 speaker; see Chapter 5]
            And the doctors found out that he had encephalitis.
L2 Student: sefala?

The L2 listener identifies a fragment that is problematic and needs 'repair', without knowing if the fragment is a lexical item or if it is the result of a boundary mishearing.

When L2 listeners have time to and are under task demands to construct a plausible interpretation for a 'mishearing', they are more likely to do so. The following two examples are from a lecture-based task with EFL students:

Lecturer: '. . . Another factor (promoting bilingualism) is migration . . .'
Student: [later in written summary statement] . . . One factor is vibration . . .

Lecturer: . . . 'There are two types of bilinguals, balanced and non-balanced . . .'
Student: [later in written summary statement] There are violence and non-violence bilinguals.

(data from Rost, 1987)

From the types of mishearings we have identified, we can see evidence of procedures for decoding sound sequences. When a cause for a mishearing is isolated, we have indirect evidence of the type of procedure used in successful decoding. It is quite likely that many mishearings go undetected, or are self-corrected by the listener, through use of contextual information.

2.8   Speaker variation

Mishearings, as we have described them, are due to the listener attending to what turns out to be the wrong set of cues. Many mishearings are attributable to noise distortion and speaker error, while others are caused by the listener's lack of familiarity with a particular lexical item or syntactic construction. An additional source of mishearing is the listener's lack of familiarity with a particular speech variety. Varieties of speech can be identified along various dimensions, such as age, setting, occupation, dialect, and individual voice settings (Saville-Troike, 1982; Wells, 1982). A listener's lack of familiarity with particular speech varieties may lead to frequent mishearings, even if the listener is a competent user of the language. We can speculate that any listener will find certain variations of a spoken language use to be relatively inaccessible, in spite of the listener's underlying competence with the language as a whole (Figure 2.11).

Of possible variations, speaker variation and dialect variation are most commonly reported as leading to problems of speech intelligibility. Variations in speaker voice quality and articulatory clarity exist among nearly all speakers of the same speech community and occasionally contribute to intelligibility problems. Problems of intelligibility are most pronounced, however, between speakers of different dialects.

Let us consider the ways in which accents (i.e. the spoken aspect of a dialect) vary. One way that accents differ is in the environments in which certain phonemes do or do not occur. This may be considered from the aspect of phonotactic distribution of phonemes or from the aspect of the phonological structures (e.g. syllable types) that are permissible. As Wells (1982) points out, phonotactic distribution (the set of phonetic contexts in which a given phoneme may occur) between dialects can be of great importance in intelligibility. One fundamental division in English accent types depends on the well-known distribution of the consonant /r/. In the rhotic accents (e.g. in most parts of North America), /r/ can occur with an overt phonetic realization in a wide variety of phonetic

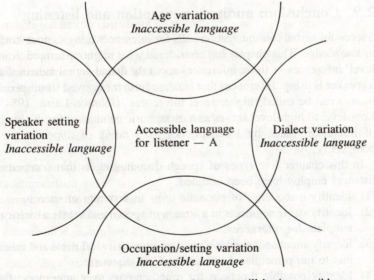

For any listener some variations of the language will be inaccessible.

FIGURE 2.11 Accessibility of linguistic variation

contexts (e.g. *farm, far, frame*), while in the non-rhotic accents (e.g. in the UK), overt phonetic realizations of /r/ are much more constrained.

Accents may also differ in the number and identity of phonemes that are used. For example, most accents of English have two distinct closed, back vowels to distinguish between 'look' and 'Luke'. In some dialects, however, there is only a single phoneme in this area. (Speakers of some varieties of English, for example, might be misheard to say 'in the mood', when they have intended to say 'in the mud'.) One can create distributional maps for how dialects differ in this respect (cf. Allen, 1976; Wells, 1970, 1982). It is probable that hearers who are unfamiliar with the accent of a given speaker need to create such a mental map of phonemic distribution in order to arrive at intelligible decodings of what is said. A hearer's initial contact with speakers of an unfamiliar dialect most often results in continuous mishearings until such systematic adjustments are made.

Accents also differ in prosodic features. Of particular importance in this respect are: **syllabification, segment duration, pace, stress**. Together, these features constitute what is often considered to be the 'rhythm' of the person's accent (Wells, 1982). Therefore, in addition to making adjustments at a segmental level, a hearer of an unfamiliar accent must learn to make prosodic adjustments as well.

2.9   Conclusion: auditory perception and listening

Successful verbal communication calls for inferences using various kinds of knowledge. This chapter has considered what might be termed 'low-level' inferences – those inferences about the actual verbal indices that a speaker is using. Inferences that become further removed from speech indices can be called 'higher level inferences' (Johnson-Laird, 1984). Low-level to high-level serves as a metaphoric continuum for the kinds of inferences made by listeners, not as a rating of importance or complexity.

In this chapter five types of speech decoding skills that competent listeners employ have been outlined:
(1) Identify a sequence of phonetic units in a stream of speech.
(2) Identify stable segments in a stream of speech and create a metrical template for utterances.
(3) Identify attentional signals a speaker gives to lexical items and relate this to the principle of 'given–new' in discourse.
(4) Identify possible functions for tone contours over utterances; for example, to indicate 'shared information' vs. 'new information' or to indicate 'question' vs. 'statement'.
(5) Adjust to speaker variation in accent or articulatory settings by

creating a 'distribution map' of the speaker's phonemic and prosodic variations.

Competent listening in English apparently depends on effective use of these interdependent skills. Although efficient auditory perception underlies effective listening, it would be oversimplifying the discussion thus far to suppose that learning to listen involves massive practice with phonological decoding alone. While it is important for learners of English to become aware of useful procedures for decoding connected speech, it is doubtful that 'fast speech rules' can be learned deductively and consciously applied in real time whenever one encounters an unfamiliar blur of sound. Rather, we should expect that learners will acquire gradually a phonological sensitivity to the new language in contexts of actual use and gradually adopt language-specific principles in decoding speech.

One conclusion for second-language pedagogy that we might extrapolate from the discussion in this chapter is the importance of developing 'selective attention'. Learner training in selective attention to phonological cues, 'attending selectively to some stimuli or aspects of those stimuli in preference to others' (Kahneman, 1973, p.3) may be useful for helping learners acquire decoding concepts in English that they may not need to employ in their first language.

2.10 Discussion questions for readers

1. Decoding sequences out of context

Ample evidence exists to support the claim that even competent listeners are unable to decode parts of an utterance which are taken out of its discourse context. As a rule, the prosodic structure which governs the individual segments must be heard in its entirety before the listener can hear the utterance as intelligible.

Audio-tape a short conversation or monologue. Play back very short decontextualized excerpts to a native-speaker listener who has not heard the full tape. Have the listener write down exactly what was heard, even when not completely sure. Write a phonetic transcription of the segment(s) you played. Compare the listener's transcription with the accurate phonetic transcription. What (if any) problems did the listener have in perception of the sounds?

2. Pause units

Audio-tape a short conversation.(You may use the same conversation you recorded for Question 1 above.) Transcribe the conversation with indications of relative pause:

]   overlapping speech from speakers
=   no pause (used when one speaker begins a turn with no
          perceptible pause following the end of the prior speaker's
          turn)
+   a short perceptible pause
+ +   a somewhat longer pause
+ + +   a very long pause

Does this representation of the time element contribute to your understanding of the conversation? If so, how? Can you suggest an alternative representation?

3. Variable realization

For each of the following transcriptions identify the connected-speech rules that are employed.

Where did you go	[wɛrdʒugo]
When does it start	[wɛnzɪtstart]
Table for three please	[teɪpfəθripliz]
It won't be but a minute	[ɪʔwõpibə rəmɪnət]
This is one of my personal favourites	[ðɪsɪzwənəmaɪ]

4. Phonological basis for mishearings

Following are some reported mishearings. The first item of each pair is what the speaker reportedly said. The second item is what the listener reported having heard. Can you identify a phonological principle that is associated with each mishearing?

I have a dental appointment — dinner appointment
They had a ten-year party for her — a tenure party
Do you know anything about four-term analogy — four
    terminology
If you enjoyed Vietnam, you'll love Angola — If you enjoyed
    meat 'n ham, ...
Where are your jeans? — Wear your jeans?
Do you own a gray Cortina? — Do you know a gray Cortina?
(from Bond and Garnes, 1980)

5. 'Frozen' mishearings

Lexical mishearings are common among L1 children, especially when children first encounter frozen, literary expressions they have never heard in normal conversation. Following is a reported example from conversations with children:

Mother: What did you learn in Sunday School today?
Child: We talked about the acts of God.
Mother: What?
Child: You know — the ax of God — it's like a hatchet.

Other examples found in the literature on mishearings are:
   of thee I sing — of the icing
   one nation, under God, indivisible — one nation, underdog, invisible
   take then thy wife and child and flee into Egypt — take then thy wife
      and child and flea into Egypt.

Have you encountered any instances of 'frozen' mishearings? Are your examples from children; from adults in their first language; from adults in their second language?

6. Metrical grids

For each of B's responses in the conversations below, construct a metrical grid that shows the expected relative stress to be given by B. What possible confusion may be created for the listener if an unexpected stress is given in one of these cases?

(a) A: What is that ugly thing on your desk?
     B: It's not ugly.
(b) A: Where's the book you borrowed from Lyn?
     B: I gave it back.
(c) A: Next, please.
     B: I'd like four cups of coffee.
(d) A: So you're quite satisfied then — with the dormitory conditions.
     B: No, on the contrary. I'm unsatisfied.
(e) A: Could I speak to Ellen please?
     B: She's not here now.

7. Schematic effects

Look at each conversation extract in which a mishearing is reported to have occurred. Can you identify what the mishearing was? What type of context effect might have contributed to each mishearing? Can you recall a similar event in which schematic effects contributed to a mishearing?

(a) [Two people are talking about a colleague]
     > Listener decodes: 'Nobody likes her now.'

(The speaker intended: 'There's nobody like her now.')
(b) [Two colleagues are discussing a report]
>Listener decodes: 'It was a horrible report.'
(The speaker intended: 'It was a tolerable report.')
(c) [An instructor addressing a class]

Some examples involving mishearings suggest that misidentifications of words occurred which could not be explained simply by phonological misestimations. In one reported case, an instructor is returning test papers to her students. The papers are in alphabetical order and as she approaches the middle of the alphabet, the instructor says, 'Barbara' and hands over a paper to an outstretched hand. The student receiving the paper, named Margaret (and not Barbara) says, 'Wait, this isn't mine.'

8. Lexical recognition

Consider the view of speech production and recognition that is suggested by the following passage from a popular novel:

> 'I've got this project I've been working on in my spare time,' he said
> ... 'Maybe you've heard about it. I've been getting people to tape-record lists of words and syllables for me.' ...
> He gave her eight yellow-boxed cartridges and a black looseleaf binder.
> 'My gosh, there's a lot,' she said, leafing through curled and mended pages in triple columns.
>
> 'It goes quickly,' Claude said. 'You just say each word clearly in your regular voice and take a little stop before the next one ...'
> She went to the desk ... and switched the recorder on. With a finger to the page, she leaned towards the microphone ... 'Taker. Takes. Taking', she said. 'Talcum. Talent. Talented. Talk. Talkative. Talked. Talker. Talking. Talks.'
> (Ira Levin, *The Stepford Wives*)

To what extent do you think it is true that as language users, we carry around with us a mental lexicon that contains words with both phonological and graphic encodings?

Notes

1. A discussion of the original motor theory of speech perception (Liberman *et al.*, 1967 and its revision, Liberman and Mattingly, 1985) is outside the scope of this chapter. The findings that led to the original theory were that acoustic patterns of synthetic speech (i.e. for speech production) had to be

modified across different contexts (e.g. Liberman *et al.*, 1952). This finding led to the notion that the 'objects' of speech perception could not be found at the acoustic surface. It was arguable therefore that some underlying phonological concept was used in decoding and encoding. In its most general form, this aspect of the original theory survives.

2. The initial exchange (A: *anyway* B: *anyway*) in this fuller transcript represents a ritualistic topic closing (in American English) in which N confirms that H has understood the topic (their meeting time) and shifts to a new topic (personal news). We can note that H's response does not come immediately, but rather follows a planning filler (Uh:::m). N's overlapping turn at the end of this segment, a sort of ratification of H's new item (getting hair cut), suggests a familiarity with the topic.

3. Hieke (1984) has suggested that second-language listeners need to learn how to restore allophonic variations to their ideal state. Presumably he suggests restoration as an awareness-raising exercise for language students, rather than as practice in an actual heuristic used by competent listeners.

4. The processes that lead to variable realizations of English phonemes are sometimes referred to as 'simplifications' of spoken English, but we must emphasize that this term itself is based on articulatory rather than acoustic evidence. For example, there are no acoustic grounds to suggest that some variants (e.g. a flapped /t/) are in any way simpler to hear than the forms they replace (e.g. an unflapped /t/).

5. For instance, fluent listeners of English can recognize that /h/ or /tʰ/ (aspirated /t/) can only initiate a new syllable, that / ʔ / (glottal stops) and unreleased stops are always syllable final, that sounds with relatively low-level sonority (specifically, the stop consonants /p/,/b/,/t/,/d/,/k/,/g/) and fricative consonants /s/,/ ʃ /,/tʃ/,/ ʒ /,/ θ /,/ f /) cannot be used as syllabics by themselves (Church, 1987; Hogg and McCully, 1986).

6. In applications for computer processing of language, Klatt suggests a sampling every 10 milliseconds is sufficient. Of course, human listeners would not be expected to sample speech as systematically, such as on a temporal basis alone.

7. A range of experiments have provided evidence, for example, that subjects will more easily recognize a word when it follows a semantically associated word (e.g. Seidenberg *et al.*, 1982).

8. It is worth noting that low-frequency items, once encountered and recognized, are more likely to be salient, and therefore more memorable. For example, the first utterance below is likely to be more memorable than the second:
   'We went to the market and bought some kumquats.' vs.
   'We went to the market and bought some oranges.'

3 Listener inference

3.0 Introduction: understanding and misunderstanding

This chapter outlines ways in which listeners form inferences as they listen. Throughout the discussion reference will be made to principles (rather than rules) that allow discourse to be interpretable to a listener. It is shown why listeners must utilize inferencing in order to make sense of discourse, and a set of procedures is given that listeners use for editing discourse in order to organize what they hear.

At the outset of this discussion, it is important to emphasize the principle of meaning as active knowledge construction, rather than as passive reception of information. Meaning in discourse is created by the listener within a personal knowledge domain. Meaning is created only by an **active listening** in which the linguistic form triggers interpretation within the listener's background and in relation to the listener's purpose, rather than conveying information. Background is then not only linguistic and pragmatic knowledge, but also a basic orientation toward the content of the discourse (Winograd and Flores, 1987). In this sense, the listener's background outlines the dimensions of what can be understood.

In the discussion of understanding in this chapter (and in later chapters), four terms relating to listener construction of meaning will be used: **acceptable understanding** (AU), **targeted understanding** (TU), **non-understanding** (NU), and **misunderstanding** (MU). Non-understanding refers to the listener being unable to draw any appropriate inference based on what a speaker has just said. Misunderstanding refers to a conflict between the type of inferences that the speaker had expected the hearer to draw from the speaker's utterances and those inferences that the hearer actually has drawn. Acceptable understanding refers to inferences drawn by a listener that are satisfactory to both speaker and listener. Targeted understanding refers to a specific interpretation that was intended by the speaker.

In this chapter, it is suggested that the listener performs the following inferential processes while listening:
(1) estimating the sense of lexical references;

(2) constructing propositional meaning through supplying case-relational links;
(3) assigning a 'base (conceptual) meaning' to the discourse;
(4) supplying underlying links in the discourse;
(5) assuming a plausible intention for the speaker's utterances.

The understanding that the listener arrives at depends in part on inferences about the **propositional sense** of what the speaker says (related to 1 and 2 above), in part on assessment of what conceptual framework must be employed to impose a **base meaning** (related to 3 and 4 above), and in part on an assignment of **interpersonal relevance** to the speaker's utterances (related to 5 above). A number of editing principles and procedures are given, by which listeners can construct meaning.

3.1 Editing strategy: estimate the sense of references

In verbal interaction, apparent discrepancies of knowledge between two interlocutors must often be tolerated in order for communication to take place. Interlocutors can typically form a satisfactory sense for a discourse without continual probing for clarification. This section provides some examples of how this tolerance can lead to acceptable understandings or to misunderstandings.

Let us take first an example of a misunderstanding. In the following extract, a native speaker (NS), Alan (A), is talking with a NNS (non-native speaker), Hiro (H), who is a native speaker of Japanese. One of the participants experiences some ambiguity about a reference ('priest' in Turns 6—8).

[after some discussion about smoking]
T1/A: Do other people in your family smoke too?
T2/H: Um, yeah, they smoke.
T3/A: Uh-huh + + +
T4/H: Um, all, um, family smoke.
T5/A: So they don't mind if you smoke, I guess + + my father would
T6/H: My father is /pri:zudu /.
T7/A: Your father is a + /prist/!? +
T8/H: Yes, he's /pri:zudu/

Having experienced this ambiguity, the listener can decide on one of of three actions: (1) tolerate the ambiguity for the time being so as not to interfere with the flow of the discourse, realizing that the ambiguity can be clarified later if it becomes important to do so; (2) assume that the speaker has made a lexical error and substitute the intended, or another appropriate lexical item; (3) skip over the problem, assuming that clarification of the ambiguous element is unlikely to assist his understanding of the overall discourse.

The misunderstanding can be traced to a referential gap in Turns 6—8: the item /pri:zudu/ was heard — or reformulated — by the listener as 'a priest'. The perceived statement 'my father is a priest' created a schematic mapping problem for Alan: he didn't expect that Hiro's father would be a priest, nor did he expect that information about Hiro's father's 'occupation' would have any bearing on the current discourse topic (family's approval of a child smoking). Because of this understanding problem, Alan initiates a **repair** sequence (Turn 7), querying whether this information is indeed what Hiro has in mind. (The use of repair will be discussed further in Chapter 4.) Hiro reiterates (or so Alan thinks) that this is the information he intended Alan to understand.

What turned out to be the source of the problem was a mishearing of 'priest' for 'pleased' — in this case due apparently in part to an intelligibility problem based on Hiro's Japanese-influenced pronunciation of 'pleased', and to the unexpectedness of the word 'pleased' to occur in this context. ('My father doesn't mind', for example, would be more likely.) Based on an intelligibility problem, the misunderstanding has a distinctive NS—NNS flavour to it.

Between native speakers of a language, understanding problems traceable to single indices in the discourse are most often due to lack of familiarity with speaker references rather than to intelligibility problems *per se*. Among more proficient speakers of a language, reference problems are likely to emerge only when a person is describing a topic with specialized jargon (such as scuba-diving, carpentry, phonology) to someone who is not familiar with the specialized terms.

Referential gaps are often, however, related to the problematic nature of lexical denotation itself, particularly the problem of referential 'fuzziness'. For example, when a person refers to a room as being *filthy* (or /sleazy/ dirty/clean/immaculate/spotless, etc.), the listener can only estimate the user's sense for the lexical item. Problems of reference are probably much more acute with verbal and adjectival expressions since, unlike nominal expressions, they most often include an element of qualitative judgement (Gairns and Redman, 1987).

Let us examine a case of estimated meaning boundaries for adjectival expressions. In some varieties of Portuguese, a speaker may use one of several terms to refer to the race of someone based on appearance of skin and hair: *branca, sarara, morena, cabo verde, preta*. When a speaker uses any of these terms, the listener might reasonably suppose that the speaker has in mind definitions for these terms that are similar to the listener's own. As a short-cut procedure for estimating the sense of the speaker's references, the listener will probably assume (if the speaker is a member of the same speech community) that the speaker will have acquired a typical componential lexical map for the terms used (Figure 3.1).

When a certain person is described as, say, a *preta*, the listener, being a member of this speech community, is likely to activate an image of someone with rather dark skin and very wavy or kinky hair. Only if evidence emerges that the speaker has a different lexical map will the speaker's use of the terms need to be clarified.

The components make up the framework against which the speakers refer to items: as long as there is no evidence of conflicting frameworks of reference, the referencing process continues without the need for clarification. If evidence of reference conflict does emerge, the interlocutors may query what sorts of components each has in mind when using certain words. In most social settings, however, interlocutors are expected to tolerate a degree of ambiguity as problematic lexical items come up in discourse. If problems of reference exceed the listener's threshold for ambiguity, the listener may be forced to seek clarification or simply abandon efforts to make sense of the discourse (see Garnham, 1986; Ellis and Beattie, 1986; Dolitsky, 1984, for a discussion).

Although problems of reference are particularly acute in NS–NNS interaction, even people assumed to be members of the same speech community experience problems of **lexical fuzziness**. For interlocutors

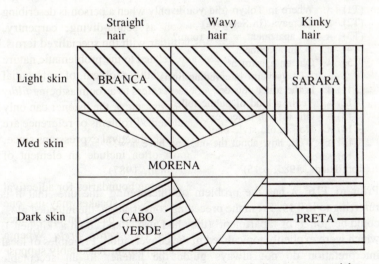

Speakers in the same speech community assume similar 'componential maps' for the words they use.

FIGURE 3.1 A model for understanding lexical references (based on Sanjek, 1971)

not of the same speech community, clarifications of lexical items are likely to be more frequent, but are none the less due to the same linguistic phenomenon — the interlocutors may not share identical parameters for referring to items, actions, events, qualities, etc.

A second source of difficulty in achieving successful reference in discourse is related to **continuity of co-references**. In any discourse the same lexical item may be referred to in different ways: as a fully repeated form (Mr Smith—Mr Smith); as a partially repeated form (Mr Smith—Smith); with a lexical substitution (Mr Smith—John—that man—the friend I was with when I met you, etc.); with a pronominal form (Mr Smith—him). Understanding discourse references is not simply a matter of constructing a feasible reference, but rather finding an appropriate gloss for the items being used in the discourse (Heyman, 1986).

Let us consider an example of how glosses for references can be misunderstood. In the following extract the listener experiences some confusion over the appropriate gloss when co-referencing is used: the listener is not sure of which of two or three candidates might be appropriate. This conversation (translated into English for this analysis) took place at the University of Hawaii between two male speakers of Japanese who had met each other previously, but were not close friends.) The understanding problem occurs at Turn 15.

(T1)   A: Where in Tokyo (did you live)?
(T2)   B: Setagaya (In Setagaya)
(T3)   A: An apartment = or a room?
(T4)   B: = an apartment
(T5)   A: Oh, an apartment . . .
              . . ./several intervening turns/
(T11) B: Is the toilet outside?
(T12) A: Yeah, a kind of public toilet.
(T13) B: Oh, a flush toilet, or?
(T14) A: No, an old style one.
(T15) B: Well, how about the one you have now?
(T16) A: . . .
(from Hinds, 1985, p.15)

Prior to T16, A has the problem of interpreting 'the one' that B is referring to in T15. From the preceding conversation, the intended gloss could be 'toilet' or 'apartment' (they had also talked about a 'kitchen'), which were explicitly topicalized in the conversation. Principles of local interpretation do not always guide the listener to an acceptable understanding. The listener can only choose the most salient gloss, whether this is the most recent topic mentioned, the first topic mentioned, or indeed a topic that has not been mentioned explicitly (but is salient from previous encounters between these interlocutors).

Resolving such problems of referential cohesion, particularly those involving anaphora and lexical substitution, frequently leads to referential problems for both L1 and L2 listeners. What seems to be peculiar about L2 listener problems with references is that the L2 listener, while fully realizing a problem exists, may not be able to trace the problem to specific references (Bremer *et al.*, 1988; Gass and Varonis, 1985). Bremer *et al.* label such occurrences **global understanding problems**: the listener cannot identify exactly where in the speaker's text the understanding problem originates and attributes the problem to the text as a whole.

Below is a summary of the types of referential problems listeners are likely to encounter. Listener strategies for dealing with these problems are suggested.

Problem: unfamiliarity with specialized jargon
Listener strategies: ignore specialized terms; tolerate ambiguity; guess meaning; ask speaker for a paraphrase

Problem: lexical fuzziness
Listener strategies: assume most common sense; estimate meaning from other speaker cues; ask for paraphrase; tolerate ambiguity

Problem: multiple co-reference possibilities
Listener strategies: select most salient gloss

Problem: unlikely reference
Listener strategies: assume speaker error; ask for clarification; tolerate ambiguity

3.2 Editing strategy: supply case-relational links within propositions

An examination of conversational texts quite often reveals that the case-relational links between items in a discourse are not explicit. For example, in the following exchange, it is not possible to identify explicit propositions in B's responses:

(T1) A: Do you live near here?
(T2) B: Yes.
(T3) A: Alone?
(T4) B: With my family.

However, it is obvious that B is being cooperative in assuring that all the propositional content is at least recoverable, even if it is not explicit.

Yes, *I live near here.*
No, *I don't live alone.*
I live with my family.

In many settings, a listener who hears a burst of speech can to some extent bypass syntactic analysis and derive information directly from the word meanings, or through an abbreviated analysis of relations among the words identified (Small and Rieger, 1982; Aitchison, 1983). The links between lexical items in a discourse text can be termed the **case relations** between items (Fillmore, 1968, 1977; Givon, 1979.)

The semantic relations between items in discourse, whether made explicit by the speaker or inferred by the listener, are typically referred to as **propositions**; propositions are said to 'carry' the information in a text (deBeaugrande, 1980). Although the term 'information' has often been used to encompass all of the speaker's assumptions that are associated with utterances, the term 'information' is used here to designate only the potential that the text has for making such assumptions accessible to the listener.

Since not all of the recoverable information can ever be explicit in any utterance (not without producing very tedious texts), it is important to realize that propositions, as units of discourse meaning, are **recoverable mental representations that link items in a discourse rather than text-defined units**. Lexical items may be unambiguous in a specific discourse and the speaker of the items may indicate the semantic relations between the lexical items used, but the necessary association of the ideas by the listener is not entirely predicted from formal features of the lexical items or the grammar of the utterance. Rather than having their meaning determined by formal semantic relationships, propositions are controlled by the links that the text user assigns to the elements they contain (deBeaugrande, 1980). Propositional content must then be constructed by the listener through **text-based inferences**, rather than fully recovered from the text.

One of the listener's interpretive tasks in discourse involves finding case-relational links for lexical items. The major linguistic-based problems for the listener in doing this relate to the interpreting of expressions in which the speaker uses ellipsis. Let us examine one case in which use of ellipsis is apparent.

Ricento (1987) points out that understanding many utterances in naturally occurring discourse requires a reconstruction of elliptical case frames. In the following excerpt, for instance, interpretation of several of the speaker contributions requires inference of case relations.

[In this exchange, A, S, and L are providing the setting for a film they have just seen for the benefit of C, who has not seen the film.]

(T1) A: Oh, maybe we should mention that it's a really ... it looks like a warm day, too, and clear blue skies and the sun is out and the ... both the man and the boy are wearing wide-brimmed hats, you know, sort of

(T2) C: like cowboy hats

(T3) S: No

(T4) L: No, sort of like, they're made sort of like, um ...

(T5) S: like a ... farmer hat

(T6) L: straw

(T7) C: Um, big brim ... or

(T8) S: straw ... big

(T9) A: big, like real ... big brim

(T10) S: Yeah, but it curves

(T11) A: Not real big, no

(T12) C: So it's more like a peasant hat than a sombrero

(T13) A: Yeah

(T14) S: Yeah

(T15) L: Yeah

(from Ricento, 1987, p.752)

What we see in this conversation extract is that most of the case relations between adjacent items (e.g. Turns 2,6,8) are not explicit in the actual text. The ellipted forms could be easily reconstituted (if necessary) through reference to surrounding turns in the discourse.

The use of ellipsis is a continuity strategy which allows the speaker to introduce new information more quickly; speakers use ellipsis on the assumption that the listener will be able to recover given items and given links between items. When the listener experiences discontinuity (that is, cannot recover the items or the links), the continuity strategy has failed and the listener must seek some kind of clarification. Lexical items that were infelicitously omitted must be reinstated; links that were assumed to be understood must be made explicit.

3.3   Editing strategy: construct a base meaning

Difficulties in making case-relational inferences are not uncommon for L1 listeners, especially for listeners in the role of bystander or overhearer (Thomas, 1985; McGregor, 1986) and particularly (as with referential inferencing) when overhearing discourse involving specialized terminology. This section outlines some of the inferencing problems that a listener encounters at this 'higher' level of inferencing.

Let us illustrate an inferencing problem with an example based on an excerpt taped from an American radio program in 1972. An overhearer would most likely have considerable inferencing problems upon tuning in to hear the following:

Guest:	so for people today it's not what's really real . . .
Interviewer:	so you're equating reality with what comes from your gut?
Guest:	yeah + uh + what do you mean by reality?
Interviewer:	you just said that what's not really real is what doesn't come from your gut
Guest:	so, yeah, if it comes from your gut.
Interviewer:	right
Guest:	then it's real . . . right

Overhearers will most likely have difficulties in estimating many lexical references and in finding suitable co-references in this dialogue ('real', 'what's real', 'gut', 'what comes from your gut'). In order to make sense of the dialogue, the hearer has to construct a general **base meaning**, or a set of unified concepts, which provides a framework for the references used. The framework defines terms in relation to each other; when the listener can retrieve the appropriate framework, the text begins to make sense.

Incorporating these aspects of listener inferencing with the notion of a cultural frame of reference, we can define base meaning for a text as the cultural and experiential frame of reference that makes a text interpretable by a listener. The following sections refer to four aspects of this rather complex notion: cultural schemata, schema and script slots, supporting data, and rhetorical genres.

3.3.1 Editing strategy: employ cultural schemata

As Labov and Fanshell (1977) have suggested, links between utterances are often not apparent at the level of form, but are implied by the speaker and inferred by the listener via **underlying propositions**. Participants in a successful conversation know what the salient underlying propositions are and can utilize them as indirect means of achieving understanding, while in an unsuccessful conversation one of the participants may not be able to identify cohesive underlying propositions. This type of misunderstanding is particularly noticeable in cross-cultural encounters. (Some cases of this kind of misunderstanding are examined in Chapter 4.)

Let us illustrate the use of underlying propositions through the following fictitious situation. There is one *Peanuts* cartoon sequence in which Linus (L), a young boy, knocks on the door of Violet (V), a girl a few years older than he is.

L: Do you want to play with me?

v: You're younger than me. [shuts the door]
L: [puzzled] She didn't answer my question.

In this misunderstanding, Linus apparently does not supply the key underlying proposition in Violet's base meaning for the event: 'Older children don't play with younger children.' This underlying proposition is not recoverable from the text alone: the real propositional meaning of Violet's utterance is not explicit. Cues in a text quite often are, as in this example, insufficient to signal the knowledge that must be activated in order for the listener to arrive at an acceptable understanding.

3.3.2 Editing strategy: fill in schematic slots

A base meaning permits expectations as to what types of inferences will be required to understand the discourse. The notion of base meaning underlies the psychological construct of a script (e.g. Abelson, 1981; Schank and Riesbeck, 1981) in which certain slots must be filled by the listener. The phenomenon of understanding through filling in the missing slots is often referred to as schematic understanding (e.g. Anderson, 1977). The key point of a schematic model of understanding is that **schemata are evoked by words in the text**. Schemata contain slots; once certain slots in a schema are filled with text information, other slots become easier to fill (Kay, 1987). The grammar and lexicon of the text create equations among the slots in a specific instantiation of a schema. (See Figure 3.2 for an example of a schematic representation.) The listener's task in understanding a speaker will involve integrating knowledge from schemata (associated with the utterance) and the propositional information available.

3.3.3 Editing strategy: fill in supporting data for claims

Within speech act theory (introduced in Chapter 1), speaker contributions to discourse are viewed as 'acts' with underlying intents. An important aspect of understanding a speaker's act is realizing the conditions which make that act plausible and 'felicitous' (or consistent with known facts). Since the most common speech acts are representative or expressive in nature (see Section 3.4 below for definitions of these terms), understanding a claim of a speaker (e.g. 'This is the best report I've seen on this topic'; 'That dessert didn't quite agree with me.') involves inferring data that support the claim.

As Toulmin *et al.* (1983) point out, whenever a person makes a claim, let us say of the sort, 'Mike will probably be late for class today', the

The utterance: 'The chef went to Fisherman's Wharf and bought some fish from some fishermen.'

Heard word — evokes » **SCHEMA** » which contains obligatory **slots**

chef	— RESTAURANT	» (food on the menus, tables, customers ...)
went to	— JOURNEY	» (traveller, means of transportation, time needed for journey, ...)
Fisherman's Wharf	— PLACE	» (conditions of the place, people living and working there, ...)
and bought	— COMMERCIAL EVENT	» (money, standards of pricing, buyer, seller, ...)
some fish	— ITEM	» (variety of items available, condition of items, owner of items ...)

(based on Kay, 1987, p.223)

FIGURE 3.2   Schematic representation of an utterance

person is accountable, if asked, to produce the data on which the claim is based. For instance, if one datum that the speaker possesses is 'It's raining' and this is already obvious to the listener, and if the listener accepts the relationship between known facts and what was said, the speaker will typically not be asked to spell out the relationship between

Data	**Claim**
It's raining	*so Mike will probably be late*
since Mike drives his car to school	
since class starts at 6 p.m.	
since rush hour is around 6 p.m.	
since drivers go more slowly in the rain	
since drivers want to be safe	
since rain reduces friction	
ground of	
argument SINCE THAT IS THE WAY NATURE IS	

FIGURE 3.3   Inferring supporting data for a claim

A 1979 interview (translated into English) between Oriana Falacci, an Italian reporter, and the late Ayatollah Khomeini

> Reporter: Imam Khomeini, the entire country is in your hands. Every decision you make is an order. So there are many in your country who say that in Iran there is no freedom, that the revolution did not bring freedom.

Comment: The reporter's claim is 'In Iran there is no freedom'; her datum is 'the entire country is in your hands'; the relationship, if made explicit, is 'If an entire country is in one person's hands, there is no freedom.' As Johnstone notes, 'this sounds acceptable to *New York Times* readers, who are used to this sort of conception of what constitutes political freedom'.

> Khomeini: Iran is not in my hands. It is in the hands of the people, because it was the people who handed the country over to the person who is their servant, and who wants only what is good for them.

Comment: Khomeini's argument also involves a claim: 'Iran is not in my hands' and a datum: 'the people handed the country over to me', which are related through a concept, if made explicit, of: 'If people put themselves under someone else's control, they have shown that they are free.'

(from Johnstone, 1985, p.172)

FIGURE 3.4 An illustration of using (and disputing) data to support a claim

the data and the claim. Still, the proposition which connects the two underlies the argument, and can be made overt, if necessary[1] (see Figure 3.3).

Misunderstandings arise when interlocutors differ as to what constitute valid supporting data for a claim.[2] Johnstone (1985), for example, considers an extended example of misunderstanding involving disagreement over what constitutes supporting data for an abstract claim such as 'The people of this country are free' (see Figure 3.4).

3.3.4 Editing strategy: use genres to generate expectations

Schema theory can be applied to explain listener understanding of single utterances (such as 'The fisherman went to Fisherman's Wharf to buy some fish'); it can also be applied to explain listener understanding of larger texts. In both cases, the listener operates on a principle of analogy, which might be paraphrased as: 'I've been in a situation something like this before, so what is happening here will be similar to what happened before' (Brown and Yule, 1983). The principle of analogy can be applied to people ('this person usually says things like that') and to places ('that's

Genre	Categories formulated by listener
Descriptions	Scope of description
	Identity of individual items
	Qualities associated with items
Narratives	Event boundaries
	Characters involved
	Causes/precedents for actions
	Outcomes of actions
Arguments	Grounds
	Claims
	Warrants
	Backing
Social conversation	Topic fields
	Plausible intentions of speaker

FIGURE 3.5 Text genres and semantic categories associated with text genres

the kind of conversation you often hear in places like that'), and to text types ('that's what usually happens in stories like that').

By using the principle of analogy, a listener can anticipate what schemata will be useful in interpreting an event or a text effectively. Adopting schema theory, we can postulate that knowledge structures will consist of categories that need to be filled with particular units from the text in question. (deBeaugrande, 1980; Meyer, 1975). As the listener identifies a particular genre (e.g. folk tales, lectures on linguistics, descriptions of a new house), schematic slots are suggested that the listener must fill in order to arrive at an acceptable understanding of the text. Figure 3.5 presents some common units associated with genres.

3.4 Editing strategy: supply plausible intention for speaker

It has been claimed that information in a discourse cannot be recovered directly from language used; the information must be inferred by way of underlying links. Editing strategies help the listener construct reasonable hypotheses about the discourse meaning. A listener with adequate knowledge of a language and adequate experience with conventions of language use (e.g. rhetorical genres) can construct an acceptable understanding of the discourse. However, even experienced listeners will regularly experience understanding problems, as not all understanding problems can be resolved solely through reliance on conventional linguistic knowledge.

The listener may attempt to arrive at an identity for underlying propositions by interpreting speaker contributions, not only on the level of **form** (what is said), but also on the level of **discourse** (what is done) and on the level of **strategy** (what is to be accomplished) (Labov and Fanshell, 1977). Speaker acts, or speech acts, then, can be interpreted as having not only decodable locutionary value, but also as having inferable **illocutionary values**. The salient relationships of these values serve as implicit links in discourse; it is through these links that a listener arrives at a relevant understanding.

Most current categorization systems for speech acts have been influenced by the work of Austin (1962), Grice (1969, 1975), and Searle (1975). Figure 3.6 presents the most commonly used classification for speech acts.

The most commonly used speech acts are those in which the speaker seeks to influence the listener at a cognitive level, to induce the hearer to believe or acknowledge an explicit or implicit proposition, to create the conditions in the hearer which will allow subsequent acts (including non-linguistic ones) to appear as felicitous. The mutual construction of belief in discourse propositions serves to create conversational coherence.

Type of act	Illocutionary point	Intended effect on hearer
I *Representative*	Commit speaker to truth of expressed proposition	Believe S's representation is valid
[examples: state, describe, hypothesize, boast, complain]		
II *Directive*	Attempt to get H to do something	Acknowledge S's desire
[examples: request, order, beg]		
III *Commissive*	Commit S to a future course of action	Acknowledge S's intent
[examples: promise, threaten]		
IV *Expressive*	Express psychological condition about a state of affairs	Acknowledge S's attitude
[examples: congratulate, apologize, thank]		
V *Declarative*	Bring about correspondence between statement and reality	Acknowledge 'new' state
[examples: resign, fire, appoint]		

FIGURE 3.6 Speech acts (based on Searle, 1975)

When the speaker does not find evidence in the listener's participation display that the speaker's intentions are being acknowledged (or that the speaker's propositions are being accepted as true), conflict arises.

Speech act theory has often been misinterpreted as suggesting that single utterances correspond to single speech acts. However, in everyday conversation, speech acts are very often achieved indirectly and are, in general, realized only over several speaking turns. An analysis of listener understanding must account for this non-correspondence of form to function and for other related issues: the indeterminacy of speaker intent in single utterances and the possibility that speaker acts may have more than one intent, or indeed, an ambiguous intent (Thomas, 1985).

For instance, in the following extract, we can see how, from the listener's (R) perspective, understanding is achieved through multiple attempts over a series of speaking turns.

(T1) c: So I was wondering would you be in your office on Monday (.) by any chance?
(T2)   (2.0 pause)
(T3) c: Probably not.
(T4) R: Hmm yes=
(T5) c: =You would?
(T6) R: Ya.
(T7) c: So if we came by could you give us ten minutes of your time?

(from Levinson, 1983, p.320)

In this example, R has probably heard c's Turns 1−3 as an indirect request (to visit R on Monday), and not as an end in itself (knowledge of R's schedule). Just as the speaker chooses social strategies (involving indirectness) to accomplish particular aims (presumably in this case to get an appointment and to appear amicable about doing so), the listener can enact strategies for interpreting the speaker's utterances.

3.4.1 Editing principle: assume speaker is being cooperative

While some speech acts require several turns to become explicit (as in our previous example), many speaker intentions are never made explicit. The **perlocutionary effect** is achieved indirectly. In handling the phenomenon of understanding in conversation, it is essential to incorporate the notion of interpreting **indirectness**. Indirectness succeeds (when it does) through mutual reference to pragmatic principles or maxims (Edmonson, 1981; Leech, 1983; Levinson, 1983; Burton, 1981).

In order for conversation to proceed smoothly, conversational participants must assume that all participants will adhere to certain **conversational maxims**, or **cooperative principles**. Speech act theorists have proposed that speakers make their contributions in the light of the maxims of quantity, quality, relation, manner, and appropriacy. Other theorists (e.g. Leech, 1983) have expanded conversational maxims to include politeness principles of agreement, approbation, generosity, modesty, sympathy, tact. Figure 3.7 sets out 'user definitions' of these maxims.

Conversational maxims, which are clearly cultural-specific (although some universal principles may hold) and culturally transmitted, can be said to constrain the speaker's action in such a way that the hearer will more likely be able to recover underlying intentions. Conversational maxims, in turn, allow the speaker to interpret listener feedback as relevant to the intention of the speaker.

For our discussion of listener inference, speech act theory is most useful in suggesting a single broad **interpretive principle** which listeners use as they listen: the listener assumes that the speaker is trying to accomplish something at a strategic level by speaking. Using the assumption that the speaker is trying to achieve an interactive effect, the listener can then consider plausible intentions for utterances. The listener can search for

---

Conversational Maxims

Quantity	Make your contribution informative and only as informative as required for the purpose of the exchange.
Quality	Say only that which you believe you have sufficient evidence to support. Do not say what you believe to be false.
Relation	Make your contributions relevant to the discourse.
Manner	Be clear, brief, and orderly.
Appropriacy	Be polite; make your contributions at the appropriate level of formality.

(based on Grice, 1975)

Politeness principles

Tact	Minimize the cost to other person; maximize the benefit to the other
Generosity	Minimize benefit to self; maximize cost to self
Modesty	Minimize praise of self; maximize dispraise of self
Solidarity	Minimize disagreement between self and other; maximize agreement and sympathy between self and other

(based on Leech, 1983)

FIGURE 3.7 Pragmatic principles for use in understanding discourse

cues — verbal, vocal, visual — for what it is that the speaker may be trying to accomplish. To take a frequently used example (from Leech 1983, p.38), if a listener hears a speaker sitting across the room say, 'Cold in here, isn't it?', the listener might reasonably construe this as a directive ('turn on the heater') that is couched in politeness tactics. In effect, 'Cold in here, isn't it?' says more than 'Turn on the heater' in that the speaker may intend to both communicate a directive and to elicit a sign of solidarity (by seeking agreement). As this example suggests, the speaker may have more than a single intent in making the utterance; at the same time, the intent that the listener recovers may not be the only intent of the speaker.

3.4.2   Editing strategy: use visual and vocal cues to infer speaker intention

Speech acts are achieved not entirely by linguistic means, but through convergences of linguistic, paralinguistic and non-linguistic cues. Listener inferences of speaker intentions then need to be based on perception of all of these cues.

In face-to-face interactions, visual cues include **gaze direction**, **body position**, and **facial gestures** (Noller, 1984). Figure 3.8 sets out the variables for each type of cue.

Another class of cues which may furnish evidence of speaker intention are **vocal cues**. These include marked variations of pitch span, tempo, loudness, articulatory setting and timing that are heard across an utterance. For a given speaker, use of marked features (i.e. other than what the speaker usually uses) may signal to the listener that the speaker is giving a special attitudinal weight to the utterance. By using cues from

---

Gaze direction: unmarked, or down, to the right or left of listener, directly at the listener, switching gaze from face to face of multiple listeners, other.

Body position: unmarked, or touching listener, touching objects, moving toward listener (distance reduction), open arms, arms crossed, body upright (attention position), body relaxed, body limp (inattention position), leaning forward, neck or arms tense, pointing/jabbing/slicing gesture, hands thrown up, arms open and down, moving head up and down, moving head back and forth, rude gesture; other movement of body

Facial gesture: unmarked, or smile, empathetic expression, head nod, frown, sneer, fearful expression, cry, smirk, shock, angry expression, disgust, glare, other

---

FIGURE 3.8 Non-linguistic cues in face-to-face communication

			Marked vocal features				
ps	vr	tmp	ld	vs	as	ap	tm

	ps	vr	tmp	ld	vs	as	ap	tm
excited	ext							
pompous	low		slow				prc	
depressed	rst	low		soft			slr	
nervous		rsd	rpd		brt	tense		
shocked	ext	rsd	rpd	loud	brt	tense		ext
affectionate		ext						ext
cold		rst				tense		
thoughtful			slow					
sexy	ext	low	slow	soft	brt		slr	
angry	ext	rsd	rpd	loud		tense	prc	
fearful		rst						

ps = pitch span: extended (ext), restricted (rst), or unmarked
vr = voice range: low, raised (rsd), or unmarked
tmp = tempo: slow, rapid (rpd), or unmarked
ld = loudness: soft, loud, or unmarked
vs = voice setting: breathy (brt) or unmarked
as = articulatory setting: tense or unmarked
ap = articulatory precision: precise (prc), slurred (slr), or unmarked
tm = timing: extended (ext) or unmarked

FIGURE 3.9 Vocal cues associated with speaker attitudes

vocal settings, the listener can make stronger inferences about the meaning of an utterance. Figure 3.9 presents a configuration of some of the vocal cues that have been associated with 'attitudes' of English speakers (Brown, 1977; Couper-Kuhlen, 1986; Crystal, 1969; Davitz, 1964).

By themselves, gestural cues, such as vocal markings, provide the basis for weak inferences about speaker meaning. When all gestural cues converge in an expected way, the listener may be assisted in drawing acceptable inferences. The influence of gestural cues in verbal communication can often be most easily detected in cases in which visual or vocal signals seem to contradict the verbal signal. Visual and vocal cues are part of the overall ostensive signal given by the speaker. They cannot be reliably interpreted as isolated signals: they suggest a convergence towards or a divergence away from the verbal signal. Perception of speaker intention, to the extent that intention can be perceived, depends on the interplay of verbal, vocal, and visual features.

3.5 Listener triangulation of speaker intention

In the view of language that has been adopted in this discussion, language use involves linguistic, ideational, and interpersonal domains. The meaning of an utterance cannot be derived without reference to all three domains. Within this view, language is a form of social action and is directed toward creating what Maturana (1980) has called 'mutual orientation'. This backdrop is essential to viewing the listener's role as more than a 'receiver of meaning'. As Winograd and Flores (1987) maintain, mutual orientation is not grounded in a representational correspondence between language and the world. Mutual orientation exists rather as a 'consensual domain' — as interlinked patterns of activity. This shift from 'language as description' to 'language as action' is the basis of speech act theory, which emphasizes the interactive nature of language rather than its role as 'representing meaning'.

As Pellowe (1986) and Sperber and Wilson (1986) point out, there are strong arguments against attempting to handle the phenomenon of illocutionary understanding entirely through a rational analysis of the intentions of the speaker.[3] One argument they give is related to the recoverability of the speaker's intention by the speaker: people often do not know why they say what they say. People often speak without having single, specific, or recoverable intentions. In addition, speakers often make remarks whose ambiguity has clear social motivation (Brown and Levinson, 1978; Thomas, 1985).

The second argument against trying to equate discourse meanings with speakers' intentions is that hearers are not passive transformers. Hearers may also have intentions. If hearers can have intentions in respect of what speakers do or say, then the detailed intention which a speaker may have cannot be guaranteed to be recovered by the hearer.

> Just as the speaker is endowed with intentions in speaking, we must assume that the listener is endowed with intentions in the context of communication. He [may or may not] choose to make an interpretation which represents as nearly as possible the speaker's point of view, to formulate what he thinks in a maximally reassuring and cooperative way. As a listener one can decide to be uncooperative, choosing not to process what the speaker is saying ... We could talk in terms of a scale of cooperativeness ...

(from Brown, 1986, p. 287)

In this view, the nature and degree of attention which the hearer gives to the speaker's remarks is determined by the hearer, not by the illocutionary force of the speaker. A hearer may intend, for example, prior to or during the speaker's remarks, to override the speaker, to discredit or embarrass or confuse the speaker, or to make light of whatever it is that the speaker says. In addition, a hearer, like a speaker, is likely to have more than one intention during any specific discourse, which can lead to simultaneous construction of two meanings for the same remark (as in the 'It's cold in here' example cited earlier). Similarly, the speaker may have two intentions, targeted for different hearers (as when a dentist says with patient and assistant present, 'I think we'd better take an X-ray', one intention might be to inform the patient of the planned treatment; another intention might be to direct the assistant to prepare to take the X-ray). Under these conditions, there is no guarantee that the meaning the hearer constructs for a speaker's remark will reflect the speaker's intention in uttering that remark. (See Thomas, 1985, for thorough discussion of multi-valenced utterances.)

A growing body of research dealing with audience as co-author of discourse meaning (e.g. Goodwin, 1981,1986; Duranti, 1986) views a speech act as incomplete, and needing reciprocal interpretations to complete its meaning in a social context. The most conservative view, expressed by Adelman (1981) and Duranti (1986), is that 'every act of understanding is active': the listener takes an active part in interpreting the speaker's message and constructing a contextually relevant sense. The most extreme view, expressed in Edmondson's (1981) 'hearer-knows-best principle', suggests that it is the listener who ultimately decides on the significance of the speaker's utterance. An intermediary view is that of 'competing frameworks': participants can offer competing frameworks with the speaker for interpretation of the talk (Goodwin, 1986).

3.6   A model of language understanding

The discussion presented in this chapter has introduced listener strategies for editing discourse that must be accounted for in modelling speech-understanding processes. This section summarizes the foregoing discussion by sketching a model of the listening process which accounts for the notions of construction of **lexical/propositional meaning**, **base meaning**, and **relevance** (Figure 3.10).

Let us now look at two brief examples of how a listener might integrate cues at these three levels. Although we cannot know the exact nature

---

A listener understanding of speaker utterance (X) is derived from converging interpretations of (i), (ii), (iii), as follows:

(i)   an interpretation of the propositional meaning of (X)
(ii) an interpretation of the base meaning of the text containing (X)
(iii) an interpretation of the pragmatic context which might have motivated the speaker to utter (X)

FIGURE 3.10   A model of listener understanding of an utterance

of the listener's mental representation of a discourse, we can infer what a discourse representation might have been through our knowledge of two factors: (a) how similar language is conventionally interpreted and (b) what the listener displays in their next turn in the discourse. Following each example is a representation of how the listener assignment of meaning for a single utterance might be achieved.

Example 1

Situation: A and B work together. They meet by chance at the photocopy machine.

(T1) A: 'You look good in that suit now that you've lost all that weight . . .'

(T2) B: 'Oh + thank you.'

Let us present what a representation of B's understanding of A's utterance, prior to her uttering 'Oh, thank you', might be:

(i) *Base meaning:* clothes and appearance is an acceptable topic for casual talk; compliments are preferred according to pragmatic principles; speaker seems to be employing supporting data (have lost weight) for a claim (you look good in that suit).

(ii) *Propositional meaning:* speaker is saying 'I look good in the clothes I am now wearing'; she's saying that 'I've lost weight'. 'All that' refers to 'a lot'? 'Now that' links these together.

(iii) *Discourse relevance:* Consider speaker intent: (a) She's saying I look good — seems like a compliment. (b) She notices that I've lost weight — seems like a congratulatory remark. Seems to be congratulating and complimenting?

What is displayed in B's turn ('Oh, thank you.')?
At this point, B apparently takes this remark as a compliment, after some initial confusion.

Example 2

Situation: B is at an employment interview in the United States.

(T1) A: [looking through the application forms] So you had all of your children in Mexico?

(T2) B: [pause] In Mexico? No, no. Here.

Again, let us present what a representation of B's understanding of A's utterance, prior to her uttering T2, might be:

(i) *Base meaning:* job interview questions often focus on family and current family status; from my application, A knows that I have children, so this question is to give him more knowledge about my family.

(ii) *Propositional level:* (a) A is asking a question about my children; I think he is asking: 'Are my children in Mexico?'

(iii) *Discourse relevance:* (a) I think A wants to know if my children are with me in America — perhaps this is an appropriate question for a job interview, but it does not seem to matter so much to clarify the precise reason for asking about my children.

What is displayed in B's turn ('In Mexico? No, no. Here.')?

B's answer 'No' could be in reply to what was (mis)understood as: 'Are your children in Mexico (now)?' Alternatively, the 'no' might be in reply at the level of discourse relevance: 'No, you need not ask any more questions about my children.'

The understanding problems of the listeners in the two above examples are different. In the first example, there is ambiguity at the level of discourse relevance — the understanding problem is not rooted in the propositional level, that is, in what the speaker actually said. In the second example, there may be ambiguity at the level of discourse relevance as well, but the misunderstanding is apparently due to misunderstanding the linguistic form of the speaker's question.

3.7 Conclusion: salience as a starting point in analysis of understanding

Since a listener's interpretation continuously changes throughout a speech event, it is not accurate to speak of sequential stages in listening, starting with speech perception. It is more accurate to think of the processes of perception and interpretation as continuous, overlapping, and mutually informing. Listening processes will be not be autonomous either; they are likely to be influenced by cognitive and emotional states as well, such as excitement or fatigue, which will, in turn, influence what the listener finds **salient** in the discourse.

This chapter has outlined editing procedures by which discourse participants use linguistic and pragmatic knowledge in discourse. A model was presented of interpretation processes at three levels (lexical/propositional level, 'base' or schematic level, and level of interpersonal relevance) and it was shown how a convergence of inferences at these three levels underlies successful listening. These discourse interpretation abilities can be summarized as follows:

(1) The ability to infer meaning by supplying links between lexical items.

(2) The ability to formulate a base, or conceptual meaning that links utterances together.
(3) The ability to formulate plausible intention(s) for the speaker in making an utterance.

The following chapter examines discourse samples to demonstrate how listeners utilize these abilities.

3.8. Discussion questions for readers

1. Discrepancies of visual and vocal cues

Consider the cases below and the difficulties the addressee might have in drawing an acceptable inference.
(a) A husband pointing and wagging his finger at his wife as he says in a loud voice:
'I just want us to be equals.'
Although the speaker says 'I want us to be equals', the pointing and finger wagging gesture suggest an authoritarian position during the utterance.
(b) A boss with folded arms, gaze directed at floor, says in a tense voice (i.e. with a tense articulatory setting):
'I don't have anything against you.'
Although the speaker's text suggests openness and lack of hostility, the non-verbal cues suggest lack of openness and the prosodic cues suggest coldness.

Can you recall any instances in which there were discrepancies between a speaker's visual, vocal, and linguistic cues?

2. Use of cues in understanding

For each of the following situations, what linguistic and non-linguistic cues (including contextual cues) have probably been used by the hearer to arrive at an understanding or misunderstanding?
(a) Mother comes running to child who is playing with a plug in an electrical outlet. She picks up the child quickly and says, 'No, no. You can't play there.'
(b) A train conductor comes up to a passenger on the train; the passenger is smoking a cigarette. The conductor says, 'I'm sorry. There's no smoking allowed in this coach.'
(c) A man is standing by the stove, cooking. He burns his finger and says, 'Ouch.' Turning to someone else in the kitchen: 'The pot holder.'
(d) A tennis coach says to a player who has just hit a ball too high. 'Keep your wrist steady.'

3. Ellipsis

In each set of braces { } insert a reference which reconstructs what (or whom) the speaker may be referring to. In each set of square brackets [ ], insert the item that has been ellipted.

(a)
A and B are arranging to invite a person to their home for dinner on the coming Friday. B was to have talked to the person during the day.

A: Did he { } call [ ]?
B: Yes [ ]. It's { } Friday.
A: [ ] Your car [ ] OK?
B: Sure [ ].

(b)
A: So, you're married, huh?
B: Yeah, yeah, [ ] about six months ago.
A: [ ] Really?
B: Yeah. [ ]
A: That's { } kind of neat.
B: Yeah, we { } went to Chicago which is where my folks live and got married there. How about you? Are you married?
A: Yeah, I'm married. It's { } been about ten years now.
B: [ ] Really?
A: Or eleven, I can't remember. [ ] Don't tell [ ] my wife, though.

Record some conversations between friends and transcribe selected portions in which anaphoric reference and ellipsis are used extensively. Show your transcript to someone, with round brackets ( ) following anaphoric references and square brackets [ ] representing ellipted segments inserted. How well can the reader 'fill in' the gaps? If possible, show your transcript to the people who were actually recorded. How well can they fill in the gaps?

Is it more or less difficult to 'fill in the gaps' when reading the transcript or when listening to the recording? Why?

4. Understanding strategies

Tape record a short interaction in which you give instructions to someone you know to perform a simple task (for example, putting some papers in a particular order, arranging some items on a table). Listen to the tape. How was the listener able to complete the task? What strategies were used? Did the listener have any problems in completing the task? Can any problem be keyed to a particular place in the interaction? If so, transcribe one place in the interaction in which a misunderstanding might be said to have arisen.

How do you characterize the source of the understanding problem?

5. Cooperative principles in conversation

Many speech acts are likely to occur in pairs (e.g. invite—accept; request—comply; assert—agree; accuse—deny). While there will be multiple possibilities for second members of the pair, there is typically one member which is preferred or expected. In each case below, a dispreferred response is given by one party. Dispreferred responses, to be heard as cooperative, require some type of perceived insertion, preface, account, or declination component to accompany them.

In each exchange, how does B respond in a dispreferred way while displaying a principle of cooperation? How is A likely to understand the response on a level of transaction and on a level of interaction?

(a) [at the end of a class, two students talking]

A: Can you give me a ride home?
B: I'm not going home right away today ... I have some errands to do downtown.

(b) [before a class, two students talking]

A: We're all getting together after class today. Would you like to join us?
B: That's nice of you. But if I don't finish this assignment tonight, I don't think I'll be able to keep up with the class.

(c) [at a perfume counter, A is a customer, B is a sales person]

A: This perfume really smells awful.
B: Well, not everyone likes it.

(d) [two strangers at a bus stop]

A: Do you have the time?
B: I'm sorry. I don't have a watch.

(e) [an interviewee (A) talking to a member of a interviewing committee (B)]

A: You do think I'll get the job, don't you?
B: Well, you know, we're in a tough position. We have to interview a lot of people before we decide — that's only fair — and it's hard for us to compare qualifications ... so I can't say for sure ...

(f) [two colleagues over lunch]

A: Monday is OK for the meeting?
B: I'd prefer Tuesday. I don't think I can have everything ready by Monday.

6. Multivalenced intentions

In each case the speaker may have more than one intention addressed to one person, or multiple intentions, one directed to one addressee and one to another addressee.

In each situation below, can you assign possible multiple intentions to the speaker's utterance?

(a) Clerk, customer, bystanders

> Customer: [holding a broken toy] I want to return this toy. It is the cheapest
> thing I have ever seen, an absolute joke.
> Clerk: OK, sir. Many customers may be unsatisfied with toys in this price
> range.

> intention to customer: _____
> intention to bystanders: _____

(b) A is talking to B and C; A knows that B's spouse is looking for work;
A knows that C might be looking for a new job.

> A: I heard that there's going to be an opening at the university.

> intention to B: _____
> intention to C: _____

(c) friends at a reception for C (Carol)

> A: [facing B; C has back to them, but is within earshot]
>   . . . Yes, Carol is one of the people in this field I have great respect for . . .

> intention to B: _____
> intention to C: _____

7. Causes of misunderstanding

Look at the lecture excerpt below and the listener summaries that follow.
Is there any evidence of misunderstanding in the listener summary? If
so, what might be a cause of the misunderstanding? See notes on
transcription conventions at the beginning of Appendix 5A.

This is a lecture on 'hierarchies of address', the principle that people
approach and speak to addressees differently based on their perceived
social status. In the lecture, the speaker uses an example of a taxi driver
talking to his customers differently depending on how old they are,
whether they are male or female, how they are dressed.

Excerpt from lecture:

50. now some people claim that there are
    universal norms/(p)
51. norms that all societies have/(p)
52. one example of a universal norm/
53. is a norm for hierarchies of address/
54. an American psychologist named Roger
    Brown
55. talks about the hierarchies of address/
56. the ways or standards of addressing/

57. the standards we use for addressing
    different people in our society/
58. as being a universal//(p)
59. let me give you an example of this/(p)-
60. recently I was in a taxi in Tokyo/(p)
61. or actually I believe it was Nagoya/(p)
62. and I hadn't been to this place/
63. and neither had the taxi driver
    apparently//(p)
64. so as we got in the neighborhood/
65. we had to stop the car/   [65: hand gesture down
                                suddenly, indicating
                                'stop']

66. and ask in turn several different people/
67. if they had ever heard of this particular
    building/(p)
68. and the taxi driver stopped and asked in
69. about four or five different people/(p)
70. a housewife in maybe her early thirties/
71. an elderly woman maybe in her seventies/
72. a businessman maybe in his forties/
73. and a group of school children/
74. say around ten or twelve years old/(p)
75. and the way that he addressed these people   [75—78 hand twirling
        was really quite different/   outward]
76. the way that he approached them/
77. the way that he opened the conversation/
78. was very different/
79. because the people were of different ages/
80. different sexes different social positions/(p)-   [79—80 hand bobbing
                                                      indicating four 'groups')
81. so this is an example of a hierarchy of
    address/(p)
82. which is a type of norm/(p)
83. and it is claimed to be a universal norm//(p)

In listener 1 summary: *Drivers ask the customers their addresses in
different ways.*
In listener 2 summary: *There are many different kinds of addresses that
taxi drivers need to know in their job.*
In listener 3 summary: *Taxi drivers are very busy and must talk to a
lot of people.*

8. Misunderstanding and non-understanding in collaborative discourse

What evidence of understanding problems is there in each turn marked
with an asterisk *?

(a) A role play at an employment office

T: hein + c'est bien ça + + bon euh+ huem+ et maintenant quel type de
+ travail vous aimeriez faire là?
(*well, that's okay, good, and now what kind of job would like to do there?*)

A*: comme le <trava> (as a <job>)

T: hem (*hm*)

A: ah parce que <trava> pas + le chômage
(*ah because don't <work>, unemployment*)

T: la + vous êtes au chômage + mais si vous avez un travail + quel type
de travail vouz cherchez, vous accepteriez?
(*there, you're unemployed, but if you have a job, what kind of job would
you be looking for, would you accept?*)

(b) A role play situation

T: ja + gut dann hatten wir die Sache fur heut' un wenn Sie also in Zukunft
noch Fragen haben kommen Sie bei mir vorbie? ja? (*good, so we're through
for today, and so if you have any questions in the future you'll let me know,
yes?*)

M: ja (*yes*)

T: <rufen Sie an? OK> (*give me a ring, OK?*) [leans back, looks at the door,
stands up]

M*: so? und jetzt muss ich geh? (*so now I have to go?*)

(from Bremer *et al.*, 1988)

(c) The following extract is from a job interview between a monolingual
Australian interviewer (an office at the Commonwealth Employment
Service) (I) and an immigrant from Cuba (J). The interview is for a job
as hospital attendant at a senior citizens' hostel in Perth:

(T1) I: Also, the hospital is a psychiatric hospital. Erm ... so, I don't know
if that's going to cause any bother to you ... or any problems at
all. Are you familiar with the term 'psychiatric hospital'?

(T2) J*: [repeats slowly in Spanish] Psiquiatri ...

(T3) I: ... People with psychological problems.

(T4) J*: [very high pitch] In my family?

(from Williams, 1987)

Notes

1. The principle of underlying propositional links operates for all instances of
understanding adjacent pieces of information, not just in conversations.
Consider how the interpretive process may work in understanding the
following connected utterances:

We had a very secure childhood even though we were very poor. My father
was a locksmith.

interpretation 1: Speaker is providing descriptive information ...
Family poor.

Poor families are usually not secure.
Base meaning = Apparent contradiction:
(This family was secure) plus
Apparently relevant data to explain this contradiction:
(Father was locksmith)

Inferential link: The profession of locksmith, while low-paying must provide steady work, and therefore a secure income.

interpretation 2: Speaker is providing descriptive information ...
Family poor.
Poor families are usually not secure.
Base meaning = Apparent contradiction:
(This family was secure) plus
Apparently relevant data to explain this contradiction:
(Father was locksmith)

Inferential link: Use of terms 'secure' with 'locksmith' and 'poor' suggests metaphorical use; possible double meaning intended to be humorous

(example from Hoffman *et al.*, 1982)

2. Morley (1987) suggests that support and warrants and backings for claims constitute second-order information that is part of the information structure of the text. From the perspective offered in this chapter, however, Morley is giving too much emphasis to text-decoding rules and too little emphasis to pragmatic procedures through which texts are used.

3. Any view of understanding which depends on a relation of hearer interpretation to speaker intention — regardless of the number of source types it includes — will be dualistic : the speaker packs messages; the hearer unpacks messages. (Pellowe, 1986)

4 Listener performance

4.0 Introduction: Displays of understanding

In the previous chapters a model was developed of the linguistic and pragmatic competence that underlies skilled performance in listening. Chapter 2 was concerned specifically with aspects of competence that allow spoken discourse to be heard as intelligible. Chapter 3 was chiefly concerned with inferencing processes that allow listeners to make sense of language in context.

The intention of this chapter is to demonstrate principles of perception and interpretation of conversational data, drawing upon methods of conversation analysis.[1] One basic observation concerning how perception of listener roles in discourse relates to interaction analysis may be reiterated here. As outlined in Chapter 1, listeners' roles can be seen to vary along a continuum from collaborative (listener and speaker) to non-collaborative. Participation strategies and interpretation orientations vary with expected degrees of collaboration; this chapter and the following one will look at listener behaviour along this continuum.

By 'collaborative discourse' is meant conversation in which all participating parties contribute verbally, even if their participation is asymmetrical, competitive, or fraught with conflict. Non-collaborative discourse (to be discussed in Chapter 5) means situations of language use such as lectures and distant presentations, such as television viewing, in which listeners have few, if any, rights or opportunities to contribute verbally to an interaction with the speaker.

Of central concern in this chapter is the issue of how the position of the listener in collaborative discourse affects **listener displays of understanding**. The view is presented in this chapter that the listener's facility in displaying signs of participation and understanding in expected ways constitutes an important aspect of listening ability. The following interpersonal aspects of listener displays of understanding will be discussed:

identifying points of transition in the discourse

organizing turn-taking
providing obligatory responses
providing 'listenership cues'

In addition, the listener's role in shaping the discourse will be discussed:

shifting to the topic-initiator (speaker) role
setting rules for interpretation
responding to speaker intent
coordinating purposes in the discourse
repairing trouble spots in the discourse
checking understanding

4.1   Listening in collaborative discourse

4.1.1   Identifying transition points in discourse

One of the principal skills which a listener must have to participate in conversation is the ability to identify a salient topic. Relevance of listener response is contingent upon the identifying of topics and transitions between topics. In order to observe how participants in discourse identify topics, we can examine how they manage the transition between topics.

In most conversational settings, interlocutors switch back and forth between the roles of primary contributor and primary interpreter. The contributor in this sense is not necessarily the person who is currently speaking, but rather the person who is currently in control of the **transactional layer** of the discourse. Occasionally this control of the transactional layer is established explicitly, as in the following segment.

> [extract from a bar-room conversation]
> (T1) Mike: Paul de Wald, guy out of =
> (T2) Curt: =De Wald, yeah I (know 'm)
>   ⌈
> (T3) Mike: └Tiffen
> (T4) Mike: =Do you know him?
> (T5) Curt: Uhhuh= I know who he i::s.
> (from Goodwin, 1986, p. 289)

In this segment, one speaker explicitly nominates a topic, seeks recognition of other participants and proceeds to elaborate. Most conversations do not exhibit this kind of clarity in selection of topic and nomination of the 'primary contributor' to the topic and the 'primary interpreters' of the topic. The distinction between contributor and interpreter is sometimes a fine one; it is one nevertheless that is important in understanding how participants make sense of spoken discourse. When we examine conversation closely we can often see how primary responsibility for the role of transaction control serves to define the exchange structure of conversation.

We can see in the following extract[2] how turn-taking is managed and acceptable understanding is achieved. Although a first glance at the extract shows a balance of speaking time, the speakers' discourse roles relating to control are not balanced in each turn. We can note that the roles of topic contributor and topic interpreter follow an identifiable turn-taking system.

The **exchange structure** in this conversation (which, one must bear in mind, is worked out during the conversation rather than being pre-planned) is roughly marked by one party assuming the role of initiator of new information, the other the role of respondent to or interpreter of the information. This shifting of roles marks a new conversational topic (Turns 4, 12, 21), as it sets a new orientation of the participants toward the conversation. If one participant lacks competence at either contributing or interpreting roles, problems may emerge around these transition points.

[two friends, both about 20 years old, American university students, are talking about their grades]
(EXCHANGE I)

(T1) A: ok (.) I can't understand (.) uh why you'd want people to have their grades sent home to their parents(.) Well I can see why you would, but why, exactly

(T2) B: well(.) simply because I feel that since my mother is paying for me (.) ah well paying for my tuition and every expense I have here (.) I feel that she has the right to know ah how my grades are (.) what her money is being like (.) invested here instead of just goofing off(.) It can be an incentive if I'm dong bad(.) she can get on my back to get me to do better or(.) I just think that parents do need to know

(EXCHANGE II)

(T3) A: when I was (.) uh checking off the thing [an item on a survey about grade reports] (.) I was thinking about the reason I went so far in the other direction was (.) was thinking why do people want that (..) then I was think the the parents always use this line of (.) you know (.) 'I'm paying for your education and you better shape up (.) and you better do better' (.) and you see with me (.) my parents don't pay (.) well they have the money to pay for me to go to school if I want to (.) but basically I'm paying for it all (.) and I talk to them every weekend (.) and I say well (.) I'm doing bad in this class (.) and I'm doing pretty good in this class (.) and they put the pressure on me anyway (.) and they see (.) they say (.) ah you know they've never

looked at my report card (.) sometime like when I got a C
once (.) and I was failing the class (.) and they wanted to
know how I was doing (.) I always said I got a higher grade
than I did (.) but if they sent a report card home to my
parents it would be like (.) you know (.) well wait do they
(.) do they (.) they don't send grades (.) they send grades to
your home right (.) but it's to you right

(EXCHANGE III)

(T4) B: well (.) I'm a freshman (.) and my grades did go home
(T5) A: do you (.) your parents (.) but it had your name on it,
            right
(T6) B: yes
(T7) A: your parents didn't open it ⌐before you did
                                        ⌊
(T8) B: to the parents of J—B—
(T9) A: did it really
(T10) B: to the parents of J— B— (.) well I know they send grades
            to freshmen (.) I well (.) to the parents of freshmen (.) I
            don't know ah
(T11) A: oh wow

(EXCHANGE IV)

(T12) B: but I didn't mind (.) I will report to my mother what I'm
            doing
(T13) A: yeah
(T14) B: I want her to know what I'm doing
(T15) A: uh huh
(T16) B: I'm spending her money
(T17) A: yeah
(T18) B: ah (.) then I don't look at it as big secret (.) my mother
            and I are very close
(T19) A: uh huh
(T20) B: and so is my dad (.) so I communicate with them all the
            time (.) and I let them know how I'm doing

(EXCHANGE V)

(T21) A: uh huh (.) but like ah you get good grades (.) I mean
(T22) B: ah (.) I've got a 4.0 I mean
(T23) A: ah (.) if you get bad grades (.) would you get like (.)
            really upset if your parents would get (.) I mean (.) but
            you see you never get bad grades

(from O'Keefe and Shepherd, 1987, p. 402)

We can note also how information is negotiated — clarified and
accepted — differently in the long turns (T1—T3) and in the short turns
(T4—T23). In the longer turns, the listener may be said to be responding
globally to what the speaker is saying, indicating general
acknowledgement of the speaker's contribution.

These longer turns are defined by the relative absence of verbal collaboration by the listener. In this friendly persuasive talk, as in most types of conversation, discourse rules are apparently in force. In this type of conversation, each participant is expected to (a) state a position and (b) wait for the other participant to state a position before negotiating specific claim(s). All identifiable speech communities (e.g. American university students) develop and maintain unspoken-rule systems for an array of conversational genres, and are to some extent defined by their knowledge of conversational rules (Hymes, 1967).

The short turn sequences are defined by frequent listener negotiating moves: the listener can be seen to be negotiating the validity of the speaker's claims and supporting data. In the shorter turns, the listener is taking a more active role in the shaping of the conversation and in the evaluation of the speaker's contribution. In these turns the listener must display an alignment, implicitly or explicitly, with the position of the speaker.

If we return to the conversation of the two university friends, we can see that even in friendly persuasive talk, listeners align themselves in degrees with the speaker's positions. Just as listeners develop back-channelling techniques, listeners must develop social strategies for appropriate expression of agreement and disagreement with others' views and for alignment with their talk. In our example here, we note an avoidance of explicit rejection of partner's views. Social talk among speakers who wish to maintain a good relationship tends to emphasize agreement, or at the very least, exhibits indirect disagreement rather than direct disagreement. Explicit rejection is avoided in face-to-face encounters (Figure 4.1).

O'Keefe and Shepherd (1987) refer to four strategies that listeners might use in aligning with a speaker's stated or implied viewpoint.
(a) **Implicit acceptance** – denial of own position (if different from the speaker's), simple agreement statements, no effort to force accounts for speaker's position.
(b) **Explicit acceptance** – offer of collaborating accounts, reinforcing backchannel signals.
(c) **Implicit rejection** – simple statement of own position (if different) without uptake of partner's position, offering of countering accounts without direct rejection of partner's view, mitigated acceptance of partner's position, modifying partner's responses to be true in an acceptable context.
(d) **Explicit rejection** – direct criticism of partner's view, depersonalizing partner's view and expressing rejection of categorical view.

FIGURE 4.1 Acceptance and rejection in persuasive conversation

4.1.2 Organizing turn-taking

While there seems to be flexibility in turn-taking and information control in free conversation, there is under the surface a remarkably systematic set of principles to organize turn-taking. The shift of conversation roles of speaker and listener (terms that will be used hereafter to correspond to 'contributor'and 'interpreter') will depend on a number of social and psychological variables. The most important of these variables are the relationship of the interlocutors, the range of topics that is expected to enter the conversations between the interlocutors, and the physical setting of a particular conversation between these interlocutors. As patterns among these variables develop, ritualistic rules for discourse may be assumed by the participants. When the interlocutors have acknowledged the introduction of the ritual, how one makes sense of the discourse is to a large extent defined by these rules.

An example of a recurring ritualistic encounter is a service encounter, say, at a restaurant. Consider how in the following extract the waiter (W) and customer (C) efficiently enter into turn-taking.

(T1) W: Good evening sir=
(T2) C: =Hello
(T3) W: What can I get for you?
(T4) C: Um+ a bowl of your chili and ⌐um
(T5) W: ⌊Um-hmm
(T6) C: I guess a glass of your iced tea
(T7) W: O:::kay

In this case, the setting and the relationship and the purpose of the interlocutors − in brief, the function of the conversation − all constrain the topic and length of turns. This brief conversation may be seen as consisting of two exchanges: 'the greeting' (Turns 1 and 2) and 'the order' (Turns 3−7). We can see that after Turn 3, the waiter readily adopts the listener's role in that the customer is controlling the introduction of new information.

The expectation that certain events must occur (here, a greeting by the waiter or waitress, an elicit for an order) and the expectation that information slots must be filled (here, the actual order of the customer) form a **script** for the conversation (as discussed in Section 3.3). Some knowledge of the schematic expectations, which are culture-specific, is essential for participating in and interpreting conversations such as this one.

The exchanges in ritualistic conversations, such as the service encounter, typically proceed in a step-like fashion. We can visualize these conversations as consisting of steps up towards a goal. Certain exchanges

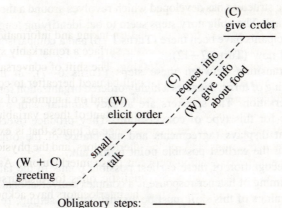

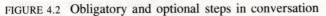

Obligatory steps: ————————
Optional steps: - - - - - - -
[W = waiter/waitress; C = customer]

FIGURE 4.2 Obligatory and optional steps in conversation

are obligatory − the vertical steps − while other exchanges are optional
− the horizontal extensions (Figure 4.2).

Even in conversations which are apparently less bound to convention
than service encounters or persuasive talk, we can note a procession of
steps:

[Ron (R) and Madge (M), residents of Santa Clara, California, are in
their 70s; they are sitting on a bench together]
(T1) R: You lived in Santa Clara very lo::ng?
          (0.5)
(T2) M: Tch!(.) Seventeen┌yea:::rs.
(T3) R: └Oh you've been here qui:::ta while,
          havenchu?
(T4) M: Hm::hmm (.) ┌Yeah, but no::t fifty! Heh-heh.
(T5) R: └Yea::h
(T6) M: Hm:hmm.
          (1.5)
(T7) R: I've seen quita few cha:::nges in Santa Clara┌m-
(T8) M: └Mm I have too:::
          I don' − I don't li:::ke it as well as I did when I
(T9) R: ┌Ye:::s
(T10) M: └came┌he:re
(T11) R: No, well └it was a sma::ler town then   not so bu::sy
(T12) M: Mm:: yeah.
(from Boden and Bielby, 1986, p. 78)

A topic structure has developed which revolves around a theme of 'the way it was'. The obligatory steps seem to be: identifying length of time the participants have been there (Turns 1–6) and a comparison between then and now (Turns 7–12).

The transition between these steps (Turns 6–7), in its smooth overlapping of turns, suggests a highly ordered organization for the genre of conversation. The speakers are already familiar with a schematic structure for this type of conversation. They produce overlaps, here alignment displays (agreements and acceptance of the other party's claims) at the earliest possible point in the talk.

This recognition of these earliest possible points in the talk and the smooth timing of listener response is a complex conversational skill. The underpinnings of this skill must be a sensitivity to setting, relationship with one's interlocutor, and purpose of conversation.

4.1.3 Providing obligatory responses

In examining both intra-cultural and cross-cultural discourse it is important to note that the rules for ritualistic encounters are often unconsciously ingrained (see Candlin, 1987a, for an elucidating discussion of this principle). When our interlocutors violate the expected rules for a ritualistic encounter, we may experience a violation of sensibilities even though an exact cause is hard to pinpoint. This sense of violation may be especially pointed when one interlocutor erroneously assumes that discourse rules are shared by another interlocutor.

Godard (1984), for example, points out some key differences between telephone-call beginnings in France and in the USA. Godard provides ample anecdotal evidence to show that callers are often heard as being rude when they skip certain steps that are considered obligatory by the answerer. In France all of the following steps are obligatory for the caller:

(1) check number;
(2) excuse yourself for intruding;
(3) name yourself;
(4) ask for your friend.

In the following dialogue between caller (C) and answerer (A), the steps are executed in expected order:

    C: [dials number]
    A: [picking up receiver] Allo?
    C: Est-ce que c'est 546 7887?
    A: Oui.
    C: Excusez-moi de vous deranger (1.0) c'est Michel (.5) est-ce que Jean est là?

In the USA, however, steps (1), (2), and even (3) may be considered optional for social telephone calls. In the following example, the caller goes directly to the key step.

C: [dials number]
A: Hello?
C: Can I speak to Joan please?
A: Yes, just a moment.

Godard points out that, in France, the listener (the person answering the telephone) may feel offended if the speaker does not provide immediate identification, and if the speaker does not offer some token apology for disturbing the household. Effective participation in a culture entails learning the expected steps for numerous rituals of this sort.

We can see in the following example how a lack of knowledge of rituals (here the adjacency pair: A: 'Is —— there?' B: 'Yes, speaking.') leads to misunderstanding.

A: Hello, is Mr Simatapung there please?
B: Yes.
A: Oh ... may I speak to him please?
B: Yes.
A: Oh ... are you Mr Simatapung?
B: Yes, this is Mr Simatapung.
(from Richards and Schmidt, 1983, p.125)

Since not all ritualistic encounters are as easily identifiable by time constraints as telephone-call beginnings, the step boundaries in a ritual may not be easy for the participants to work out. Nevertheless, even in open-ended conversation, the participants will often set up routine exchanges that require overt recognition (or 'ratification') by the other participant. For instance, in the following segment, a continuation of an earlier excerpt, we can see how the listener ratifies the speaker's contributions.

R: Mm, yeah, we::ll I remember when the bowling club had, you remember, that section at McCo:::nnell's Pa:rk?
M: Yea:h
R: It was a smoo::th green — the texture, I mean
M: Uhhuh
   (.03)
R: Well, it's no:t like tha::t anymore
M: No.
(from Boden and Bielby, 1986, p. 79)

Not only does the listener ratify the content of the speaker's utterance, but again she does so at the earliest possible points.

In summary, timing of listener response itself is an aspect of listener

> Listeners will attend to any of these cues or to a convergence of two or more of these cues.
> (1) Intonation — an onset of terminal rise or fall in intonation signalling the end of a clause.
> (2) Drawl — a drawl on a syllable, signalling a possible end of a clause.
> (3) Sociocentric sequence — the presence of a stereotyped expression, typically following a substantive statement, such as 'y'know, but uh ...'.
> (4) Pitch/loudness — drop in pitch and/or loudness.
> (5) Gesture — termination of a hand gesticulation used during the speaking turn

FIGURE 4.3 Cues for listener response

performance that can reveal the listener's orientation to, and understanding of, the talk at hand. Listeners who have developed a knowledge of discourse rules begin or attempt to begin their (verbal or non-verbal) responses around **points of transition relevance**, rather than continuously or randomly throughout the conversation (Sacks *et al.*, 1974).

Points of transitional relevance in a conversation are often constituted by clausal boundaries, that is, at the completion of a grammatical clause containing a subject—predicate combination (Duncan, 1972). However, a multitude of cues are apparently used by speakers to signal transitional opportunities, places in which the speaker is willing to cede the floor. These cues might be considered traffic signals for listener interruption (Beattie, 1983; Duncan, 1972; Harrigan, 1985) (Figure 4.3).

4.1.4 Providing 'listenership cues'

In all language communities listeners are expected to provide appropriate **back-channelling signals** to interlocutors to indicate that they are listening. In face-to-face encounters, listener back-channelling is virtually continuous in verbal, non-verbal (e.g. nodding), and/or semi-verbal (e.g. 'mm', 'whew', 'tch') channels.

Without appropriate back-channelling, a conversation is likely to break down or simply stop, since the speaker is unsure that the listener is actively attending to and interpreting the discourse. In order for conversational maxims to be maintained (see Section 3.4), the listener must provide appropriate recognition that the discourse is being edited and that acceptable inferences are being drawn.

Consider how in the following example, from Japanese, the interlocutors provide numerous back-channelling signals.

[three women are talking about their children at school]
A: Mukashi no hito iun ja nai? (*People used to say that all the time, right?*)
B: Um, so so so. (*yeah, right right*)
    ıDemo, honto so yo. (*but really, it [was like that]*)
C: Um, um. (*um, hmm*)
B: Yochien no toki, sugoku itagaru ko ga ite, yappari (*when [I] was in kindergarten, there was this kid who was always complaining about this pain, you know ..*)
C: Um (*yeah*)
B: Donna sensei no toko ittemo, kekkyoku seichoki de (*all the doctors said it was just a matter of growing up*)
C: Um (*right*)
B: Baransu ga torenai toki no (*seems to be related to coordination and ..*)
C: Um (*right*)
B: Itami ga okorutte (*[just] at that time, it seemed to hurt*)
C: Um, um (*right*)
B: Sooyo (*Really*)
(from LoCastro, 1987, p. 109)

Here the listeners (A and C) provide continuous verbal and semi-verbal 'listenership cues' (Gumperz, 1983), and presumably also appropriate non-verbal cues (nodding, maintaining eye contact with the speaker, etc.) as culturally appropriate. Appropriacy of listenership cues will vary from culture to culture. Variables influencing appropriacy may include: intimacy with the speaker, familiarity of speakers with the physical setting, the emotional charge of the conversational topic.

One important observation about listener back-channelling is that back-channelling behaviour itself does not necessarily indicate the listener is understanding the discourse at a transactional level. These cues tend to be used interactively to demonstrate that the listener is aligning with the intent — the presumed intent — of the speaker.

A related aspect of providing listenership signals is in explicitly **prompting the speaker** on how to continue a conversational topic. This may be in the form of formulaic prompts (e.g. 'Oh, really') or specific referential questions. We can see in the following example how the listener provides topical prompts for the speaker to continue.

[from a television talk show]
(T1) A: omimai wa tokidoki itte masita kedo ne (*[we] used to go to see [him] in the hospital sometimes, but ...*)
(T2) B: ee. Tokyo de ... (*Um-hmm. in Tokyo?*)
(T3) A: Ee, ee. Tokyo desu kedo, ano, nanka, kazoku de, zen'in de ne, nanka, tonikaku, ashita zettai ikenakya ikenaitte iu ki ni natte, anoo, sore de, sono maa, minna de itta wake desu yo (*right, right. It was in Tokyo, but, you see, um, in the family, everybody, um, what, anyway, I thought we'd better go the next day, and uh, then, well, we'd all better go*)

(T4) B: Ee. Toku ni sore hodo sepatumatta jotai de wa na ...   (*Right,*
            you mean even though a special reason wasn't ...)
(T5) A: Ja nain desu   (*right, there wasn't*)
(T6) B: Ah soo   (*Oh, I see.*)
(from Szatrowski, 1987, p. 430)

In this example, the listener practically co-narrates this part of the story
in that she makes the ellipted segments in A's discourse explicit. Finally,
however, she provides a listenership cue (Turn 6:'I see') as if the speaker
had narrated the story alone.

As in this case, the listener may be ratifying more than the informational
layer of the speaker's contribution. A listener may also ratify what is
taken to be an interactional layer of the discourse, that is, the intention
of the speaker in making a particular contribution at the time. For
example, B's Turn 6 ('I see'), if heard as referring to the transactional
layer of the discourse alone, might be taken by the speaker as redundant
or condescending. Rather than ratifying the transactional content of the
speaker's utterance, B's 'I see' can be taken as ratifying A's intention
in bringing up the previous point (apparently, there was something
mysterious or strange about her intuition). B's cue here serves as a kind
of interpersonal support for the speaker.

As a listener can respond to both interactional and transactional layers
of information, the verbal responses that a listener provides may be at
times ambiguous. In some ritualistic encounters in Japanese, for example,
the listener is often expected to respond to the interactional layer rather
than the transactional layer.

[A is an instructor talking to B, who missed the previous class]
A: Konakatta deshoo?   (*You didn't show up, did you?*)
B: Hai.   (*Yes [that's right]*)
A: Dakara, moo .. doo suru ka ...   (*So then ... what are we*
       supposed to do?)
B: Hai.   (*Yes*)

In B's final turn 4 the 'yes' response can be taken to ratify A's intended
disciplinary action. B is not expected to respond to a superior's actual
request for information, but is rather responding to A's right to continue
the ritual disciplinary action.

4.2   Listener shaping of discourse: cooperation and conflict

The listener may of course do more than ratify a speaker's contribution
and provide prompts for the speaker to continue. The listener may also
shape the discourse by indicating which parts of the speaker's talk are
to be further developed. Similarly, a listener can shape the discourse

by challenging the speaker's contribution, either the informational value of the contribution or the speaker's right to make that contribution.

First let us consider some examples in cooperative conversation. In the following excerpt from a conversation among friends, S is currently in the speaker's role in the conversation; D and P may be identified as listeners.

(T1) S: 'Cause they were built near the swamp . . . We used to go . . .
          hunting frogs in the swamps . . .
(T2) D: Where was it? Where was yours?
(T3) S: In the Bronx.
(T4) P: In the Bronx. In the East Bronx?
(T5) D: How long did you live in it?
(T6) S: Near the swamps . . . Now there's a big cooperative building.
(T7) P: Three years.
(T8) D: Three years.
(from Tannen, 1984, p. 67)

In Turn 2 there is an attempt by the listener to elicit additional information, and a direct transactional response by the speaker. In the remainder of the segment it is not so clear that the speaker takes up the listener's directives for shaping the discourse. In Turn 4 there is another attempt by a listener to elicit specific information where the elicit is not directly taken up by the speaker. Another example of an elicit is in Turn 5. Here, the elicit is taken up, but not by the original speaker.

4.2.1   Shifting to the role of topic-initiator

As has been suggested, much of the functional talking (e.g. in service encounters) that we do is within definable social rituals, in which there are clearly defined roles of speaker (information controller) and listener (interpreter). In casual talk, it has been suggested that the participants readily select definable roles as well. One of the unspoken norms regarding speaking/listening roles in casual talk may be that of symmetry: participants are expected to distribute these roles more or less equally over an extended conversation.

In two-party conversation between friends, the roles of speaker and listener are often quite symmetrical. In the following extract, a casual conversation between two friends, P and D, there are balanced contributions and listener back-channelling and ratification.

(Exchange I)
(T1) P: What I've been doing is cutting down on my sleep
(T2) D: Oy!
(T3) P: and I've been . . . and ⌐I s . . .

(T4) D: └I do that too but it's painful

(T5) P: [Yeah, five, six hours a night and . . .
(T6) D: Oh god, how can you do it? You survive?
(T7) P: Yeah late afternoon meetings are hard . . . ⌐but outside
              ⌊
(T8) D: Mmm
(T9) P: of that I can keep going pretty well

(Exchange II)
(T10) D: Not sleeping enough is terrible . . . I'd much rather not eat
              than not sleep
(T11) P: I probably should not eat so much, it would . . . it would uh
              . . . save a lot of time.
(T12) D: If I'm like really busy I don't I don't I don't eat . . . I just
              don't eat but ⌐I
                           ⌊
(T13) P: ⌐I I tend to spend a lot of time eating and
              preparing and
(T14) D: Oh, I never prepare food . . . I eat whatever I can get my
              hands on
(T15) P: Yeah
(from Tannen, 1984, pp. 22–3)

Within the overall symmetry of speaking time for each participant, we
can notice a shift of roles in initiating topics. At Turn 10, D introduces
a new topic element 'eating', and thus takes on the initiator/developer
role for the next several turns. We can surmise that this conversation
might continue in the same vein, with the topic-initiator role switching
back and forth following several turns of topic development and topic
ratification.

What these last examples suggest is that in collaborative conversation
listeners have purposes in discourse beyond understanding the
transactional content of a speaker. They may indicate that they are
listening and acknowledging the speaker's right to the floor, they can
provide prompts for the speaker, they can ask elaborative questions about
the content of the speaker's talk, and they can make contributions that
are relevant to the content of the speaker's talk.

4.2.2 Setting rules for interpretation: reformulating a speaker's contribution

An additional and important conversational management role that listeners
play in collaborative conversation is to **reformulate** the speaker's talk.
Reformulation can be based on cooperative or conflicting intentions of
the listeners. In NS–NNS conversation, we often find a NS or another
speaker of the target language reformulating the discourse with a
cooperative intent.

N: have you had the sweater on?
R: yeah
N: yeah? [=encouraging elaboration]
R: two three day
N: uhhuh [confirming tentative understanding]
R: + + and wash
N: ah, mm
R: and [makes gestures with hands: 'small']
N: I see+ you mean it got smaller [offers reformulation]
(from Bremer *et al.*, 1988)

This type of formulation, which is quite common among second-language teachers and their students (see Section 8.6), serves as a ratification of the speaker's attempt to communicate. This confirmation move allows the conversation to continue.

Listener reformulations may not always be motivated by cooperative attempts to understand what it is that the speaker is saying. In the example below, in which B and C are police officers, and M a complainant, we see how a speaker's contribution can be rejected.

(T1) C: we'll take a statement off you and then you're quite free to
(T2) M: right mm hh I don't want to end up in the river
(T3) C: leave the station all right like
(T4) B: this is Reading nineteen eighty it's not bloody Starsky and
          Hutch/ end up in the river/ what's the matter with you
(from Candlin, 1983)

In this extract, Police officer B rejects the speaker's claim (that she might 'end up in the river' for filing a complaint) and reformulates her contribution: her view of the event is regarded as being imaginary (as in a television show, not in the real world); her competence is called into question ('what's the matter with you?').

In asymmetrical situations, such as police—client, doctor—patient, and teacher—student interactions, challenges by 'the inferior party' may be difficult to formulate and maintain beyond a single turn. This may be so because the superior party often **sets the rules of interpretation**. The superior party may be someone who has an elevated social position, someone with temporary situational control (e.g. a mugger), or someone of equal status but with better language skills. (See Adger, 1986, for some interesting examples of this last type of interaction among native-speaker and immigrant children in Canadian schools.)

An example from an asymmetrical context demonstrates how a person in a position of power, here a psychotherapist (T), can keep an interlocutor, the patient (P), guessing about which rules of interpretation are in force, first responding to an information agenda and then to a therapeutic agenda.

P: I want permission to go home and stay there from Friday to
    Saturday.
T: But it is occupational therapy on Saturday. I think you ought to
    participate in that. I guess that is more important for you now than
    permission to go home. What do you think?
P: I don't think the occupational therapy is that important.
    [pause, no answer from T]
    Well, may I have permission to leave then?
T: This is typical for your way of behaving, do you know that?
P: OK. Then I won't ask for permission. I will not go home.
T: Why? Why don't you want permission?
(from Maseide, 1987, p.76)

From the therapist's perspective, the purpose of the conversation was
not to respond to the explicitly introduced problem − this is treated as
a surface topic. A deeper topic, apparently the right of the patient to
make certain decisions, was on the therapist's priority agenda. Once a
deeper topic is recognized, its development takes precedence over all
other topics. The distinction between surface and 'deep' topic is
presumably directly linked to therapeutic knowledge to which the patient
is not privy. The rules of interpretation, the right to recognize and pursue
certain topics, are controlled by the therapist.

The notion of ceremonial communication suggests that specific stylistic
rules underlie the interpretation of the discourse in a specific community.
Someone who is unfamiliar with the rules for discourse interpretation,
in spite of apparent linguistic competence, is unable to perform
successfully in these verbal rituals.

In virtually all settings, stylistic rules of participation will influence
interpretive frames that listeners use to arrive at acceptable
understandings. Knowledge of stylistic rules affects the likelihood of
acceptable understandings.

Some of these stylistic rules will relate to linguistic form, some will
relate to ideational content, and some to sequencing of turns. In the
following interview situation, in which a white middle-class Australian
(WMCA) (DE) is interviewing a South East Queensland Aborigine
(SEQAB) (A), we see an example of apparent stylistic rules in linguistic
form.

(T1) DE: Were you very young then?
(T2) A: Eh?
(T3) DE: You were very young?
(T4) A: I was about 14.
(T5) DE: Your husband was a Batjala man?
(T6) A: He was a Batjala.
(T7) DE: And where was he from again?
(T8) A: Beg pardon?
(T9) DE: He was from further south, was he?

(T10) A: He's, he's from here, not far from X station.
(from Eades, 1987, p. 94—5)

Although the conversation proceeds in the intended direction (of DE), it is not without trouble spots. The question reformulations that are necessary (T1/T3 and T7/T9) are apparently due to a mismatch of questioning styles between WMCA and SEQAB varieties of English. The normal, expected SEQAB strategy is to present information (even if the information is entirely speculative) and then ask for confirmation. The normal questioning strategy (i.e. asking direct referential questions) adopted by WMCA can create interpretability problems for the listener (Eades, 1987).

4.2.3 Responding to speaker intent

Cross-cultural encounters are not the only type of encounter in which stylistic differences sometimes lead to misunderstandings. Differences in styles of speaking and interpretation also affect success of communication among people of the same sociocultural background. According to Holmes (1987), some differences are due to **predispositions the listener may have** towards certain types of people and certain types of conversational topics. Some listeners may be predisposed to respond only to the transactional layer of information in a speaker's contribution, while ignoring the interpersonal layer, whereas others may respond only to the interpersonal layer and ignore transactional content.

Holmes, in the following example, suggests that M may have ignored the possible interpersonal goal that the speaker had, and responded only to the transactional layer:

W: You've got a radio there then
M: Yes [pause] I've been trying to get the weather
W: I've been trying on mine but I can't get a thing
M: mm
W: We really need to know before we leave [pause] we're on bikes you see
M: mm
W: I've got a handicapped kiddie too [pause] we're from Hamilton and we're cycling to Taupo [pause] where are you going then
M: Taupo
(from Holmes, 1987, p. 28)

Holmes reports that M's responses continued in this fashion — for the most part monosyllabically — for a few more turns until he finally said:

M: look I'm sorry I can't get a thing we must be too hemmed in.

and then ended the conversation politely.

Holmes underlines the pragmatic principle that skilled conversational participants not only observe conversational maxims of quantity and quality but also simultaneously try to observe maxims of politeness (see discussion in Chapter 3):
(1) Give addressee options ('maxim of deference'),
(2) Make addressee feel comfortable ('maxim of solidarity').
In the example above, the listener is judged to be unskilled in that, although he is cooperative (i.e. attends to information), he does not take into account politeness principles (i.e. doesn't attend to rapport).

While insensitivity to speaker intentions can lead to misunderstanding, hypersensitivity to the intentions of speaker comments may also lead to misunderstanding. In the following two examples reported by Holmes, the husbands reported feeling misunderstood by their wives. They claimed the informative intent of their utterances was misinterpreted.

> [at a camp site]
> Man: Sally's still awake, but the others are asleep
> Woman: I suppose I should have sent her down earlier
>
> Man: ooh that lump of porridge is sitting in my stomach
> Woman: Sorry I won't give you so much tomorrow
> (from Holmes, 1987, p. 29)

In both cases the men claimed they had intended to be informative and descriptive, but had been heard as critical of their wives' prior actions. The women, Holmes suggests, considered the explicit information content of the men's utterances as inadequate (i.e. not worth saying) in some respect, and proceeded to examine the contents for affective and interpersonal content.[3] It is possible that the listeners assumed that the primary content of the utterances was likely to be affective rather than descriptive. She goes on to propose an interpretive rule with which many middle-class New Zealand woman seem to operate: scan every utterance for possible critical intent (Holmes, 1987, p.29).

4.2.4 Listener and speaker coordination of purposes

Coordination of intent, or mutual acceptance of the other party's intent, is vital in collaborative discourse. Misunderstanding occurs when a listener does not understand the speaker's specific intent in making certain comments or pursuing a certain line of discourse.

In the following interview, B apparently does not realize the overall intent of the speaker's questioning.

> [from an employment interview]
> A: can you tell me about the welding that you learned?

B: yes there is a+acetylen welding acetylen gas welding and electronic
     welding
A: hm sorry and what
B: electronic arc welding
A: electric arc welding
B: yes
A: right yes
B: yes and gas welding
A: and you did some gas welding right? can you tell me about
B: yes
A: the gas welding you did?
B: (it was it) + + one is oxygen gas and the other one is acetylene +
     is both working with copper rod + there
A: hm + hm
B: I work
A: yes? what sort of things did you do what sort of things did you
     weld?
B: is make some + + angle you know just practise our welding + is
     roughly made job there (not proper —
A: hm well the welding we do here as you know is erm + mig
     welding + do you know what mig welding means?
B: yeah + + no
A: well it's er + + it's welding with a gas flux + right
B: (yeh)
A: we did
B: yes they (they is) I think + + production work
(from Perdue, 1984, p. 78)

It appears that the interviewee may not fully understand the purpose
of the discourse: for the interviewee to present the best possible view
of his/her training and background and willingness to apply that to the
new job. In the conversation segment here the interviewee tends to dwell
on details of description, rather than on his ability. Further, the
interviewee apparently does not see that one purpose of the interview
is for him to elaborate. The author notes that out of 70 questions in the
interview, the interviewee gave a one-word answer to 27 of them; another
14 were four words or less.

In a similar interview situation, reported in Williams (1987), the
interviewee responds to a request for assurance as a request for
information.

[M is a Balinese man]
I: And did you have to use a till? Did you have to ring the money up
     on a till or a register?
M: Ah, no. No, I don't.
I: So, you've never had to actually take cash and ring it up on a
     register and put the money in the drawer.
M: Oh, no.
I: You realize that would be involved in this particular job?

M: Yeah.
I: Would that worry you at all?
M: Yeah!
I: It would worry you?
(from Williams, 1987, p. 173)

'Would that worry you?' is syntactically a yes/no question, but it must be interpreted in this setting as inviting only a 'no' response, with some qualification if necessary.

A similar type of misunderstanding occurs in the following interview. The resulting interpretation made by the interviewer turns out to be unfortunate for the interviewee.

[M is a Balinese man]
I: Erm ... this place that you have in Fremantle ... this is a
     permanent address? You're staying there permanently, are you?
M: Yes.
I: And you are over in Australia to stay, or would you like to travel
     later on? or ...
M: I think I would like to travel.
I: You would like to travel? Er, where would you like to go?
M: Europe.
I: Europe. ... mm ... any idea when ... when you would like to
     go?
M: Erm ... depend when I get the job, you know.
I: Good OK. ...
(from Williams, 1987, p. 174)

There is apparently a misunderstanding of the intent of I's Turn 3, asking about travel. M perhaps interprets this as a personal question about his interests (possibly leading to some solidarity with the interviewer), unaware that in a job interview all questions potentially gauge the candidate's suitability. M apparently fails to interpret the interviewer's questions in this light, and, as it turns out is labelled 'not stable enough' for the job.

In the following example, reported by Gumperz (1983), we see a case of mutual misunderstanding of the interactional layer, although it is hard to pinpoint the source in the text itself. In this excerpt, an opening phase of a conversation, we see how expectations of the participants differ.

A, a trained teacher born in Pakistan, has been referred to a language centre funded by the British Department of Employment because his communication skills are judged to be lacking for high-school teaching in Britain. Both participants agree on who controls the power in the interview—counselling session, although their expectations of what is to be accomplished in their first meeting apparently differ.

A: exactly the same way as you, as you would like to put on

B: oh no   no
A: there will be some of the things you would like to

B: yes
A: write it down
B: that's right, that's right
A: but uh ... anyway it's up to you (1.0)
B: um ... (high pitch) well ... I .. I Miss C.

A: first of all
B: hasn't said anything to me you see (2.5)
A: I am very sorry if she hasn't spoken anything
B: (softly) doesn't matter
A: on the telephone at least
B: doesn't matter
A: but uh ... it was very important ... uh thing for me
B: ye::s Tell, tell me what it is you want

A: um
   um, may I first of all request for the introduction please
B: oh yes sorry
A: I am sorry (1.0)
B: I am E.
A: oh yes (breathy) I see ... oh yes ... very nice

B: and I am a teacher here at the Centre
A: very nice

B: and we run=
A: =pleased to meet you (laughs)
B: different courses (A laughs) yes, and you are Mr.?
A: N.A.
B: N.A. yes, yes, I see (laughs) Okay, that's the introduction (laughs)
A: would it be enough introduction?
(from Gumperz, 1983, p. 175)

Gumperz points out that the interviewee had intended for the teacher to provide appropriate certification for him rather than to recommend actual language courses. His request for 'an introduction' is apparently intended to allow the teacher at the centre to recognize his problem and respond to his implied request. The teacher's understanding of his request for an introduction is apparently to provide one's name and occupation. Although it is difficult to identify precisely where in the conversation the misunderstanding has started, we can see that after several exchanges (A: 'Um, may I first of all request for the introduction please?') something is seriously wrong. The interpretive frames of the two interlocutors, that is, their perceptions of the purpose of the interview, are different.

4.3   Listener queries and listener repair

During collaborative conversations, listeners may query various aspects of the discourse. We use the term **query** to refer to questions, statements, and non-verbal reprises through which the listener indicates non-understanding (a lack of uptake) or confusion. Queries are seemingly motivated by the listener's desire to **repair** an understanding problem, rather than to tolerate ambiguity and continue or to override the trouble.

Global query: the listener indicates an understanding problem, or desire for elaboration, related to overall text or task and not specifically connected to the recent text

Examples:
'I don't understand. Can you speak more slowly?'
'Do you want me to remember all of this?'

Local query: the listener identifies a portion of the discourse text as a trouble source. This may be a specific lexical problem, or a problem with the form of an expression.

Examples:
'What do you mean by "into the other one" (repeating a phrasing)
'Eccentric?' (repeating a lexical item)
'I don't know that word.'

Transitional query, usually a hypothesis formation or a forward inference: indicating trouble with macrostructural organization or prediction of information

Examples:
[Having just heard a reference to Greek Street in a series of directions] 'I don't know where Greek Street is.'
[Having just heard a fact that doesn't fit in with one's prior understanding.] 'So why did she do that?'

FIGURE 4.4   Listener queries as a function of discourse organization

Figure 4.4 categorizes queries from a cognitive perspective, with listener repairs corresponding to local, global, or transitional (local to global) representations of the discourse. It is important to note, of course, that these categories are functional rather than formal: the form of the query itself does not necessarily indicate the representation trouble the listener is experiencing.

Listener queries can also be categorized from a formal perspective in which the surface discourse features of the listener query are identified

Metalinguistic query (not explicitly related to the immediate discourse)	A:	You'll have to take this down to the complaint department.
	B:	I don't understand. Can you speak more slowly?
Minimal query (generally connected to immediately preceding discourse)	A:	Take this slip up to personnel on the sixth floor.
	B:	What?
Reprise of trouble source (explicitly connected to immediately preceding discourse)	A:	If you have your health form finished, take it to Room 312.
	B:	Health?
Elicitation query (linked to immediately preceding discourse, listener asks for information not yet given)	A:	Can you take this to Room 312 please?
	B:	Is that the personnel office?
Overriding (asking a question or making a statement which apparently ignores the immediately preceding discourse)	A:	I would like you to answer all of the questions on side 1 …
	B:	Can we open the window?
Topic switches (developing a given aspect of the discourse topic, but not the present topic)	A:	I thought that most of the people I talked to at the job interview were friendly, but there were two very rude people, especially …
	B:	I had an interview once too.
Avoidance of trouble source (ending the current source of communication difficulty without resolution)	[not easily illustrated by formal features]	
	A:	I didn't have any problems with the written test, but the interview was more than I had expected.
	B:	Oh, you have many interesting experiences.

(Adapted from Bremer *et al.*, 1988)

FIGURE 4.5 Listener queries

(i.e. the form of the discourse prior to the listener query) (see Figure 4.5). This procedure is perhaps more reliable, although both functional and formal perspectives are necessary in order to characterize listener queries (and other responses).

4.3.1   Checking understanding

Because neither speaker nor listener can ever be fully aware of the inferences that the other is making, listener checking is routine in all types of information exchange, even among competent speakers of a language. Consider the following example.

(T1) F: When did you want her to come do:::wn?
(T2) S: Oh any time between now and next Saturday, hhh
(T3) F: A week from (.5) this coming Saturday?
(T4) S: Yeah.
(T5) F: hhhh Oh:::
(from Heritage, 1984, p. 318)

F's Turn 3 does not reflect a lack of understanding ability, but rather the pragmatic skill of checking possibly ambiguous information.

We can formulate from this sample a typical sequence involving an understanding check:
(1)   A (the speaker) produces an utterance segment requiring 'repair' (here: 'Saturday')
(2)   B (the listener) initiates a check (here: 'A week from this Saturday?')
(3)   A provides a confirmation/disconfirmation (a repair)
(4)   B acknowledges the confirmation/disconfirmation ('Oh')

This sequence as illustrated in the extract may be considered efficient in that the listener offers a hypothesis-type check ('A week from this Saturday?') rather than a global query (e.g. 'What?' or 'Can you say that again?'). The sequence becomes longer – and introduces potential for new problems of understanding – when the listener does not offer a hypothesis (concerning his/her current state of understanding).

Although understanding checks are both necessary and common in NS–NS discourse, they are all the more necessary (but not necessarily more common) in NS – NNS discourse since references are often not immediately recognizable to the NNS. Conversation between NS and NNS often involves lexical 'push-downs', in which one party in an interaction (typically the NNS) experiences non-understanding of references in virtually every listening turn, as in the following example.

T: wieviel ham Sie in Italien verdient?   (*How much did you earn in Italy?*)
M: wie viel?   (*How much?*)

T: in Italien wieviel ham Sie verdient?   (*In Italy how much did you earn?*)
M: hams? (*Did you?*)
T: wieviel haben Sie in Italien verdient?   (*How much did you earn in Italy?*)
M: verdient? (*Earn?*)
T: wie hoch war der Lohn?   (*How much was your pay?*)
M: Wie hoch 'e alto'? (*How much is 'e alto?'*)
(from Bremer *et al.*, 1988)

Here the clarification sequence is repeatedly initiated, but never satisfactorily completed: each cycle creates new problems of non-understanding. It is evident that the problem of understanding is the responsibility of both participants once either of the interlocutors topicalizes a repairable segment in the discourse.

4.4 Conclusion: traces of development in listening in collaborative discourse

From the samples of collaborative discourse reviewed in this chapter, one can summarize the range of skills and strategic responses that constitute effective listener performance in collaborative discourse. A range of skills has been described:

(1) Recognizing indicators by speaker for introducing a new idea or a ritualistic exchange; for changing topic, providing emphasis or clarification or expansion of points, indicators for expressing a contrary view.
(2) Maintaining continuity of context to assist in predictions and verification of propositions in the discourse.
(3) Identifying an interpersonal frame that suggests speaker intention towards hearer.
(4) Recognizing changes in 'prosodic gestures' — pitch height, pitch range, pitch patterns, pause, tempo — and identifying inconsistencies in speaker use of these gestures.
(5) Identifying ambiguity in speaker utterance, speaker contradictions, places in the discourse in which the speaker is providing inadequate information.
(6) Differentiating between fact and opinion; identifying uses of metaphor, irony, and other 'violations' of conversational maxims.
(7) Identifying needed clarifications of topics and ideas.
(8) Providing appropriate feedback to speaker.

In terms of development of listener skills, we can expect that as acquisition progresses, the language learner uses these various identifying and recognizing skills more often and over a range of discourse types.

These skills will be reviewed and recontextualized in Chapter 6 in the discussion of development of listening ability.

Following the discussion in this chapter, strategic listener responses in collaborative discourse can be summarized as follows.

(1) *Identifying points of transition in the discourse and shifting to the topic-initiator (speaker) role.*
STRATEGY: skilled listeners will try to identify points at which they can switch to speaker role.

(2) *Organizing turn-taking and providing obligatory responses.*
STRATEGY: skilled listeners will look for places in discourse routines in which they are expected to participate in socially appropriate ways.

(3) *Timing of listener response and providing listenership cues.*
STRATEGY: skilled listeners will provide appropriate cues to the speaker that they are following the discourse.

(4) *Prompting the speaker and indicating which aspects of the discourse are to be developed.*
STRATEGY: skilled listeners will provide prompts to the speaker for continuing the discourse.

(5) *Aligning with the speaker's claims.*
STRATEGY: skilled listeners will provide cues to indicate how they align with the speaker's statements and intents.

(6) *Reformulating the speaker's contribution.*
STRATEGY: skilled listeners will evaluate the speaker's contributions and reformulate them when they conflict with listener goals.

(7) *Setting rules for interpretation.*
STRATEGY: skilled listeners will be aware of power asymmetries in the discourse and recognize when a 'superior' party is enforcing interpretative rules.

(8) *Responding to speaker intent.*
STRATEGY: skilled listeners will identify a plausible speaker intent when interpreting an utterance.

(9) *Coordinating purposes in the discourse.*
STRATEGY: skilled listeners will afford recognition to the speaker's intent in participating in unequal encounters.

(10) *Querying and repairing.*
STRATEGY: skilled listeners will identify parts of discourse needing repair and will query those points when appropriate.

(11) *Checking understanding.*
  STRATEGY: skilled listeners will utilize gambits for checking their understanding when appropriate.

In terms of development of listener strategies, it might be expected that problems of understanding will become more easily defined as acquisition progresses. For example, learners will be expected to move from using primarily global queries and local queries to using more transitional queries in repairing discourse. One would expect that the learner's discourse strategies, such as repair strategies, will progress towards effective management of understanding problems:

(1) The learner's range of strategies for dealing with non-understandings will increase and will be used more effectively over time.
(2) Misunderstandings and smoothness of encounters: there should be a general trend towards fewer misunderstandings, and towards smoother encounters when misunderstandings need to be rectified.

Chapters 6, 7, and 8 attempt to incorporate these features of listener participation into a pedagogic design.

4.5 Discussion questions and projects

1. Understanding problems

Record a conversation between a native speaker and a non-native speaker of a language who has not attained target-like proficiency.

How do the interlocutors indicate understanding problems? What types of understanding problems do they repair? What types of understanding problems do they not repair?

2. Interactional variables in listening

Some SLA researchers have claimed that adjustments in interaction are probably more important for making language understandable to L2 learners than are text simplifications.

Tape record several conversations between NS and NNS (enough to provide at least 50 exchanges). Transcribe the entire conversations, or select parts of the conversations which reflect interactional adjustments by the NS to make the conversation more understandable. What features of interaction adjustment can you identify?

3. Development of listener strategies

Bremer *et al.* (1988) have noted that a learner's problems of understanding in the target language (TL) become more easily defined as acquisition progresses. At the beginning stages of acquisition learners tend to have 'global' problems with the interpretation of utterances, while at later stages, problems tend to be more locally identifiable.

Select an L2 learner whose development of listening ability over an extended period you wish to study. (Alternatively, you can choose yourself as a subject if you are currently learning a second or foreign language.) How could you observe this learner's listening behaviour in classroom and/or non-classroom settings over a period of, say, six months?

What kind of data would be the 'richest' — capable of providing the most evidence of the listener's developing listening ability, and the interaction of listening ability with other language abilities? In what situations would you wish to gather data? How would you gather the data? Can you gather data in a way that will make successive observations comparable? How would you analyse your data for evidence of developing listening skills and strategies?

4. Cultural studies

Goodenough (1957) proposed that a description of a culture should properly specify what it is that a stranger to a society would have to know in order to perform appropriately any role in any scene staged by the society. If we take this notion seriously, we should be able to discover 'rules' for performance through systematic observation of 'cultural scenes'. These 'rules' would be 'learnable' by 'strangers' and, one might presume, they should be 'teachable' to some extent.

Select a **commonly occurring event** involving spoken discourse that may be difficult for 'strangers' to learn. This event may be defined by function (what the participants are trying to accomplish, e.g. saying goodbye to guests at a party) or by time of occurrence. This may be an event that involves L1 speakers only, L2 speakers only, or both L1 and L2 speakers.

Tape record at least two of the same type of events and transcribe a comparable segment of each one. Are there any identifiable interaction routines; information routines? How did the interlocutors utilize cultural knowledge to fulfil their roles? Are there any implications for 'successful listening' in this situation? Can this 'successful listening' behaviour be learned by a 'stranger'? How?

(Possibilities include: scheduled student consultations with a classroom instructor, or with a medical doctor, etc.; a telephone call to an operator or sales agent asking for specific information; small talk among students at the beginning of a class period before the instructor enters; asking for information at a shop.)

5. Clarification

McTear (1985), in studies of L1 acquisition, notes that requests for clarification are 'a type of conversational repair mechanism in which the listener diagnoses a problem and requests clarification', and the speaker of the 'repairable' utterance carries out the repair. (These are distinguished from 'other corrections', in which the listener both diagnoses the problem and carries out the repair.)

Audio tape a conversational session in which one person is giving directions to another person. Transcribe the tape and identify sequences involving requests for clarification. Which of the types mentioned by McTear are used most often?

1. Non-specific request for repetition:

   A: do you like his big brother?
   B: what?
   A: do you like his big brother?

2. Specific request for repetition:

   A: do you like his big brother?
   B: his what?
   A: his big brother

3. Specific request for confirmation:

   A: do you like his big brother?
   B: his big brother?
   A: yes

4. Specific request for specification:

   A: do you like his big brother?
   B: which one?
   A: the one with the curly hair

5. Potential request for elaboration:

   A: I saw his friend
   B: when?
   A: this morning

6. Potential request for confirmation:

   A: I saw his friend
   B: this morning?
   A: yes

Notes

1. For background on conversational analysis, and particularly concerning speculation about the universality of types of participation, the reader is

referred to Goffman (1974, 1981). Goffman speculates that the following turn types may be universal: openings (and noticings), closings (and pre-closing moves), turn-taking signals, back-channel signals, repair systems (clarification requests, etc.), bracket signals (asides), and pre-empt signals.

2. Some conversation analysts who are interested in how prosodic features of discourse (timing/overlapping of utterance, pauses, lengthenings of vowels, etc.) affect turn-taking will use more detail in transcription that analysts who are interested primarily in lexical content. I will base my transcripts on the system and level of detail given within each source.

3. This interpretive rule parallels the rules proposed by Sinclair and Coulthard (1975) to account for pupils' correct interpretations of teacher directives. Ervin-Tripp (1972, p. 169) combines and refines these principles into the following rule: Those utterances will be interpreted as directives which break topical continuity in discourse, and which refer to ... prohibited acts ... or social rules. Examples would be' Somebody's talking' or 'I see chewing gum' ...

5   Listening in transactional discourse

5.0   Listener understanding in transactional discourse

In collaborative discourse, listeners can enact strategies for understanding
overtly and evidence of understanding can also to some extent be
displayed in listener turns at talk. In many settings where the listener
cannot or does not interact with a speaker, however, as when watching
a television programme or listening to an announcement on a train
platform, clarification strategies cannot be enacted directly and listener
understanding is not normally displayed to the speaker. Listeners can
of course achieve acceptable understanding of discourse in such non-
collaborative settings, settings in which the listener's purpose can be
characterized as primarily **transactional** rather than **interactional**. This
chapter examines listener performances and listener strategies in
transactional discourse. It focuses on those aspects of understanding and
non-understanding that can be inferred by listener performance on tasks
that have tangible outcomes. In this discussion, the cognitive skills that
underlie effective listening in transactional discourse will be defined.

The discussion in this chapter will be in reference to situations involving
extended listening, situations such as classroom lectures in which a
participant is expected to listen continuously for up to a few minutes
at a time. The chapter begins by outlining ways in which listener
understanding can be inferred in transactional discourse, and considers
in some detail three types of evidence of listener understanding utilizing
examples from second-language learners. The evidence to be considered
is that which is available in performance outcomes on retrospective (post-
listening) tasks, such as summarization and multiple-choice (m/c) answers
to questions, in the performance on prospective (pre-listening) tasks, such
as predictions, and in performance in on-line (while-listening) tasks, such
as note-taking and selective completion activities. The term 'task' is used
in this chapter to refer to 'pedagogic tasks', which are defined by Breen
(1987) as 'any structured learning endeavour which has a particular
objective, content appropriate to the setting or event the learner is
involved in, a specified working procedure, and range of outcomes for

those who undertake the task'. In subsequent chapters, distinctions will be drawn — often absent in discussions of the term 'task' in the applied linguistics literature — between pedagogic tasks, testing tasks, and real-world tasks.

5.1   Access to listener understanding in non-collaborative discourse

It is a well-established principle in memory research that intervening stages between experiencing an event and recalling the event inevitably distort one's memory of the original event (Loftus, 1975). Moreover, our schematic expectations about what certain events should include tend to colour our memory of an event. What is elicited by recall questions about an event, then, is not entirely reliable evidence of what a person has initially understood (Figure 5.1).

This interactive phenomenon will be displayed in any extended listening event, such as listening to broadcast news (Findahl and Hoijer, 1982). In most instances, a person viewing a televised news programme would not be expected to perform an overt task to demonstrate an understanding of the news. However, if, following the news broadcast, the viewer were unexpectedly given several written questions about the broadcast, we can expect that the viewer's performance would be influenced by factors other than simply recall of information from the news broadcast itself.

Following the discussion of Brown *et al.* (1985), let us consider a possible portrayal of the intermediate stages between putative understanding of what the newscaster has said and the task response that the listener/viewer would have to produce:

(1) The listener has to interpret the language and images in each news item and construct a representation of these items in memory.

(2) The listener has to construct an interpretation of the 'task instructions' (the questions) which specify what kind of response is required.

(3) The listener has to understand how to relate what is required by the task to the type of language input (i.e. how much information to

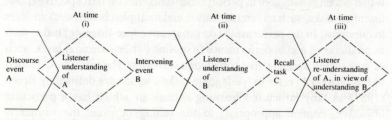

FIGURE 5.1 Intervening factors in recall tasks

include in the answer to the question about the news item, how much additional information to draw into each answer, how to present that information).

(4) The listener has to produce a task response. If the response is considered inadequate, the reason may lie in the listener's inadequate or inappropriate performance at any one of these four stages, separately or in combination.

Access to listener representations of texts is limited to either **listener accounts** of their listening process (either 'on-line' commentary or 'after the fact' recollections), or **task performances** which reveal specific aspects of text understanding. Whether accounts or task performance are utilized as evidence of listening processes, distorting variables will be encountered. First, process accounts and performances on tasks are both socially mediated by the relationship between the listener and the person who will be evaluating (or even is simply in the presence of) the listener's performance. We can visualize the listener's problem of listening representation and form of expression of this representation as involving a 'targeted' audience or task interpretation (Figure 5.2).

Second, any listener account or task performance involves production ability, which is to some degree independent of listening ability. In L2 settings in particular, performance data concerning understanding will be distorted, in part through L2 speaker/writer errors and omissions in the account or task. In order to gain access to what an L2 speaker or writer has understood of a target-language message, we cannot avoid relating the various types and the extent of message adjustment to the

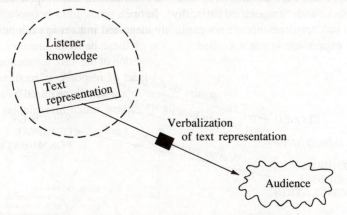

A listener's verbalization of understanding is always 'targeted' at an audience.

FIGURE 5.2 **Verbalization of understanding** (based on Chafe, 1977)

well-formedness, acceptability, and appropriateness of the actual messages he/she produces (Varadi, 1983). Thus in interpreting L2 understanding data, we must attempt to ascertain whether error-free or appropriate speech (or writing or non-verbal response) was achieved at the expense of abandoning or compromising the learner's optimal meaning, on the one hand, or whether, on the other hand, errors are largely due to the learner's refusal to compromise his or her optimal meaning despite the gap that may exist between this optimal meaning and the learner's encoding capabilities in the target language.

5.2   Types of tasks

Taking listener and task variables into account, we can view listener response as likely to contain three sources of distortion. One source will be the amount of veridical verbal representation of the input that is required by the task. Another source will be the amount of time between listening and task performance. A third will be the amount of original production that is required in the task performance (Figure 5.3).

One source of distortion in tasks is the degree of production required of the task performer. In this respect, task responses can be viewed on a continuum from 'open' to 'closed'. Recognition tasks, in which a listener must choose from alternatives presented by a test-writer, are the prototype of a closed task, which may be called a task of 'fixed difficulty'. In m/c recognition tasks, the salient information points of a text are pre-analysed and the linguistic options for expression of the points identified are pre-set. Free summarizing tasks, in contrast, are more 'open' tasks, or tasks with 'unspecified difficulty'. In open tasks, links between text and task requirements are not explicitly identified and a range of options for expression is not specified.

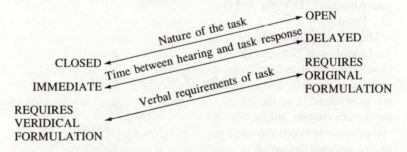

Task conditions constrain listener performance and thereby introduce distortion in interpreting a listener's response.

FIGURE 5.3   Sources of distortion in interpreting of listener responses

Another source of distortion is the time of the task response. Tasks that require responses during the text listening may provide constraints on the listener different from those that require responses after text listening. Responses after listening are subject to intervening conditions that affect memory for detail, whereas responses while listening are subject to conditions of time pressure that may affect one's ability to reflect upon the meaning carried by the overall text. Both conditions constrain the listener's response. Both sources of possible distortion must be taken into account when we interpret listener responses.

The following sections present sample performances on these different types of tasks (open and closed), which are performed with different focuses on the text: on-line tasks (performed while listening), retrospective tasks (performed after listening with a focus on organization and recall of the text), and prospective tasks (also performed while listening but with a focus on predicting subsequent parts of the text).

5.3 On-line tasks

An **on-line** task is an activity performed while listening. First an open task, note-taking, will be examined, and then a closed task, a grid completion.

5.3.1 Open task: note-taking in lectures

Examining listeners' note-taking may provide some evidence of how they focus on information during parts of a lecture. However, as research on note-taking has shown, there is not likely to be a clear correspondence between quantity of notes and quality of understanding, nor will there necessarily be a correlation between quality of notes and quality of understanding[1] (DiVesta and Gray, 1972; Dunkel, 1985; Chaudron *et al.*, 1988).

The lack of correspondence is due in part to limitations of our attention. As Lindsay and Norman (1977) have pointed out, there is a paradox in selecting what to note down as important: note-taking is a decision to defocus the text, and to focus on the act of writing. Listeners who are most attentive to the lecture, and possibly understanding more of the lecture content, might take the fewest notes. In order to achieve a compromise between the need to attend to the lecture and the need to record selected information, experienced note-takers learn a type of shorthand and thus minimize the time they must focus on writing. The notes themselves become a simplified register (Janda, 1985) that the listener must later translate into formal register.[2]

Experienced listeners will take notes in accordance with their expectations for subsequent tasks (Dunkel, 1985; Chaudron *et al.*, 1988), and to compensate for their limitations of memory. For example, if the listener knows that there will be a list of questions on historical facts following a short lecture, the listener's attention during the lecture may be tuned to recording new historical facts.

Without prior expectations about subsequent tasks, however, note-taking, like most other listener behaviour in non-collaborative discourse, is likely to vary unsystematically, thus providing only an idiosyncratic view of listener encoding processes (Rost, 1987). As such, although we can observe differing styles in note-taking, it is unlikely that we will find consistent correlations between product categories in listener notes and text content, and only occasional correlations between note quality (e.g. inclusion of key words) and listener performance on tests. (Chaudron *et al.*, 1988; Rost, 1987; Dunkel, 1988, provide a discussion of this question.) Figure 5.4 provides some correspondences between listener notes and text content.

Topic-relation notes:
1. Topicalizing − writing down a word or phrase to represent a section of the text
2. Translating − writing down L1 equivalent of topic
3. Copying − writing down verbatim what the lecturer has written on the blackboard (overhead projector, etc.)
4. Transcribing − writing down verbatim what the lecturer has said
5. Schematizing − inserting graphics (e.g. diagrams) to organize or represent a topic or relationship

Concept-ordering notes:
1. Sequence cuing − listing topics in order, numbering
2. Hierarchy cuing − labelling notes as main point (key finding, conclusion, etc.) or example (quote, anecdote, etc.)
3. Relation ordering − left-to-right indenting, using arrows, dashes, semi-circles, or = signs to indicate relation among topics

Focusing notes:
1. Highlighting − underlining, placing a dot or arrow in front of a topic, circling a topic word
2. De-highlighting − writing in smaller letters or placing topic inside parentheses

Revising notes:
1. Inserting − drawing arrow back to earlier note, inserting with caret
2. Erasing − crossing out old note.

FIGURE 5.4 Types of correspondences between listener notes and lecture texts

Appendix 5B provides two examples of note-taking, based on a lecture segment for which the transcript given in Appendix 5A at the end of this chapter. One example provides a view of a listener who is selectively topicalizing sections of a lecture, providing relational cues, and highlighting particular points. The other example is from a listener who seems to be transcribing bits of the lecture (at a very rapid rate), without much apparent ordering, contrary to the canons of effective note-taking.

With appropriate expectations, a listener's notes may serve as a useful external store of information that the listener hopes to reconstruct or elaborate upon when performing or preparing for a task. Whether or not the listener can reconstruct useful information from those notes, however, is probably dependent on the degree to which particular items in the notes relate to the overall representation the listener has of the text at the end of the lecture or during subsequent review sessions, rather than at the time of writing them down (DiVesta and Gray, 1973).

5.3.2 Closed task: completing an information grid

The on-line task performances of listeners in closed tasks are easier to interpret than on-line performances in open tasks such as note-taking, because they force the listener to enact selection strategies in real time. In this section we will look at a commonly used type of closed task, a grid completion (Figure 5.5). Closed tasks of this type, of course, are still subject to the attentional paradox that affects note-taking: the listener must at times focus on the act of completing the grid rather than on the listening text. However, when graphic elements of the task require minimal visual interpretation and therefore allow maximal attention to the spoken text, and when completions are limited to minimal writing, completion tasks may provide useful evidence of listener attention and

Fill in the grid as you listen.

	Eat	Don't eat
French		
Chinese		
Americans		
Indians		

On-line tasks force the listener to select and prioritize information while listening.

FIGURE 5.5 Grid completion while listening

understanding. (Chapters 7 and 8 will provide further discussion of this type of task.)

5.4   Retrospective tasks

Retrospective tasks are those which require responses formulated after listening to a text. Before introducing examples of this type, however, let us consider the cognitive processes that retrospective tasks require.

Forming a cognitive representation of a text is the basis for listening task performances. Any representation that a listener constructs of a text can be thought of as both reductive of and additive to the text. It is reductive in the sense that the listener cannot retain in memory a verbatim representation of a text for more than several seconds.[3] The representation is additive to the text in that the listener must bring in background information and assumptions in constructing a coherent representation.

Representations may be usefully classified by the types of text cues that the listener uses in making inferences about text meaning. The type of representation of a text that a listener constructs depends firstly on listener orientation to the text and secondly on the type of understanding problem presented by the text and the task.

(1) **Verbatim** representations are often necessary, as when one needs to recall specialized terminology or names or numbers. For the representation of any text some verbatim 'text anchors' are essential. For many academic tasks, particularly those requiring definition or explication, verbatim representation of key parts of a text are essential. Verbatim representations of extended texts are difficult to retain, since rehearsal is needed to keep items intact in short-term memory (cf. Miller, 1962; Neisser, 1982).

(2) **Propositional** representations of text are called for in representing the gist of a text. In order to form a propositional representation, the listener must select information from a text and reduce the information to a generalization which can be later modified (Schank, 1982).

(3) **Schematic** representations are formulaic ways of representing a text without assigning a specific semantic relationship (e.g. case relationships of agent, object, etc.) to items in them. Schematic representations are anchored by what is already available as background knowledge; unknown 'slots' in the representation are left unfilled and can later be elaborated upon if necessary in subsequent task requirements (Chafe, 1977).

(4) **Argument** representations can be seen as functional models of a text: they account for what the speaker is trying to do in the text

— typically persuade the audience of the acceptability of a certain idea or fact (Schmalhofer and Glavanov, 1986).

In forming and updating a text representation, listeners most probably use all of these types of representations to varying degrees, depending on preferred styles for dealing with specific texts and tasks. In extended listening the listener must balance new and old information in order to update a cognitive representation of the text as the speaker continues to talk. In non-collaborative discourse the listener may not be able to arrive at acceptable understandings on a turn-by-turn basis, but must carry forward representations of the text even if understanding is flawed or incomplete.[4]

5.4.1 Strategies for updating representations

When, as listeners, we experience difficulty in updating our representation of the speaker's text, we can enact strategies for constructing plausible interpretations of what we are hearing. Listeners in non-collaborative discourse, having no access to the speaker for clarification, need to compensate for their lapses of attention and inability to interpret various segments.

The following is an outline of some cognitive strategies listeners may use in transactional discourse:

(1) **Context implication:** Utilizing a principle of local interpretation, listeners depend on contextual cues to generate relevant links between two or more propositions in the text.

(2) **Generalization of ambiguous segment:** Using a principle of analogy, the listener assumes that an ambiguous segment is consistent with what is already known of the text.

(3) **Selection and prioritization of inferences:** Relying on the principle of discourse relevance, listeners identify salient lexical items or propositions and give priority to inferences based on these items and propositions.

The following sections present some examples of listener performance on retrospective tasks and suggest how strategy use is reflected in task responses.

5.4.2 Open task: summarizing

Evaluating summaries poses problems in that a summary writer often has myriad choices of what information to abstract and a range of strategies in how to present it. Evaluating summaries by L2 writers poses additional problems, since proficiency-related difficulties load on to normal summarizing difficulties.

A key part of evaluating summaries is identifying instances of text-amending strategies. Summary-writing strategies that have been identified include:
(1) The zero strategy − verbatim or nearly verbatim repetition of text propositions.
(2) Deletion/selection − selection of parts of the text in verbatim form with juxtaposed or internal items deleted.
(3) Addition/invention − adding items to a summary that were not in the text.
(4) Reduction/generalization − combining two or more lexical items or propositions into a single item or proposition (Fløttum, 1985; Brown and Day, 1983).

Let us proceed to an examination of some actual listener performances on a retrospective summarizing task (Figure 5.6). (Refer to Appendix 5A at the end of this chapter for a transcript of the lecture which is being summarized.) Scales which have been devised for evaluating summaries generally utilize these criteria:
(1) Effectiveness of summary at reflecting text content: identifying a topic and main idea that are neither too general nor too narrow. (Scoring by a cloze entropy technique allows the scorers to arrive at a realistic range of expected responses. In a cloze entropy technique, tasks are given to a mastery group (e.g. native speakers in a university class). A range of responses of the mastery group are considered within the range of acceptability, or 'correct'.)
(2) Including facts which support the main ideas.
(3) Overall fluency and cohesion of the summary text.
(4) Originality in wording.
(See Angell and Young, 1981; Zabrucky, 1986; Fløttum, 1985; Brown and Day, 1983, for elaboration of these criteria.)

A group of L2 listeners has heard an eight-minute lecture segment on video tape (see Appendix 5A at the end of this chapter). Following are selected summaries (with original spellings, punctuation, wording); comments concerning possible representations the listeners had formed are provided after each summary.

Sample 1
THE DEFINITION OF THE TERM IS, YOU IMAGINE SNAILS WHEN YOU HEARD OYSTER, AND THEN LOCUSTS, THEN FISH, THEN SNAKES, YOU CAN IMAGINE. THE EXAMPLES OF NORMS ARE FOOD, CLOTHES, HABITS, WAYS OF TALKING, WAYS OF TREATING PEOPLE. ESPECIALLY ABOUT CLOTHES, YOU CAN FIND THE PEOPLE'S LEVEL AND HIREACHY.

Comment:
This would be considered an ineffective summary of the entire
lecture in that it accounts only for the first part of the text. This
suggests that the listener experienced an overload of information and
retained a somewhat coherent representation of the first minute or so
of the lecture. The listener did not attempt to generalize the other
parts of the lecture based on this initial understanding. We can see
evidence of verbatim recall from the first part of the lecture.
However, one lexical item at least, 'hireachy' (hierarchy), seems not
to be recalled in any meaningful context − evidence of a limited
context-implication strategy.

Sample 2
NORMS INFLUENCE OUR BEHAVIOR IN ALL AREAS: FOOD,
SPEECH, CLOTHES, AND HABITS. PSYCHOLOGIST R. BROWN
POSITS A UNIVERSAL NORM. ONE EXAMPLE OF THIS WAS
HIERARCHIES OF BEHAVIOR − WE MODIFY OUR SPEECH
ACCORDING TO PERCEIVED HIERARCHICAL BASED ON AGE, SEX,
AND POSITION. BROWN DISCUSSES NORMS FOR COMPLEX SERIES
OF BEHAVIORS − RITUALS.

Comment:
This would be considered an adequate summary in that it accounts
for main points throughout the lecture segment heard. The summary
writer prioritizes, generalizes, and makes explicit links between
propositions.

Sample 3
THERE ARE MANY INFLUENCES ON BEHAVIOR. FOR EXAMPLE,
FOOD. UNIVERSAL NORM, AND ADDRESS. FOOD, CLOTHES,
HABITS, WAYS OF TALK INDICATES NORM. DR. BROWN'S
UNIVERSAL NORM HIERARCHIES OF ADDRESS (AGE, SEX ...)
GREETING AT DOOR.

Comment:
The writer leaves the links between successive propositions rather
inexplicit. Without explicit links, the summary appears as little more
than a list of items heard, although there is evidence that the listener
has selected important lexical items in the text.

Sample 4
WHAT IS SOCIAL PSYCHOLOGY? HE GAVE EXPLANATION, IN
DETAIL, OF SOCIAL PSYCHOLOGY.

Comment:
Although the writer apparently exercises a generalizing strategy, the
summary is obviously far too general. The writer uses a rudimentary
context-implication strategy: the writer knows that the lecture is part
of a series on social psychology.

Sample 5
STUDY OF SOCIOLOGY INCLUDES INFLUENCE. INFLUENCE IS
MADE UP WITH NORMS. IN SOCIETY PEOPLE SHOULD OBEY THE
NORMS AND RULES OF THE WAY TO ACT, FOR INSTANCE THERE
A RULE IN BRITISH HOUSEWIVES WHEN THEY VISIT NEIGHBORS.
Comment:
This summary writer provides clear links between propositions and
attempts to give an illustration. Throughout the summary we see that
the summary writer has problems with clear usage, a factor which
often affects the interpretation of information in non-native
speaker/writer texts.

Sample 6
EACH SOCIETY HAS WAY FOR SURVIVAL. SOCIAL PSYCHOLOGY
STUDIES THIS WAY. I DON'T UNDERSTAND THIS TOPIC.
Comment:
This summary shows the equivalent of a global reprise in
conversational settings: *I don't understand.* (See Chapter 4 for a
discussion of reprises.) Although reprises are generally not
considered appropriate in written summaries, we can suppose that
many listeners wish to query parts of the text as the speaker
proceeds. Not having the chance to obtain clarification, the listener
apparently experiences an information overload and cannot form a
coherent generalization of the text.

Sample 7
NORMS SOCIAL PSYCHOLOGY
CULTURE AND BEHAVIOR
ONE'S BEHAVIOR VARIES WITH COUNTRIES
Comment:
This summary resembles notes of a lecture. No links are given
between items and the first two lines do not express a proposition.
However, we can speculate that an experienced writer, utilizing just
these notes and task directions, might be able to compose a more
acceptable summary of the text by elaborating from background
knowledge.

FIGURE 5.6   Sample summaries

5.4.3   Closed task: multiple-choice selection

Closed tasks, such as written multiple-choice (m/c) tests, differ from
summarizing tasks in that the listener is given a new text (i.e. the written
test) and is asked to integrate a representation of the first text (i.e. the
lecture text) with this text. This contribution of the new text is often
overlooked when m/c tests are used as measures of 'listening
comprehension'. (The term 'comprehension' is used here to refer to a
restricted concept of understanding: identifying propositions in a text.)

Given the loading factor of comprehension of the new text, it is not surprising that researchers find consistent correlations among most probe-type measures of passage comprehension (Chaudron *et al.*, 1986).

Individual items on m/c tests may be considered as selected probes of text representation rather than indications of the listener's understanding of the overall text. However, correct responses on probe test items do not necessarily indicate text understanding either. Because of chance factors on m/c tests, all subjects, even those who did not hear the lecture text (e.g. were not present at a lecture), will obtain some correct answers. 'Test wiseness' (i.e. the comprehension of the 'test as a text') will contribute further to some subjects obtaining correct answers. Given these two contributions to test scores, a large number of items are usually required to reveal any systematic variance among test takers.

In spite of the error of measurement associated with m/c tests, by eliciting introspections of test takers in selecting a right versus a wrong answer, we may be able to infer something of a subject's text representation and retrieval strategies. For example, let us consider a single item on a m/c test:

- People from Iran eat beef, but they don't eat pork. People from India eat pork, but they don't eat beef. This might be an example of:
  (a) a role reversal
  (b) a cultural norm
  (c) a basic element of survival
  (d) a complex series of behaviors

To derive the correct answer (b) (as based on the lecture text in Appendix 5A), the listener must have a distinct representation of the concept 'norm'. How would a listener who chose (a), (c), or (d) go about making those choices? A 'wrong' choice on a m/c test indicates that the test taker finds one of the distracting items a more plausible (or equally plausible) match. The test taker's cumulative knowledge about the topic being probed (in the test item here, why people in some countries eat a certain food while people in others do not) may be more salient than the information recently provided in the lecture. In short, the test taker did not find the information in the lecture and test item more salient than what he/she already knew. Assuming this is a valid test item, a listener who misses the item would need more background information, or a different orientation to the concept, or more practice with the test format to make the concept of 'norm' more salient.

Performance on closed tasks provides some evidence of selection of strategies during listening. A wrong answer is evidence, albeit indirect, that the listener has made inferences based on links between unmatched items from the text, and, as a result, has not formed an acceptable representation of the relevant part of the listening text. We assume that a test taker who chooses (a), (c), or (d) in the preceding item did not form a schematic representation of the targeted topics in the lecture text.

5.5 Prospective tasks

Listener performances on **prospective tasks**, that is, on tasks involving predictions, provide another indirect type of evidence of listener text-representation strategies. In this section we will look at samples of prediction protocols following segments of a narrative in order to demonstrate plausible prediction processes (Figure 5.7).

In this experiment, listeners were presented a narrative in a live setting. During planned pauses in the narrative, the listeners were asked to write a prediction of the next part of the story. (See Appendix 5C at the end of this chapter for the full narrative text and the continuation of the prediction protocols.) Analysis of their predictions was performed to find evidence of context implication and generalization strategies.

Based on this brief examination of listener performance in prospective tasks, we can observe that listeners can and do make inferential extensions

---

Coding student predictions:
CI: context implication
GEN: generalization
UN: unrelated or unclear; or restatement of given fact

The story
My friend John was engaged to get married to a woman named Diane/and Diane had to go overseas/to study for one year// and their plan was to get married/ when she returned///PAUSE ONE/

Student predictions
PG: While she was away, an unexpected thing happened. (CI)
MG: While she was out of the country, he fell in love with the girl. (CI)
YT: John will go to see Diana. (GEN)
MK: But she didn't come back for long time. (CI)
MA: But he don't like that plan. (CI)
RK: After Diane going back, John and Diana will marry. (GEN)
MM: John asks her 'What happened with you?' (GEN)
MZ: John will wait for her. He said, 'I will wait for you one year' (UN)
TH: She talks to (UN)
YK: She was glad to go there and she told him her experience on her letter. (GEN)
AK: But she said she wants to stay longer in abroad. So John got very upset. Because their marriage is gonna put off. (CI)

Comment:
MZ's and RK's predictions are generalizations of what has come before; that is they express direct continuations of the text rather than impositions of contextual knowledge.

Story continuation
but when she was gone/ John met another woman/ named Carol/ and Carol and John became very friendly/ and they started dating/ and they even decided during one of their school holidays/ to take a trip together// to some tropical countries///PAUSE TWO/

Student predictions
PG: While they were there, John met Diane. (CI)
MG: Diane will notice the change in her fiance. (CI)
YT: Diane will be angry. (CI)
MK: John have met Diane there unfortunately. (CI)
MA: He enjoys very much. (UN)
RK: They will enjoy the trip. John will love Karl more. (GEN)
MM: Diane wrote a short letter to him. (CI)
MZ: In the trip John find out several bad points of Carol. he getting dislike her. (CI)
TH: They spent happy time then they fall in love. (CI)
YK: He was confusing if he told her the truth or not. (CI)
AK: When Diane knew about it she got really angry. (CI)

Comment:
MA's prediction is unclear, or very weak. It does not involve much contextual implication. RK shows a confusion of referents; this can create further misunderstanding later on in the story.

Story continuation
and John wrote a letter to Diane/ and explained this to her/ that they would be traveling together/ and Diane was very upset about this///PAUSE THREE/

Student predictions
PG: She decided not to marry John and broke off the engagement. (CI)
MG: Diana decided to write a letter to John, 'not to go'. (CI)
YT: She will write a letter to him too. (GEN)
MK: But also she had another steady who was very nice and good looking. (CI)
MA: Diana looks like interested in that. (UN)
RK: But John will annoy about Diane and Carol. (UN)
MM: Diane wrote a short letter to him. (CI)
MZ: Diane was not really upset so she said to him 'You can date with her but don't forget your wife should be me.' (CI)
TH: She gets angry about it, so she said to him she will come back. (CI)
YK: She wanted to go back to John but she didn't because she knew he won't change his feeling. (CI)

AK: Diane told John that she wants to think about their
     marriage. (CI)

Comment:
MA's prediction again involves weak inferences. RK's prediction
shows some ambiguity, which could lead to non-understanding in
following segments.

Story continuation
so when they returned from their trip to these tropical countries/
John became very sick/ developed a very high fever/ and he had to
go to the hospital//PAUSE FOUR/

Student predictions
PG: John will not be able to get married because of illness. (CI)
MG: What kind of disease did John get at the tropical island? (CI)
YT: He will have to go hospital long days and need a lot of
     money. (CI)
MK: He was thin because his sick was so bad. (CI)
MA: [no prediction]
RK: Carol will often come to the hospital and she'll make John
     vigorous. (CI)
MM: He goes to heaven. (CI)
MZ: The doctor said to John you're very serious sick so you need
     treat sick long time. (CI)
TH: Both women want to he recover him then their feel very bad
     each other. (CI)
YK: When Diane heard that, she went to see John, and she met a
     girl who is John's girlfriend. (CI)
AK: Diane heard about John's sick, she came back to the states.
     Because she was really worried about him. (CI)

Comment:
The only protocol which shows lack of context implication is that of
MA, whose prior two predictions suggested a build-up of
misunderstanding.

FIGURE 5.7 Prediction protocols

of the text as they listen. Prediction involves using a context-implication
strategy in which the listener projects schematic expectations onto the
text. Since many types of schematic completions are possible at transition
points, the quality of predictions will in most cases be only a weak
discriminator for listening ability. Beyond indicating that a listener has
crossed a threshold of text understanding at which he/she is able to
generate some prediction, the verbalized prediction that a listener makes
will reflect writing and speaking (performance) strategies as well as text
representation (cognitive) strategies.

5.6   Traces of development in listening in non-collaborative discourse

From a psycholinguistic perspective, the development of listening ability in transactional discourse involves a capacity to construct and update representations of spoken texts of increasing length and complexity and, of equal importance, a strategic competence in attending to requirements of tasks. Development of listening ability in transactional discourse also involves a growth in expectation of the range of topics likely to be introduced in a particular kind of discourse and an increase in the listener's intent to make more information in the text salient.

As in collaborative discourse, listeners in non-collaborative discourse may enact various editing strategies to update their representations of the discourse. These are:

(1) **Formulating propositional sense for a speaker's utterance**. This includes the sub-skills of:
   (a) deducing the meaning of unfamiliar lexical items;
   (b) inferring information not explicitly stated, through filling in ellipted information, making bridging inferences;
   (c) inferring links between two or more propositions.

(2) **Formulating a conceptual framework that links utterances together**. This includes the sub-skills of:
   (a) recognizing indicators of discourse for introducing an idea, changing topic, emphasis, clarification and expansion of points, expressing a contrary view;
   (b) constructing a main idea or theme in a stretch of discourse, distinguishing main points from supporting details;
   (c) predicting subsequent parts of the discourse at conceptual levels;
   (d) identifying elements in the discourse that can help in forming a schematic organization;
   (e) maintaining continuity of context to assist in predictions and verification of propositions in the discourse;
   (f) selecting cues from the speaker's text to complete a schematic prediction.

5.7   Discussion questions and projects

1. Learnability and teachability of listening skills

In our discussions of listener performances, we have suggested a number of interdependent psycholinguistic and sociolinguistic skills that underlie listening competence. Instruction aimed at the development of listening skills should account for the following principles.

(1) Listening ability is knowledge-based:
   (a) The listener uses pragmatic knowledge to estimate sense of unknown or unclear items and to make predictions about discourse events.
   (b) The listener uses procedural knowledge to accomplish tasks based on what is understood.
   (c) The listener remembers and represents discourse meaning in a usable form.
(2) Listening ability is interaction-based:
   (a) The listener identifies understanding problems − detecting meaning problems in speaker's contribution; identifying inadequacy of speaker's message for task at hand.
   (b) The listener demonstrates understanding or non-understanding in an appropriate way.
   (c) The listener, in some settings, collaborates with an interlocutor to arrive at acceptable mutual understanding or to accomplish collaborative task.

To what extent do you think these knowledge-based and interaction-based skills are transferable from a learner's L1? To what extent are they teachable? They are apparently transferable and learnable for many L2 learners, but to what extent can formal instruction facilitate their development or use in the TL?

2. Text variables in listening

Chaudron (1983) and Chaudron and Richards (1986) explored the text variables of topic restatement vs. anaphoric reference. They were interested in seeing if the use of topic restatement in pre-recorded lectures facilitated understanding of an expository text. Understanding was measured by successful completions of cloze paragraphs immediately following the presentation of a 10−15 second text segment.

Choose a text variable that you think could affect L2 listener performance with expository, narrative, or descriptive texts.

Propose a hypothesis concerning the likely contribution of this variable to understanding in a specific non-collaborative discourse setting.

Outline a study that might support a hypothesis that your text variable affects listener performance.

Consider specifically: who are your subjects? What type of text and task outcome would you use in the study? How would you assess 'listening success'? What procedures for interaction and negotiation, if any, would be allowed?

3. Styles of lecturing

Brown and Bakhtar (1983) categorized different styles of lecturing in university settings. Tape record (video is preferable) two different lecturers. How do they differ in lecture style? How might each style affect the understanding of L1 listeners? How might each style affect the understanding of L2 listeners?

4. Listener introspection

Murphy (1985) has proposed that L2 listening in non-collaborative settings can be investigated, experimentally, in an interactive context. He gathered data for his study of listener strategies in an interactive context, in which student listeners stopped an audio-taped lecture and gave comments. Murphy classified listener comments as text-based or knowledge-based. What types of comments do you think he classified as each? What problems could there be with a dichotomous categorization of listener comments?

Outline an investigation of listener commentary or 'stream of consciousness' while a subject (native speaker or non-native speaker) is listening to a pre-recorded tape. How can you design procedures to assure a replicable administration with other subjects? How can you usefully classify the listener's comments?

5. Training studies

Process—product studies, in which the short-term effects (the 'product') of a training procedure (the 'process') are investigated, may be of considerable relevance to classroom teachers.

Select a specific listening-related problem that L2 students (who you currently teach or have recently taught) have experienced. This might be a problem of skill in making discourse 'intelligible' or 'interpretable'. Try to state the problem as specifically as possible.

Outline a training study that would provide specific training procedures for dealing with the problem. What is the basis of the training procedures — an infusion of cultural or linguistic knowledge? Guided practice? Procedures for increasing learner awareness of strategies?

How would you discover if the training procedures were effective — in the short term and in the long term?

6. Background knowledge and performance

Findahl and Hoijer (1982) studied the problem of comprehension of broadcast news among native speakers (of Swedish). They investigated comprehension by viewers who had varying degrees of background knowledge. They found that comprehension (as measured by free-recall tests) was a result of an interaction between the listeners with their prior knowledge, the content, the form of presentation of the broadcast, and the subject's prior experience in the experimental setting.

Similarly, Rost (1987) studied the problem of understanding of recorded lectures among L2 learners. He investigated the effects of prior presentations of related material on understanding (as measured by post-listening summary tasks). He found that understanding of new topical information was related to prior presentations of content.

Outline a training study (preferably one that is feasible for a group of language learners with whom you have contact) in which you control for a variable of prior presentation or training.

7. Triangulation

Video-tape a student—teacher interaction (with the permission of both teacher and students) during a language class sequence in which the teacher is explaining a new concept to one or more students.

Replay the tape to the teacher and students separately and interview them concerning what is going on in the actual sequence. Compare the teacher and student accounts. What, if any, behavioural cues (including language) were interpreted by the teacher or student differently from what was intended?

8. Coding listener predictions

Using the system given in this chapter, code listener predictions to a narrative in which the speaker pauses at transition points in the story. You may wish to start by completing the codings of the protocols presented in Appendix 5B.

If possible, compare your codings with those of another rater. Where do you differ? Why?

Appendix 5A: The social psychology lecture transcript

Notes on transcription conventions: the numeral in the left-hand column indicates number of pause from beginning of lecture; underlined word or phrase indicates place of perceived tonic prominence; (p) at end of line indicates pause unit with falling ('proclaiming') intonation, pause units without (p) indication are uttered with rising or level tone; phrase at right indicates gestures used by speaker; column at right indicates time elapsed (minutes:seconds)

1. hello everybody / (p)
2. today I would like to continue
   our discussions of social psychology /   [1–3 eye contact with audience]
3. by talking about some of the
   major influences on our attitudes /
4. and on our behaviors / / (p)
5. I think the place to start is by introducing
   the idea or the concept of a norm /
6. n o r m / (p)
7. and I'm sure you're all familiar with this
   concept /
8. a norm is an accepted or expected
   standard of behavior /
9. or standard of thinking in a given group
   of people / (p)
10. and we find that all groups of people have
    norms /
11. or an array of things / (p)
12. for basic things like the food they eat /
13. the clothes they wear /
14. to much more complex types of /
15. behavior and decisions / / (p)
16. I would like to give you an example
    of a norm / (p) –
17. OK first I'm going to give you some
    names of some food items / (p) –
18. see if you've heard of these /   1:00
19. or have eaten these before /
20. here they are oysters snails
21. locusts fish pork beef snakes / (p)
22. OK now all of these are food items /
23. that are part of the norm within given
    societies / (p)   [23–27: hand bobbing in front of body in cadence]
24. for example, Americans eat oysters /
25. but they don't eat snails OK / (p)
26. the French eat snails /
27. but they don't eat locusts / (p)
28. the Zulu in Africa eat locusts /
29. but they don't eat fish / (p)
30. the Egyptians eat fish /
31. but they don't eat pork / (p)
32. Indians will eat pork /
33. but they won't eat beef / (p)

34. Russians will eat beef/
35. but they won't eat snakes/(p)
36. the Chinese will eat snakes/
37. and they don't eat oysters for example/(p)
38. do you see what I mean/ —
39. that different types of food are part   [39: cupping hands
                                                     together)

   of one group's norm/
40. but not another group's norm/(p)
41. so that each group has different norms/
42. for things like food/ (p)   2:05

43. OK now that it seems in every culture/
44. we do have standards for these kinds of
   things/
45. that relate to the very basic elements of
   survival/
46. such as food/(p)
47. and our basic habits such as the way that
   we get dressed/
48. the way that we talk to people/
49. in different situations//(p)
50. now some people claim that there are
   universal norms/(p)
51. norms that all societies have/(p)
52. one example of a universal norm/
53. is a norm for hierarchies of address/
54. an American psychologist named Roger
   Brown
55. talks about the hierarchies of address/
56. the ways or standards of addressing/
57. the standards we use for addressing
   different people in our society/
58. as being a universal//(p)   3:00

59. let me give you an example of this/(p) —
60. recently I was in a taxi in Tokyo/(p)
61. or actually I believe it was Nagoya/(p)
62. and I hadn't been to this place/
63. and neither had the taxi driver
   apparently/(p)
64. so as we got in the neighborhood/
65. we had to stop the car/   [65: hand gesture down
                                                    suddenly, indicating 'stop']
66. and ask in turn several different people/
67. if they had ever heard of this particular
   building/ (p)
68. and the taxi driver stopped and asked in
69. about four or five different people/(p)
70. a housewife in maybe her early thirties/

71.   an elderly woman maybe in her seventies/ 4:00
72.   a businessman maybe in his forties/
73.   and a group of school children/
74.   say around ten or twelve years old/ (p)
75.   and the way that he addressed these people [(75–78: hand twirling
                                                                    outward)
       was really quite different/
76.   the way that he approached them/
77.   the way that he opened the conversation/
78.   was very different/
79.   because the people were of different ages/
80.   different sexes different social
       positions/(p)   [79-80: hand bobbing
                                                          indicating 'hierarchy']
81.   so this is an example of a hierarchy of
       address/(p)
82.   which is a type of norm/(p)
83.   and it is claimed to be a universal
       norm//(p)

84.   OK now so far I have mentioned norms
       about about very basic things/(p) –
85.   I've mentioned some norms for things like
       talking/
86.   things like eating/(p)
87.   and these are rather simple norms/(p)
88.   there are of course more complex ones/
89.   which involve a series of actions/
90.   or a series of behaviors/ (p)
91.   and these norms are called rituals//(p)
92.   all right rituals are a set or series of
       actions which/   [92–3: fist opening
                                                          and closing]
93.   take place in a certain order/
94.   and they together form a certain kind of
       norm// (p)
95.   one example of this is quoted by a British
       psychologist named Michael Argyle/(p)
96.   Argyle had studied the rituals in various
       societies/
97.   including British society/
98.   and he has identified a number of steps/   [98–99: flat hand motion
                                                          indicating 'steps']
99.   that take place in different rituals/(p)
                                                          5:20
100. one ritual that I'd like to mention is
       called/ –
101. is what he calls the new neighbor
       ritual/(p)
102. all right in the new neighbor ritual/

103. as he calls it/
104. we have a typical type of/   [104—5: hands held as if
                                                   surrounding object[
105. set of behaviors// (p)
106. when a new family moves into a
     neighborhood/
107. shortly after that/
108. the housewives in the immediate area will
     come over to the house/
109. and through a series of actions/
110. introduce themselves to the new housewife
     in the neighborhood/ (p)
111. and according to Argyle these are the
     steps/
112. OK these are the steps in this particular
     ritual/(p)
113. first there is the invitation/
114. an old neighbor invites the new   [114: hand gesture,
                                               indicating (come')
     neighbor to come over/(p)
115. OK that's the first step/
116. the second step is that there is the greeting
     at the door/(p)
117. hello how are you please come in/
118. the visitor is invited into the house/
119. that's the third step/ (p)
120. the fourth step the visitor has to
     admire the house/
121. gee that's a lovely/   [121: eyes open wide, face
                                               miming (admiration')
122. lovely furniture you have here/(p)
123. next the hostess will serve tea and
     biscuits/(p)
124. then they will sit down/
125. and will exchange information/(p)
126. essential in this exchange/
127. they must exchange information about
     their husbands/
128. what their husbands do/
129. where their husbands work/
130. what their husbands like to do in
     their free time/(p)
131. and finally/
132. after a fixed period of time/
133. maybe fifteen minutes is appropriate/
134. the new neighbor must take the initiative/ [134:points and wags
                                                 index finger]
135. and say it's time to go/(p)
136. gets up/
137. says farewell/

138. we'll have to see each other <u>again</u>/(p)
139. OK now these <u>steps together</u> form what
    we call/
140. a <u>ritual</u>/
141. or a ritualized <u>norm</u>/(p)   7:00

142. OK <u>not only</u>/
143. in a ritual <u>not only</u> must all the steps
    <u>be there</u>/
144. but they must be there in a <u>certain</u>
    <u>order</u>/(p)   [144–5 flat hand motion
                                                        indicating steps']
145. for example in the <u>new neighbor ritual</u>/
146. the hostess won't <u>immediately</u> serve tea
    and biscuits/
147. without giving a <u>tour of the house</u>/(p)
148. nor will the person who <u>comes to the</u>
    <u>house</u>/
149. <u>immediately</u> start talking about her
    <u>husband</u>/(p)

150. OK the point here is that in <u>a ritual the</u>
    steps must be there/
151. and must be there in a <u>certain order</u>/(p)
152. Argyle the British psychologist and <u>others</u>/
153. claim that it is <u>knowledge of rituals</u> that
    make/
154. us <u>skillful</u>/(p)
155. that <u>make</u> us socially <u>skillful in a given</u>
    <u>society</u>/(p)
156. so learning the rituals is part of learning
    to be an <u>acceptable member</u> of our
    <u>society</u>/(p)   8:00

(from Rost, 1987)

Appendix 5B: Sample notes

Sample (i)

NORM — STANDARD
 | (clothes, food...)

(Universal) norm (R. Brown)
    example: address
                (taxi driver)
  norm — (ritual) (more complex)

M. Ar----?

ex. new neighbor / typical

hello - invite - lovely - husband -

good-bye -

ORDER!

learn norms ——→ society member

Sample (ii)

discussion social psychology / influences

attiluds

    concept of norm   fraimiliar concept

norm accepted   thinking in group

all groups of people   anythings

foods, clothes.   complex example

food items eaten   oysters pork snakes

societies American Snails

French la custs Zulu - ... Chinese

    different foods   pork norm
    different norms

    every culture standards elements

    habits situations universal norm

    American - Brown   used for

    Addressing taxi in Tokyo

Appendix 5C: The story transcript

Full text of narrative referred to in Section 5.5 and continuation of the prediction protocols.

The narrative:

My friend John was engaged to get married to a woman named Diane/and Diane had to go overseas/to study for one year// and their plan was to get married/ when she returned///PAUSE ONE/ but when she was gone/ John met another woman/ named Carol/ and Carol and John became very friendly/ and they started dating/ and they even decided during one of their school holidays/ to take a trip together// to some tropical countries///PAUSE TWO/ and John wrote a letter to Diane/ and explained this to her/ that they would be traveling together/ and Diane was very upset about this///PAUSE THREE/ so when they returned from their trip to these tropical countries/ John became very sick/ developed a very high fever/ and he had to go to the hospital///PAUSE FOUR/ and Diane heard about this/ and she returned to the United States/ because of the/ because of John's sickness/ and Carol and Diane met at the hospital/ and both of them were trying to help John to recover///PAUSE FIVE/well it turned out that John developed this disease called encephalitis/ which caused some slight brain damage/ and he developed amnesia/ there were several things he simply couldn't remember///PAUSE SIX/and so Diane and Carol were both trying to help him/ recover his memory/ and he couldn't remember Diane at all//he could only remember Carol/ and so his engagement broke off/ and eventually John married Carol///PAUSE SEVEN/

Continuation of the prediction protocols (from Section 5.5)

(after Pause Five)

PG: The two girls become friends and leave John.

MG: They realized they really cared for each other. John knew he loved Diane more.

YT: Two women will become friend, so John will wonder.

MK: In spite of their cares, John was getting bad gradually.

MA: He thanks Diane's behavior.

RK: John will be very glad to come Diane.

MM: He becames well.

MZ: John realizes Diane is good. So he decided never gonna lose her.

TH: [no prediction]

YK: John thought he still love Diane and he decided to say other girl.

AK: John was so happy. Because Dian came back. He realized he loves Diane best.

(after Pause Six)

PG: John starts a new life without Carol or Diane.

MG: The two thought it is a real pity that he lost his memory.

YT: The fact will be that John tell a lie.

MK: They abandoned John because in fact they were not so kind

MA: Diane feels very sad.

RK: Diane and Carol both will be sad.

MM: His doctor also became a sick.

MZ: But he still remain Diann's warm heart movement.

TH: Diane feels sad, but she decide to look his behind.

YK: Both of girls tried to put his memories only themselves.

AK: Even after he lost the memory of Dian, he is falling love with her again.

(after Pause Seven)

PG: Diane was heartbroken and went abroad again to pursue her studies.

MG: [no prediction]

YT: Dianna will have new boy friend soon.

MK: Diane killed herself to spell him.

MA: Diane continue crying

RK: Diana will go back her homeland. John and Carol will become happy.

MM: He and Carol have a happy life.

MZ: Diann is really love John. So she go away from John, and she back to her school to find other men.

TH: [no prediction]

YK: Diane was very sad but she met another guy who was in the hospital at same time of John was there.

AK: After his marriage with Carol, he thinks he's always looking for someone. Diane is still waiting him even she doesn't get married.

Notes

1. There are two (potentially complementary) trends in applied linguistics research relevant to note-taking (and other listener behaviour) in academic settings. One trend (exemplified in Chaudron *et al.*, 1988, and Dunkel, 1988)

is characterized by searches for correspondences between the heard texts, lecture notes, and task content. Another trend (exemplified in Benson, 1987) is characterized by attempts to situate listener behaviour, including note-taking behaviour in classes, in a macro-context of the learner's goals, study techniques, and 'support system' for passing the course. Given the unclear results of the former approach, the latter, if done with proper ethnographic methods (see Watson-Gegeo, 1989) is more likely to yield insight into this type of listener behaviour.

2. Second-language textbooks promoting note-taking skills often take it as given that learners must develop a shorthand form for recording information. However, to the extent that the note-taking process is taught as 'text driven' (i.e. based on the information in the text) rather than 'purpose driven' (i.e. based on what the learner needs to know and how the learner is likely to benefit from text), the learners are being encouraged merely to perform a parody of 'real life' note-taking. See Dunkel and Pialorsi (1982), Mason (1982), Lynch (1982) for differing approaches to the teaching of note-taking.

3. Memory is a broad term for the representational system of experience (Leont'ev, 1973). It is assumed that different 'parts' of this system (presumably correlating to neural networks) can be defined in terms of their processing functions and capacities. Primary memory is identified as that which supports ongoing processes at the centre of attention. Transient memory of physical perceptions (perceived in 'iconic' memory and temporarily stored in 'short-term' memory), which is used as a 'buffer' for primary memory, is on the order of ten seconds (Miller and Johnson-Laird, 1976). Typically, within this limitation, a person (in a first language) can retrieve verbatim only the prior clause of an utterance (Jarvella, 1971).

4. Updating one's representation involves integrating new information into the existing semantic framework in memory (Ehrlich, 1982). Listeners cannot fully separate what they learn through this updating process from what they already know — the 'I-knew-it-all-along' effect (Fischhoff, 1982; Goethals and Reckman, 1982). This effect occurs because while the listener updates a text representation, the listener updates simultaneously background knowledge of text-based content as the speaker continues talking. As a result of this simultaneous updating, it may be impossible for the listener to recover text representations exclusively when attempting to recall the text.

6 Development of listening ability

6.0 Introduction: listening and language learning

This chapter focuses on principles of developing listening ability. It begins by formulating what listening ability is, based on aspects of listening performance discussed in Chapters 2, 3, 4, and 5. There follows a review of educational and language acquisition principles upon which listening development is based.

6.1 Characterizing listening ability: enabling skills and enacting skills

In describing what a successful listener does, one can easily postulate a number of component skills in each language domain that might underlie performance, just as one can postulate a number of logically separable eye−body coordination skills that might underlie kicking a football through two goal posts. The appeal of taxonomies to instructors of a complex skill is clear: taxonomies enable one to chart out a plausible sequence for controlled practice by someone who is to learn the skill; taxonomies also allow one to analyse apparent 'deficiencies' in performance of the overall skill.

Analytic taxonomies of language skills, however, have three decisive disadvantages as bases for teaching or testing. First, by interpreting a taxonomy as the underpinning of successful learning, teachers and students may be misled into spending inordinate amounts of time practising 'specific skill outcomes' (e.g. phoneme discrimination) to perfection with little concern for transfer of the skill to target listening situations (cf. Bygate,1987; Anderson and Lynch, 1988). However, language learning is a complex psycho-motor skill and evidence from skill-learning research has suggested that this type of skill is better learned when aspects of the skill are practised in 'clusters' rather than in minimal units (Welford, 1968). The conventional belief that a learner of a complex skill will benefit from a systematic presentation of discrete skills and step-by-step practice and will later be able to put the skills back together is one that applied linguists have begun to challenge (Long and Crookes, 1987).

Second, language skill taxonomies often confuse skills that can be developed with analytic procedures that any language user, regardless of proficiency, will need to follow. For instance, some skill taxonomies will make explicit all the procedures that a listener must inevitably perform when encountering spoken language, such as 'use background knowledge'. Listing all possible procedures typically fails to clarify the distinction between psycho-motor skills that can be developed for language-use situations and knowledge that is part of a person's general analytic competence (Henzell-Thomas, 1985).

Third, many taxonomies (e.g. Munby, 1978; Richards, 1983) seem to imply an order of learning. However, there are no empirical data to suggest that skills are developed in a linear sequence and that the simplest skill must be developed before the next simplest skill can be undertaken (Hatch, 1983). Synthetic approaches which imply proceeding step by step are probably based in part on a testing paradigm which orders the likelihood of learner success on discrete language items.[1] Rather, skill deficiencies, which are definable by taxonomies, tend to be exhibited in clusters, rather than in step-like sequences. Skill development within one group of skills is most likely to proceed from directed attention to or awareness of the most salient skill in that group (Fleishman and Quaintance, 1984; Levine *et al.*, 1973; Farina, 1973).

In sum, the potential danger of any skill taxonomy in language education is that it may be interpreted as suggesting a 'product syllabus'. Learners may be expected to display the 'products' of the taxonomy, which correspond to the behaviours of target-like users of the language. SLA research of the 1980s has shown, however, that language development for most learners (at least in the structural domain) does not correspond to simple increments of target-like products (see Long, 1985; Larsen-Freeman and Long, 1990 for a review). There is not likely to be an ideal or prescribed order of development of language macro-skills (listening, reading, speaking, writing) either, whether these skills are referenced to structural, ideational, or interpersonal domains.[2] It is plausible, however, based on a broad view of language development, to propose a hierarchy of listening skills, where within a cluster one skill would appear to be *most salient* (Figure 6.1).

In this taxonomy, I propose that development of the uppermost skill in each cluster subsumes development of several sub-skills. Instruction in listening is most profitably geared toward the development of these more global skills.

Emphasizing perception:

(1) *Recognizing prominence within utterances*
   includes the sub-skills of:
   (1a) Perceiving and discriminating sounds in isolated word forms (phonemes, especially phonemic contrasts; recognizing phoneme sequences, allophonic variants).
   (1b) Discriminating strong and weak forms, reduction of unstressed vowels, modification of sounds at word boundaries (assimilation, elision, liaison); phonemic change at word boundaries; allophonic variation at word boundaries.
   (1c) Identifying use of stress and pitch in connected speech: for indicating boundaries of information units, rhythmic patterning; showing emphasis, providing contrast.
   (1d) Adapting to speaker variation.

Emphasizing interpretation:

(2) *Formulating propositional sense for a speaker's utterance*
   includes the sub-skills of:
   (2a) Deducing the meaning of unfamiliar lexical items.
   (2b) Inferring information not explicitly stated, through filling in ellipted information, making bridging inferences.
   (2c) Inferring links between two or more propositions.

(3) *Formulating a conceptual framework that links utterances together*
   includes the sub-skills of:
   (3a) Recognizing indicators of discourse for introducing an idea, changing topic, emphasis, clarification and expansion of points, expressing a contrary view.
   (3b) Constructing a main idea or theme in a stretch of discourse; distinguishing main points from supporting details.
   (3c) Predicting subsequent parts of the discourse at conceptual levels.
   (3d) Identifying elements in the discourse that can help the listener form a schematic organization.
   (3e) Maintaining continuity of context to assist in predictions and verification of propositions in the discourse.
   (3f) Selecting cues from the speaker's text to complete a schematic prediction.

(4) *Interpreting plausible intention(s) of the speaker in making the utterance*
   includes the sub-skills of:
   (4a) Identifying an interpersonal frame that suggests speaker intention toward hearer.
   (4b) Recognizing changes in 'prosodic gestures' — pitch height, pitch range, pitch patterns, pause, tempo — and

identifying inconsistencies in speaker use of these gestures.
(4c) Identifying speaker contradiction, inadequate information, ambiguity in speaker utterance.
(4d) Differentiating between fact and opinion; identifying uses of metaphor, irony, and other 'violations' of conversational maxims.

Enacting skills

(5) *Utilizing representation of discourse to make appropriate response*
        includes the sub-skills of:
(5a) Selecting salient points from information given for use in a task.
(5b) Reducing and transcoding information from spoken source to other forms (often written form, such as note-taking).
(5c) Identifying needed clarifications of topics and ideas.
(5d) Integrating information from text and other sources.
(5e) Providing appropriate feedback to speaker.

FIGURE 6.1   Enabling skills and enacting skills in listening

6.2   The problem of developing skill: quality of response and scope of interpretation

Two central principles are put forth in this chapter. The first is that development of listening ability involves the balanced enactment of linguistic, ideational, and interpersonal domains of language. The second is that formal instruction in listening should aim both to present learners with increasingly challenging listening texts and pedagogic tasks and to induce the learner to resolve points of non-understanding and misunderstanding.

As Resnick (1984) notes, a theory of instruction cannot pass directly from statements about 'expert knowledge' to prescriptions for instruction. First, we need to know what the processes of knowledge construction are so that we can propose principles for learner approaches to texts and tasks and principles for instructor intervention. Based on these principles, and informed by the learning goals of particular students, we can outline a method for grading listening texts and tasks as well as a method for instructor intervention in listening activities.

Growth in a learner's listening ability entails a progressive increase in the sheer amount of language the learner can handle at one time. Development of listening ability also entails a progressive increase in the range of events that the listener is capable of interpreting sensibly. The intention in this chapter is to expand upon the notion that the development of listening ability also involves an awareness of difficulties in understanding and an intent to change instances of non-understanding and misunderstanding into acceptable understanding.

To some extent, then, the development of listening ability will be **quantitative**, involving increasing knowledge, and to some extent **qualitative**, involving the appropriate selection of responses. Specifically, as the learner gains knowledge of phonotactic rules, grammatical sequences, and cultural scripts, his/her capacity for understanding increases. At the same time, as the learner develops a repertoire of responses and pragmatic rules for selecting appropriate responses, performance improves. The latter point will be examined in more detail in the following section.

A theory of development that describes only the knowledge that is needed in skilled listening is not adequate to account for gains in listening ability. As many L2 learners can attest, an increase in listening capacity does not necessarily entail an increase in listening performance − the ability to use relevant knowledge to make sense of language under reciprocal and temporal constraints − that is, with actual interlocutors and 'in real time'.

A complementary model of growth in listening ability is needed, one that addresses the listener's ability to make relevant interpretations of language in actual social contexts. The development of listening performance involves not only an increase of knowledge but also sustained attempts at purposive encounters with spoken language.

In order to improve performance, the listener will need to develop strategies for increasing a repertoire of responses and for addressing non-understandings and misunderstandings that occur. The development of listening strategies will tend to be cyclical: the learner applies an old rule for interpretation and evaluates the outcome of the event in which the rule is applied, **revises** old rules for interpretation, **elaborates** old rules for interpretation, or **constructs** new rules for interpretation in similar situations in the future, or in repairing the current situation. This development is contingent on the learner gaining linguistic, schematic, and pragmatic knowledge, but the key difference between knowledge development and performance development is that performance development involves evaluation by the listeners of their relative success in using that knowledge.

Listening development can take place only if the learner is able to evaluate the quality of response. As long as the listener can compare current responses to a language event with more favourable responses (in a sense, this is to compare current interpretations with those of more proficient users of the language), listening development can occur.

Listening instruction will seek to assure that conditions for this development are present.

At beginning stages of development, the comparisons are somewhat easy for the learner to make. At later stages they may become harder if the learner, having achieved a 'survival level' of competence, fails to take note of (or to show interest in) how current responses differ from those of more proficient users. Until the L2 learner achieves a target-like competence, the learner faces the continual problem of what Klein (1987) calls 'matching?': finding the discrepancy between one's current understanding of an utterance (or any event) and more target-like understanding.

It is not being claimed here that there is a single, correct TL 'understanding' of each utterance that a learner hears, and that the learner should strive for 'correct comprehension'. Learning to listen is a continuous process of the listeners' attempting to increase their capacity to interpret and respond to language events. The developmental process is continual in the sense that every act of understanding widens the ability to understand. This leads to the well-known hermeneutic circle: what we understand is based on what we already know, and what we already know comes from being able to understand.

Two questions emerge that are important for pedagogy. How can the learners find useful comparisons between their current interpretations and responses to the L2 event and those which might be more favourable, or 'acceptable'? How can the learners increase the quality of their interpretations and responses?

The development of knowledge and access to recurring encounters with increasingly challenging language are both necessary conditions for the development of listening ability. They are, however, not sufficient to assure development. In order to develop fully, the listener must experience 'intake' of language in its interpersonal domain: the listener must experience directly the effects of language understanding.

Recall the view developed in Chapter 3: language is fundamentally a form of human social action and is directed towards creating what Maturana (1980) and Winograd and Flores (1987) have called 'mutual orientation'. Mutual orientation is realized as interlinked patterns of activity between interlocutors, rather than as a representational correspondence of ideas.

In the discussion of the interpretation of speech acts it was stressed that speech acts create commitment on the part of both speaker and hearer. To elaborate the views of Winograd and Flores, who see commitment as the basis for language understanding, language is embedded in a social structure. Within that social structure, a person is a user of language through involvement in generating commitments through speaking and listening.

The development of listening ability, if it is to be more than a quantitative development of recognition of language forms and the comparison of plausible interpretations of spoken texts, must account for the development of generating commitment through speech events. What this means is that the development of listening skill must involve a growing initiative on the part of the learner to interact with and make commitments with other speakers — through 'authentic use' of the target language. Achieving intake of language in this interpersonal domain must be seen as a process driven by listener intent.

Listening development involves growth in skills and strategies underlying expert performance; this development must be viewed in light of listener intent to understand. Instruction will involve a principled theory of intervention that seeks to set listener intent into motion.

6.3   Developing the quality of response: listener strategies

Conscious strategies to bring more of a language event into focus are the means by which listeners maximize their performance. Through strategy use, learners can understand as much as possible and respond as appropriately as possible given their current capacity in the L2. Adoption of strategies cannot effect miracles of understanding; the activation of viable strategies will at best take one as far as current knowledge allows (Varadi, 1983).

Figure 6.2 lists a proposed set of listener strategies. Each strategy entails some movement from a current state of knowledge or current orientation to another.

6.4   Developing the scope of response: task support

A view of classroom activity as comprised of pedagogic tasks provides useful insight for formal language instruction, as well as for the identification of aspects of listening development that can be incorporated in that instruction. Here, the term 'task' is used in a rather specific pedagogic sense, to refer to a unit of teaching/learning activity which involves relevant instructional variables to be manipulated by the learners using some kind of data. Learning tasks are considered units of pedagogic planning in that instructors can identify in advance those variables that are likely to affect learning focus and learning outcomes in classroom activities (Breen, 1987; Nunan, 1988, 1989; Samnda, 1989). Task

(1) Movement from always adopting 'high risk' strategy (i.e. assuming that current understanding is correct without checking if it is) to adopting 'low-risk' strategy (i.e. assuming current understanding needs to be checked), when appropriate (Chapter 8 provides further discussion of risk strategies).

(2) Movement from treating all listening tasks with the same 'risk' orientation ('high' or 'low' risk) to adopting flexible orientation depending on purpose.

(3) Movement from extrinsic orientation (i.e. following procedures only) to tasks to personal orientation to task (i.e. attending to personal goals).

(4) Movement from requiring clear phonetic representation of all parts of an utterance to accepting ambiguity (and constructing plausible phonetic representations).

(5) Movement from identifying non-understandings (NU) as a general non-understanding of entire utterance or segment (e.g. 'I don't understand anything') to identifying sources of the non-understanding.

(6) Movement from dependence on local clarification of NU (e.g. 'What was the last part of what was said?') to hypothesis formation about how much was understood (e.g. 'Did you say ... or ...?'). In other words, to move from the representation of an utterance as a non-understanding to a representation of the utterance as having a plausible meaning.

(7) Movement from attempting to attend to all information equally and later sort out important information to predicting relevant information in advance and attending to confirmations of it while listening.

(8) Movement from trying to attend to and represent one proposition to attending to more than one proposition.

(9) Movement from viewing listening success as entirely the responsibility of hearer to collaborating with the speaker for clarification.

(10) Movement from attempting to understand all aspects of discourse immediately to postponing aspects of non-understanding for possible later clarification.

(11) Movement from waiting for completion of text or utterance before inferring necessary knowledge links to predicting the knowledge framework which will assist understanding.

FIGURE 6.2 Strategies for listening

planning for the language classroom is useful in that it can clarify instructor choices in creating conditions which influence student learning.

In Chapter 8 the view is presented that learning tasks and projects that link tasks are a sound basis of a language curriculum, and one which allows for contextualized development of language skills. The subsequent sections of this chapter present a detailed characterization of the variables in tasks, in order to demonstrate the degree of control that instructors have in any pedagogic task.

Based on Candlin's (1987b) descriptive framework, we note that any language classroom activity can be characterized as consisting of the following identifiable elements:

(1) **Input:** what learners are provided, have access to, or are expected to have available (including prior knowledge) as they proceed in a learning activity. Input is often closely associated with learning **materials**.

(2) **Setting and roles:** how learners are expected to interact with language data. 'Role' refers to what power, rights, and obligations learners have *vis-à-vis* other learners and instructor (this includes access to information needed in the activity and authority over use of information). 'Setting' refers to whom the learners interact with (critically, who they are grouped with as fellow participants). Setting and roles are often associated with teaching **methodology**.

(3) **Procedures:** what the learners actually do during the activity. This may involve answering questions, completing tables requiring information or opinions, taking notes, following directives, etc. Procedures are sometimes associated with learning **routines**.

(4) **Outcomes:** what the learners produce or, in some sense, take away from the activity. This may include an immediate outcome (a product of the activity) and a projective outcome (a mental representation which is to carry forward). Outcomes are often associated with **assessment** and **evaluation**.

(5) **Monitoring:** what is being attended to by learners and instructor as the activity progresses. Monitoring may be considered to correspond to the meta-cognitive and meta-linguistic processes of both learners and teachers during a learning activity. Monitoring is often associated with teacher **intervention** and teacher **correction**.

(6) **Feedback:** what signals are provided to learners to indicate degree of success/failure, future direction. Feedback may be considered to be related to what is to be remembered: the aspect of the task which is carried forward for future learning. Feedback is often associated with **guidance**.

6.5   Input as a task component

Input includes materials and language data that the learners are to attend to or manipulate during the task. Input selection requires consideration of abstractness of content, cultural aspects of the content, number of information points, media support provided, length of the extract, and level of linguistic difficulty. None of these considerations alone, however,

Degree of difficulty

Static descriptions	—	Dynamic narrations	—	Abstract expositions

(few elements which may be difficult to distinguish)

(new information is not dense; includes repetition and redundancy)

(new information is dense; does not include repetition and redundancy)

(many elements which may be difficult to distinguish)

FIGURE 6.3 A framework for estimating difficulty of input for listening activities (adapted from Brown et al., 1984)

can predict the difficulty that a learner will experience, since text difficulty relates to affective factors of learner interest and motivation, and does not take into account support provided by the task.

The difficulty, or listenability, of a text for a particular listener (which deBeaugrande, 1980, defines as the proportionality between processing effort and obtainable knowledge while listening) must take into account more than the listener's familiarity with text topics and text organization. A least-effort principle alone is inadequate to explain text-processing difficulty since listeners may expend more effort on a difficult text provided that the text offers useful and informative insights. Also, texts which are vivid or interesting may be easy to understand even though they contain unfamiliar content or difficult text features (e.g. complex syntax and low-frequency, technical vocabulary).

In classroom settings, listener reactions to texts and tasks are sometimes better understood in terms of fairness than in terms of difficulty (Alderson and Urquhart, 1988). Listeners who expect a text to be at a certain level of content abstractness and a task to be in a certain format may not find a text which is difficult by structural criteria to be especially difficult.

Individual listeners will vary with respect not only to preference for and ability to understand certain conceptual information, but also in preferences and abilities with text types along the concrete—abstract continuum. Brown and Yule (1983b), emphasizing that listening difficulty cannot be entirely determined by textual criteria, provide a model of predictability for the difficulty of a text. They combine two scales, one for types of input and one for the complexity of information within any single type of input text (Figure 6.3).

6.5.1 Authenticity

An additional concern in selecting input for listening activities is the nature and source of the input, as well as the purpose of the audience for whom the input is intended. Widdowson (1979) highlights the difference between the first concern − the text itself − and the concerns of learner use of the text. Genuineness is a characteristic of the text itself and is an absolute quality. Authenticity is a characteristic of the relationship between the text and the reader/listener and has to do with appropriate response (see Candlin and Edelhoff, 1982).

Many language educators (e.g. Besse, 1981; Riley and Zoppis, 1985; Underwood, 1989) point out that there is great advantage in using pre-recorded texts of native speaker conversations and native speaker−oriented programmes in the classroom because of the genuineness they provide. However, some educators argue that, paradoxically, genuine texts do not lead to authenticity of purpose for the learners (Candlin and Edelhoff, 1982). As such, the real-life conditions of listening that the instructor seeks to create in the classroom may be lost with 'genuine' texts. Some teacher trainers therefore encourage only the limited use of recordings in their classrooms, for example, when it is important to draw attention to dialect differences or features of settings in particular locales (Ur, 1984).

'Real-life listening' (a term used by Ur, 1984) is contingent upon the reality of the learner as listener, rather than on genuineness of discourse input. Ur maintains that: (1) real-life listening allows listener sufficient access to environmental cues; (2) listening segments come in short chunks; and (3) listening requires some show of reciprocity and typically requires frequent listener response.

6.5.2 The use of pre-recorded texts

For a variety of reasons (not least of which is the fact that EFL throughout the world is taught mainly by second-language speakers of English, many of whom do not have or do not feel they have adequate command of spoken English), many language instructors use pre-recorded audio and video tapes for the purpose of helping learners develop listening skills. Audio and audio−video texts are also needed in task-based syllabuses to provide stepping stones in the task (see Chapter 8).

In selecting pre-recorded texts, one consideration is the variety (dialect and accent) of English to be used. Strevens (1987) suggests that instructors should use one of the main varieties of English − standard British or standard American − and use consistently texts of that variety. Other varieties of English may be introduced, he says, for specific purposes.

Another consideration is continuity. When using pre-recorded texts (i.e. audio or video recordings), instructors face a problem of involving the learners more closely in the sphere of participation. As McGregor

(1986) notes, in order to bring the eavesdropper into the discourse framework — which is where authentic information is being exchanged — it is necessary to provide a frame of reference by which the listener can establish who the participants in the original exchange are and what they are perceived to be doing from their own point of view. As such, it will generally be preferable to use texts in a series in which the context has been established, or texts recorded in familiar contexts, over recorded texts selected simply on the basis of immediate interest value or content.

6.5.3 Speaker style

One other aspect of input that deserves consideration is speaker style. This will include observable aspects of delivery as well as less tangible affective factors.

Brown and Bakhtar (1983) report on an extensive study of speaker styles in classrooms and note five categories based on the the type and degree of situational structure they provide. For instance, 'visual speakers' provide full notes and diagrams on the blackboard for students as they lecture; 'exemplary speakers' repeat main points, stress main ideas and frequently summarize; 'oral lecturers' tend to provide highly structured packages of information with explicit definitions of terms; 'amorphous speakers' provide unstructured streams of consciousness and frequently abandon their original purposes; 'eclectic speakers' tend to extemporize and frequently digress, taking up ideas which may be only tangentially related to the aims of the lesson. At the end of their analysis the authors give a clear message to lecturers regarding audience design: that they must take into account content type, student background, and student learning style in selecting a speaking style.

Beebe (1985) reports on the importance of speaker style in classrooms as well, emphasizing the affective nature of learner solidarity with the speaker. She claims that solidarity with the speaker crucially affects learner motivation and attention. Therefore instructors must be sure to choose 'the right stuff' when bringing taped material into their listening classes.

6.5.4 Simplification of texts

A final aspect of input to be considered concerns simplification, altering or planning text features and topics in order to make the input more accessible to learners.

The most compelling argument against the instructional strategy of simplifying language texts for learners concerns the long-term negative effects of habitually making things easy for learners. In most language classrooms, input is often carefully selected and edited by an instructor, presented in short or simplified segments; syntactic and morphological elements are often previewed. Guided language learning of this nature is assumed to be potentially shorter, less stressful, and more efficient than the 'authentic' type of language learning in spontaneous acquisition, as the learners are spared the necessity — and also deprived of the rewards — of undertaking difficult and uncertain means of trying to make sense of the language they hear.

Another potent argument against simplifying texts comes from those who see language classrooms as places of inquiry: if we simplify and thereby remove culturally rich features of the language, are we not undermining the process of student inquiry? It would seem that if learners are being shielded systematically from those very cultural features that they are seeking to explore, we are indeed short-circuiting the entire educational process by continually simplifying and diluting texts. The primary use of authentic (unaltered) texts is consistent with the notion of an encounter syllabus for language learning (Candlin, 1981). This approach holds that for a text to be useful to L2 learners for **transfer of learning strategies to target situations**, texts must be presented 'as is', i.e. as aimed at audiences in situations in which they normally use such texts for communicative or information-gathering purposes.

Although guided instruction can be beneficial for developing listening skills, if the guided presentation continually distracts the learner from the principles of linguistic—pragmatic matching used in natural settings, or if the guided presentation provides a distorted view of culturally embedded texts, our seemingly beneficent pedagogic simplifications may create real developmental difficulties.

We must balance these arguments with the learning principle that **language data must be made accessible in some domain** before students are able to understand. In order to make language more accessible to a listener, the speaker can effect 'easification' in any of the three language domains we have postulated: linguistic, ideational (schematic), or interactional. Many language educators who have explored the notion of text simplification have focused primarily on the linguistic domain, exploring the possibilities for easification of text structure. Figure 6.4 presents some of the most commonly identified easification strategies that speakers use. Note that most adjustments that have been studied in experimental settings are in the linguistic domain (see Chaudron and Parker, 1987, for a review). There has been less experimental investigation of simplification strategies which enter the ideational and interactive domains of language.

In phonology
slow down speech in order to allow L more time to process the
language, more deliberate articulation in order to allow L to identify
ideal phonemes more readily, pause more between phonological
phrases in order to allow L to identify salient boundaries of
constituents

In morphology
use verbs in base form so that L has less syntactic processing to
perform

In syntax
omit unstressed words (e.g. copula) in order to avoid L problems
with destressed syllables, use topic reinstatement rather than
anaphoric reference in order to allow L to keep references clear,
avoid complex constructions

In text structure
use paratactic connections between utterances ('and', 'then', etc.)
rather than hypotactic connections ('in spite of', 'although', 'the one
who' . . .) in order to avoid continuity problems, topicalize familiar
items (i.e. state familiar items first) in order to allow ideal given—
new pattern of processing, explicitly signal new topics, provide
frequent repetition and rephrasing of key propositions

In vocabulary
avoid low-frequency words in order to avoid L search for new
words, provide paraphrase or simple definition for new words

In communication strategy
avoid tangential topics or topics likely to be unfamiliar, recycle
topics frequently, mark clearly any major topic shifts, structure short
turns to ensure listener response

In paralinguistic features
use more of intonation range to provide contrasts to listener; provide
gestural cues for redundancy

FIGURE 6.4 Conversational strategies for making language (potentially)
more accessible to listeners

Instructors need to exercise caution when using interpersonal
modifications such as these with their learners. In introducing these
modifications, the native speaker is guided — consciously or not — by
hypotheses concerning the learner's current language skills and current
level of understanding of the discourse. As Klein (1987) points out, in
introducing modifications, the teacher may err in three ways. Firstly,
the teacher's modifications may hinder comprehension if the
modifications alter the intended message. Secondly, the learner may
interpret them as a sign of social distance and condescension, and feel

insulted in being addressed in a simplified register. Thirdly, the modifications may introduce non-target-like discourse which provides the learner with false models of language use and thereby undermines the purpose of instruction. (See Anderson and Lynch, 1988, for further discussion.)

6.6   Setting and roles as task components

Setting refers not to overall classroom setup *per se* but to the interactive setting that individual learners are part of. Decisions about setting relate to grouping of learners for maximal practice of the listening strategy being focused on. **Role** refers to the rights and responsibilities of individual listeners in controlling the activity and the flow of information in the task. Decisions about roles relate to determining who is in possession of information needed for task completion and who has authority over the information that is used in the task.

Setting and roles need to be prescribed in a task design. They will be related to the domain of listening that is emphasized. Collaborative settings are necessary for practice of interactive listening skills (such as using comprehension checks and confirmation signals, requests for clarifications). For transactional listening tasks in which individual learners are separately responsible for collecting and interpreting information, less collaborative settings may be appropriate. However, even in lecture-type settings it is important to create opportunities for clarification and questioning in order to assure that learners are indeed actively engaged in listening. A prolonged absence of interaction can indirectly encourage a serialist approach to a task (Pask and Scott, 1972), in which learners simply follow procedural guidelines (e.g. take notes) and obtain minimally appropriate outcomes.

The interrelationship among settings, roles and task outcomes is often overlooked in task planning, while much greater attention is given to selection of input materials. However, it is easy to demonstrate that even in tasks dealing with identical informational content, an alteration of learner rights and responsibilities for the flow of information and for the choice of procedures in tasks can affect what students learn (cf. Barnes, 1976; Wright, 1987).

Careful designers of classroom tasks will then consider questions such as: Who is controlling information flow? (Are there possibilities for students to gain this control?) Who is responsible for completion of activity? (Each individual learner? Each member of a group contributing equally?) These questions are critical since it would appear that the creation of active information-controlling roles for learners in listening activities helps to create a balance among the ideational and interactive aspects of listening performance. Brown *et al.* (1985) refer to the necessity of setting up helpful conditions to ensure learner success in classroom exercises. One's prescribed role in an activity may be considered as one of these conditions.

6.7   Procedure as a component of task design

Procedure refers to the sequence of actions that is carried out by the participants in a task. Procedures essentially specify what is and what is not to be done. Decisions about procedures must answer these questions: What variations in procedures are acceptable? Which variations are encouraged and which are not to be tolerated?

Although 'procedures' is used here to refer to the observable behaviour of learners, instructors are obviously most concerned with the underlying skills and strategies that are reflected in the procedures, and should therefore devise procedures which encourage specific listening strategies or enabling skills, and which allow for useful feedback on the use of the targeted skills or strategies.

Well-devised procedures will attempt to promote the selection of appropriate risk strategies and take into account the required level of response by the learner. Procedures which require greater levels of response from students — either cognitively, linguistically, or interactively — make a task necessarily more complex, even if all other features of the task are held constant.

6.7.1   Questions as the basis of inquiry: a typology

If tasks are seen as problem-based, procedures may be seen as manifesting the process of inquiry into the problem. Although question-answering itself is a procedure, questions can form the basis for various procedure types. Activity frames (such as grids or charts or tables) which assist students in focusing on various aspects of the text can be thought of as reformulated questions. This section presents some typologies of questions.

Question typologies reveal the range of cognitive and affective demands that questions might impose. Candlin *et al.* (1974) proposed five types of questions that can be asked or implicitly incorporated into procedures:
(1) literal questions concerning factual data, word meanings, recognition of ideas;
(2) reorganization questions concerning analysis, synthesis, classification, reorganization of information;

Least difficult question type ———— Most difficult question type
< replicative — echoic — synthesis — oblique — surmise >
Least integrative work ———— Most integrative work

Replicative	— answer replicates or repeats the text word for word
Echoic	— the answer echoes the text although it may differ lexically or grammatically
Synthesis	— the reader/hearer must connect and conflate a number of identifiable bits of information
Oblique	— the reader/hearer must infer a fact which follows from something mentioned explicitly in the text
Surmise	— the reader/hearer must infer a fact or idea, but not from an explicit statement in the text

FIGURE 6.5 Grading of questions in terms of response required
(based on Gerot, 1987)

(3) inferential questions concerning conjecture, hypothesis, and prediction;

(4) evaluation questions requiring students to draw on prior knowledge to make judgements on validity, accuracy, acceptability, or worth;

(5) appreciation questions concerning language appreciation, significance, communicative value, and stylistic features.

The proportion of the inferencing based on the text alone diminishes as one goes up the scale.

Responses to questions can be considered along a continuum of inference: from **echoic** (whose answers are self-evident, such as those to display questions or directives to reproduce information explicit in a text) to **integrative** (answers that are original and must be constructed from background knowledge sources and text information (Figure 6.5) (cf. Nix, 1983; Gerot, 1987).

The difficulty of a question can also be considered from the aspect of the space for choice that is provided. A simple syntactic continuum of yes/no questions, either/or questions, W/H questions, illustrates the fact that some questions are procedurally easier to answer, irrespective of the knowledge that is called for in answering them.

Because questions are so widely used in language classrooms, often as prompts to elicit shows of student understanding, it is important for task designers to consider various continua of cognitive difficulty. Questions are extremely powerful devices for guiding selective listening and for assisting listeners in forming representations of text segments, particularly when they are posed in advance (Figure 6.6).

A. Definition
- (suitable modality) Define...
- Give a definition of...
- What does —— mean by...
- What does (term) mean?
- What is/are (term)?

B. Example
- Give an example of...
- Can you name one type of...

C. Significance
- What is the significance of ...
- Why is ...important
- What is the importance of ... for...
- Tell what the role of ... is
- Who was ...?

D. Physical image
- Describe what (...) (must have) looked like
- Give a description of...

E. Function/purpose
- Tell me the function (purpose of)...
- What is ( ) used for

F. Sequence and state changes
- What happened after...
- Tell me about what happened to ...
- Describe what (...) did...

G. Similarities and differences
- What's the difference between... and ...
- Compare ... with ...
- How do... differ in (trait)
- Why is ... different from...

H. Classification
- How many kinds of ... did you find
- What groups of ... would be suitable for...

I. Cause/result
- What caused ....
- What factors contribute to ...

J. Familiarity with argumentation
- Why does —— insist on ...
- What justification does —— give...
- Explain why...

K. Evaluative thinking
- What do you think is the key ...
- Give another explanation for...
- Do you support (this) opinion...

(based on Horowitz, 1986)

FIGURE 6.6 Cognitive difficulty continuum for questions as prompts (examples of formulaic wordings follow each type)

Appropriacy of questions will depend on text type, content, and organization, as well as on learner needs and abilities. Simply suggesting that learners should pay attention to, focus on, or think about pre-set questions during a listening task is often ineffective in L2 classroom settings.

6.8   Outcome as an aspect of task design

Outcome refers to a recognizable evaluation point in a learning activity. Doyle (1983) says that learning tasks should specify the 'products students are to formulate'. Usually the product is represented by something tangible that the learner produces (e.g. a completed grid, a list of notes or questions), although an outcome may be something quite intangible, such as a shift in attitudes or mental representation.

Clear outcomes are critical in structured learning activities, since they allow learners and instructors to be accountable for what has transpired and to plan for subsequent tasks based on the instructor's evaluation (or co-evaluation by learners and teacher). Clear outcomes of listening activities are vital from a developmental standpoint because, as has been stated, one central question in a qualitative view of listening development is: how can the learner find useful comparisons between current interpretations of the L2 and those of competent users of the target language? Outcomes allow learners to make their interpretations tangible and thereby make comparisons between their current interpretations and those of the instructor or of other learners, or their own later (and earlier) responses on the same task.

Time of the outcome is a vital concern in listening practice, since delays in completion of a task require the learner to use recall skills that are not directly related to interpreting discourse in real time (cf. Carroll, 1972; Fredericksen, 1972). In general, instructors concerned with development of listening strategies should specify outcomes that immediately follow chunks of spoken input, and should provide some method of allowing the learners to check their outcomes quickly.

Outcomes need not be considered with any finality as evidence of learning; they should rather be seen as tentative representations of current understanding. Current representations of L2 learners are often based on non-understandings and misunderstandings, caused by the multitude of perception and interpretation effects discussed in Chapters 2, 3, and 4, and compounded by the distinctive anxiety that learners often report experiencing when listening in their L2.

Because revision and elaboration of current understanding is the topic of L2 listening instruction, instructors must be prepared for the range of possible learner outcomes for a task. Only by realizing possible causes of misunderstandings and non-understandings that lead to partially acceptable outcomes can the instructor draw attention to strategies for re-understanding the task. As such, it is vital that instructors are able to interpret both acceptable and unacceptable outcomes as evidence of appropriate or inappropriate listening strategies. Outcomes should then be graded to allow for successive encounters with the language data presented.

Successful task outcomes are not necessarily evidence that the task performer has learned the information contained in a text, nor are unsuccessful task outcomes necessarily evidence that the task performer has not learned useful information, or hierarchically more important information contained in a text.[3]

It has been claimed that text understanding cannot be measured additively. It is contended that listeners do not cumulatively comprehend texts by decoding information units sequentially and arriving at some percentage of total understanding of the speaker's text. An individual's understanding will be related to what aspects of the text are congruent with prior knowledge and expectations. Listeners who find a text highly discontinuous with their prior knowledge and expectations may learn more than listeners who already know a great deal about what the speaker is saying. This observation underlines the importance of having tasks that can make appropriate outcome demands for learners at different levels of skill (or allow for different solutions depending on skills and strategies of learners) and the necessity of having multiple exposures to the same or similar texts in order to allow learners to approach text meaning in stages.

6.9   Monitoring as an ongoing aspect of a task

Monitoring refers here, in the context of task design, to the attention of the teacher to the learners' performance, particularly to the strategies and skills the learners are employing. A vital aspect of instruction in listening is finding and recording evidence of learner use of skills and strategies in tasks.

The monitoring of skills and strategies is to some extent informed guesswork since the instructor does not have direct access to what the learner is thinking. Successful monitoring by the instructor will usually involve knowing the learners well in order to better interpret non-verbal behaviour. Successful monitoring will also involve the learner in triangulation of the instructor's judgements.

Assuming that the instructor is monitoring for effective use of skills and strategies, decisions that the instructor may make based on what is observed include:

(1) giving advice about strategies;
(2) reformulating procedures (e.g. introducing a practice routine);
(3) providing new input (to one or more learners);
(4) altering settings;
(5) changing roles of learners;
(6) noting areas for further practice, later mention, future tasks, etc.;
(7) stopping the activity.

Instructors obviously will want to intervene only at appropriate points during the task procedure, rather than at the time they make apparently significant observations about the learners' performance in the task.

6.10   Feedback in tasks

Feedback refers here to an explicit highlighting of what has been learned or what is being learned, and potentially an application of what has been learned. Questions related to feedback include the following:

(1) How do learners know they are doing (or have done) well or poorly on the task?
(2) Does successful performance on this task lead the learner to another task?
(3) Will appropriate feedback be given in the context of a subsequent activity?
(4) Will post-listening activities provide feedback by expanding into cultural areas or by examining linguistic aspects of the task?

Feedback is a critical stage of any learning activity since it formalizes what type of learning is expected. Oller (1987) suggests that a testing/feedback/evaluation component of some type should be included in every activity in order to provide tangible references for the learning process. Because feedback has consequences for adjustment of learning strategies, where possible, the task should allow for co-evaluation by learner and teacher, rather than evaluation solely by the teacher (Nunan, 1988). Feedback includes learner evaluation of the activity as valuable or helpful, whether the learner is satisfied with outcome, and how the learner and teacher intend to proceed in subsequent learning tasks.

6.11   Conclusion: criteria for task validity

Good listening instruction is first and foremost good instruction, that is, it creates the conditions for meaningful learner involvement, outcomes, and evaluation. Good task design for listening development will likewise be first good task design: it will account in advance for variables that are likely to affect student learning.

Figure 6.7 summarizes the foregoing discussion of task design in the form of a checklist of what may be considered to constitute good teaching practice.

In order to be considered most instructionally useful, a listening task should, where possible, consider the following.

Overall considerations

(1) The task should be based on, derived from, or have transparent applications toward real-world tasks that the learners are expected to perform.

(2) The task should be consistent with valid approaches to language learning that are acceptable to the learners. In cases in which tasks make new demands on learners or suggest learning styles that are unfamiliar to learners, the new demands and procedures must be considered as primary aspects of the task.

(3) The task should take into account major factors that are likely to influence complexity.

    (3a) Speakers: the pace of the speaker, the accent of the speaker, the number of speakers to listen to.

    (3b) Content: the linguistic structure of utterances within the segment, the accessibility of the rhetorical structure of the segment, the amount of redundant information and signals which reinforce this rhetorical structure.

    (3c) Support: visual aids, print, prior reading material, prior presentation.

(4) The task should require attention to the information conveyed through speech; focus should be on listener construction of meaning (rather than on analysis of formal features of the utterance) and negotiation of understanding if initial attempts at understanding are not satisfactory.

(5) The task should encourage the use of the listener's prior knowledge and use of environmental cues in interpreting speakers' utterances.

Input considerations

(1) The task should provide a 'problem source' that is interesting enough to engage the learners, and rich enough in linguistic and ideational content to allow different learners to apply skills and strategies at their own level of competence, and to project learning outcomes onto significant issues of learning. Texts which are projective onto larger cultural issues and important personal issues for the learners are likely to be of most value.

(2) Tasks should use appropriate input material, whether from the teacher or other speaker(s), or from recorded audio or video sources, in consideration of learner attention, motivation, and prior context, rather than only in terms of 'linguistic difficulty'.

(3) Tasks should provide contextualized samples of speech that are intelligible, exemplifying natural features of spoken language (pause, hesitation, on-line composing features of syntax and vocabulary selection), utilizing a commonly known dialect and accent; present appropriate cues to contextualize the sample.

(4) Tasks should present input material in appropriate sizes of segments or chunks and at a pace which allows both continuity and frequent learner response or directed feedback to the speaker.

Role and setting considerations

(1) Tasks should allow learner groupings (settings) and roles (rights to control information and task procedures) which are appropriate for the purpose of the task.

(2) Task sequences should allow learners to assume a range of listener roles (eavesdropper, audience, participant).

Procedural considerations

(1) Task procedures should call for continual listener response.

(2) Task procedures should include ways of dealing with non-understandings and possibilities for negotiation.

Outcome considerations

(1) The task outcome should be appropriate to the input in terms of complexity. (Conversely: The text chosen should be appropriately focused for the task outcome.)

(2) The outcome should be stated in terms of a listening construct that is identifiable by learners and instructor.

Monitoring and feedback considerations

(1) Task or instructor should provide encouragement and motivation for learners throughout the task and should reward sincere efforts at accomplishing the task.

(2) Intervention by the instructor in the task should be timed to occur only at appropriate transition periods in the task.

FIGURE 6.7 Checklist for planning tasks

6.12   Discussion questions and projects

1. Listener intent

Consider the notion of 'listener intent' — do you find that the development of intent is an important concern in listening development? To what extent is the issue of listener intent amenable to empirical research?

2. Enabling skills

Interview a language learner about the difficulties or challenges the learner experiences in situations calling for listening ability. List as many specific points as possible. Later, attempt to classify the reported difficulties into the categories of enabling skills given in this chapter.

Which are more commonly reported — those in the 'salient skills' category or those in the 'sub-skills' category? Why might this be so?

3. Listening strategies

Keep a diary for one week of the situations you are involved in as a listener. These may be situations in which you are using your first language or a second language.

Make notes of the variables that might be relevant:

place;
number of speakers;
your role (addressee, overhearer, etc.);
what goal(s) you achieved in the interaction;
how you achieved the goal(s);
any problems you had as a listener;
what you did (if anything) in attempt to address the problem.

After one week (in which you will presumably have at least 10–20 self-reports/observations), look for patterns in the diary accounts. Do you see any evidence of strategies — successful or unsuccessful ones? Can these be related to the strategy list in this chapter? If not, how can the list be revised?

4. Task design

Visit a language classroom of a colleague (or have someone visit your classroom if you are currently teaching). Record on tape at least 30 minutes of class activity. In reviewing the tape, can you categorize the overall activity in terms of individual 'tasks', with components of input, setting and roles, procedures, outcomes, monitoring, feedback? Which are most obvious? Which are least obvious? Which seem to be missing altogether?

Show the results of your observation to the teacher (or if a colleague is observing your class, have the colleague show you the results). Are there any category occurrences which the observer and instructor disagree on? Does the instructor view this classification system as helpful for planning or evaluation? Why or why not? Would the learners benefit from this classification system? Why or why not?

5. Classroom questions, test questions

Analyse a 15-minute segment of classroom discourse, preferably in a class which is emphasizing the development of listening skills. List all of the questions asked by instructor and students. Which of the question types proposed in Sections 6.9 and 6.11 are most often used by the instructor? (Consider separately Gerot's system of inferential types and Horowitz's system of text-probe types.) Which by the students? To what extent is this a function of the text; of the task; of the teaching style of the instructor; of the learning style of the students?

6. Principles of task design

Review the list of considerations for task design provided in Section 6.11. In designing tasks for a particular group of learners, would you find any of these considerations problematic? Why?

Notes

1. An example of this reasoning might run as follows: 'Beginning-level listeners are more likely to be able to discriminate phonemes /s/ from /f/ presented in isolation than they are to note correct information (such as times in a train departure announcement); therefore, we should teach beginning-level learners phoneme discrimination first.' This reasoning fails in terms of a type of external validity: the classification system does not address the objectives for which it was designed (Fleishman and Quaintance, 1984).
2. One can find general pedagogic prescriptions for listening (and other macro-skill) instruction in 'stages' in various books and articles on teaching methodology, such as Rivers and Temperley (1984). Prescriptions for language-teaching methodology often seem to me to be based on tradition, expectation, and the belief that activities that learners can perform with minimal linguistic error must be good for them. This debate concerning decisions about syllabus content based on what the learners can do versus what needs to be learned (and what is learnable) is crucial in the language teaching profession. The issue will be taken up further in Chapter 8.
3. In a discussion task reported by Rulon and McCreary (1986), some learners who had heard a lecture on the American Revolution claimed that the Revolution had taken place on British soil, and had spent considerable time discussing the lecture without having this misconception corrected. Are we to infer that the learners had misunderstood the lecture or is it feasible that the learners did not find information about location to be important in the context of the discussion?

7 Assessing listening ability

7.0 Assessment and sampling

Issues of skill development, as discussed in Chapter 6, are closely related
to issues of skill assessment. The relationship is based on the notions
of criterion-referencing and grading: if a skill can be developed over
time, reliable judgements of 'how much' of the skill has been acquired
can be made at suitable points in time and reasonable criteria for grading
a performance (in terms of quantity and quality) can be articulated.

It is axiomatic that assessments of skill attainment which are referenced
to specified domains of language use are more relevant to test users than
those which are not. For example, a numeric score intended to signify
a person's ability in listening is of little value, even if it is referenced
to a group's norm (e.g. a native-speaker norm), without reference to
criteria in some topic domain (say, mechanical engineering) and to
behaviour within a situational domain (say, summarizing a presentation
at a convention for mechanical engineers).

The assessment of a learner's ability for any macro skill, such as
listening, is necessarily based on a judgement of quantity and quality
in a limited **sampling** of performances. Only to the extent that the
selection of samples is a fair representation of a person's performance
in a specified domain can we consider that our assessment is meaningful.
This chapter outlines several broad issues related to preparation and use
of listening tests and the interpretation of test results. First, key concepts
related to validity are reviewed. Then the variables in language testing
tasks are outlined in order to see how test specifications reflect a test's
validity (and therefore its utility). Finally, a band scale for characterizing
listening ability is proposed.

7.1 Purposes of testing in education

From a practical perspective, testing is a critical area in language
education as results of testing often influence the future of learners, the
professional evaluation of instructors, and the direction of curriculum

design. Testing has long been an active arena for debate among applied linguists, many of whom contend that current language-testing practices often provide inaccurate information about learner ability and instructor ability, and are therefore an unstable basis for programme evaluation.

A central issue in this debate concerns the purpose of testing. Most testing and assessment programmes now in place in formal education are for purposes of reporting on learner status (e.g. by providing **norm-referenced** information on learner ranking) rather than for purposes of learning (e.g. by providing **criterion-referenced** feedback to students in order to help them formulate learning objectives in achievable steps) (Black, 1986). Thus, while concern over testing may provide indirect instrumental motivation for learners ('I want to pass the test so that I can get on with what I really want to do'), the testing process itself — in design, administration, scoring, feedback — may not reflect needs of learners and teachers for assessment of how well learning goals are being reached. In other words, testing may influence both learner and instructor concern over the results of instruction, rather than provide input for planning, revision, and refinement of **pedagogic tasks**, which are the heart of the process of instruction.

7.2   Questions of reliability and validity

Reliability is a measure of the degree to which the same assessment procedure is likely to give consistent results. In order for a test to be reasonably reliable, error of measurement (the variation in test results among test-takers that does not represent true differences between individuals, but rather represents differences among the examiners, differences in testing conditions, differences among the discrimination values of test items) must be reduced. In order to increase reliability, the various aspects of test content and test administration need to be restricted. Test writers will seek to delimit the test content to that which can be most clearly defined and to select only those testing conditions that can be effectively controlled. Tests which prove to be most reliable will typically have very refined 'specifications' for content and format. (See Henning, 1987, for further discussion of reliability and detailed instructions on calculating reliability coefficients.)

While it is a necessary first condition for interpretation of a test, high reliability is sometimes achieved at the expense of other criteria that make a test useful. Language educators frequently express concern that many major language tests may be more reliable and administratively efficient than they are valid and relevant to the needs of examinees and teachers (Duran *et al.*, 1987). The requirement that test writers (and testing organizations) achieve high reliability in test results versus the concern of teachers and test takers for maximal relevance of test to the learning situation is a complex issue in language teaching.

Decisions about testing a group of learners will involve a compromise over issues of test reliability and validity. For instance, we know that listening discrimination tests are likely to have higher reliability than listen-and-recall tests (Allen and Davies, 1977), but this does not mean that listening discrimination tests are 'better' listening tests for all purposes. The value of the reliability must be weighed against the need for useful information about the ability in question. The following paragraphs consider several aspects of validity. (See Alderson and Hughes, 1981 for more thorough definitions.)

Face validity (or subjective validity) is the degree to which test users consider the test will measure the ability it claims to measure. (For example, if a group of teachers considers that the language used in Test A, designed to measure learners' ability to listen in academic settings, does not truly reflect the language used in academic settings, the test has reduced face validity.) Face validity is based on how fair the test is from the test user's vantage point — that is, the degree to which testing tasks resemble pedagogic tasks and real-world tasks and means of evaluation resemble those used in pedagogic and/or real-world settings (Figure 7.1). A non-technical question that captures the gist of this issue is: does the test appear to be a reasonable and fair test to all test-takers?

Content validity is the degree to which the items in the test adequately reflect samples of the ability to be assessed. (For example, if test items are drawn directly from tasks the learners have engaged in and if the test items represent samples of all the tasks the learners have engaged in, the test has high content validity.) This will include the notion of **procedural validity** — the degree to which responses are 'authentic', or appropriate to the type of input. Questions that may capture this issue are: do the decisions (and behaviours) that the test taker has to make (and perform) resemble those to be made (and performed) in natural conditions? Are the test-taking conditions and targeted behaviours similar to those of the teaching situation?

Empirical validity (or validity in reference to another measure) is the degree to which results of the test correlate with results or rankings on another measure. (For example, if a group of learner results on Test A, designed to assess ability to listen to English in academic settings, correlate highly with the results on Test B, designed to assess ability to listen to English in social settings, Tests A and B have empirical validity, relative to each other.)

Construct validity is the degree to which the test reflects and attempts

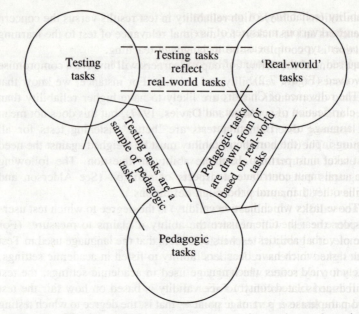

FIGURE 7.1 The interrelationship between testing tasks, pedagogic tasks, and real-world tasks

to incorporate theoretical notions of the ability being tested. An empirical issue related to construct validity is suggested by a basic question: does the test distinguish effectively those who have gained the targeted skills and utilized targeted strategies from those who have not?

Ecological validity is the degree to which a test can be conducted and evaluated with available resources. (For example, if Test A can be carried out using only a tape recorder, paper, and pencil and has responses that can be evaluated on a dichotomous (right or wrong) scale, it might be considered to have higher ecological validity than Test B, which requires placing the learner in a live lecture, video taping the learner, and two raters later analysing the learner's note-taking behaviour.)

The question of appropriate trade-off in types of validity is obviously complex and no test can meet all criteria concerning validity. Priorities in test design must be observed from the outset. If test writers ignore relevant questions of validity until the reliability of a measurement is ascertained, the resulting test is likely to be unacceptable.

Throughout the history of language testing, testing researchers have been careful to define the types of tasks that tend to produce the greatest stability (reliability) of measurement. Chaudron (1985), for example, examined various measures of listening ability and suggested relationships between type of measurement, the amount of language processing required, and the amount of language encoding the test-taker's response involved (Figure 7.2).

The relevance of Chaudron's scheme for the testing of listening is in its clarification of construct validity within an input—output orientation to language use. The scheme attempts to estimate the relationship of testing input (the horizontal dimension) to the cognitive operations the test-taker must perform. In other words, the scheme estimates how much the aural input contributes to test performance and the degree to which skills other than aural processing are required (the vertical dimension).

Those tasks which have been labelled as closed tasks — requiring a response near the time of listening and requiring a response with minimal use of verbal abilities — will (it is predicted) yield reliable test scores.[1] The tasks which have been labelled open tasks, on the other hand, are likely to yield scores which may not be accepted as reflections of listening skill as an isolated construct. For example, if a learner is asked to recall and paraphrase a part of a spoken text, the learner's verbal encoding (spoken or written) ability is reflected in the response. Separating out the listening aspect of the recall performance from the speaking aspect of that performance with any degree of certainty is virtually impossible

	(Closed)			(Open)
	Less encoding required (Non-verbal)	—	(Oral)	More encoding required (Written)
(Closed) Less 'understanding' required	signal detection pattern recognition pattern matching		echoic response imitation	
				partial dictation listening cloze cloze recall
	motor response selecting NV response			
More 'understanding' required (Open)			paraphrasing recalling text	
				written recall
				comprehension question response

Vertical dimension (left column) suggests 'degree of understanding' of speech that is required; horizontal dimension suggests amount of linguistic encoding of response that is required.

FIGURE 7.2 Dimensions of response to spoken input (adapted from Chaudron, 1985, p. 288)

(as discussed in Chapter 5). It is still possible to produce reliable measurements of performances on open tasks (through establishing clear criteria for responses, training raters, etc.), but only when the criterion measures recognize the influence of other skills involved in the tasks.

Although judgements of the value of listening-skill tests primarily on the basis of statistical reliability are defensible on scientific grounds, such judgements are questionable in terms of educational principles. The key problem with an approach that overemphasizes reliability is that it may unwittingly sacrifice important aspects of content validity. The unfortunate effect on pedagogy (which is not necessarily intended by the test writers) is that the test users − language teachers and learners − may come to accept that listening ability amounts to whatever can be measured reliably by a published audio-based test. Assessment of listening and the teaching of listening skills in a realistic context, in which other skills are used, is a more suitable direction.

7.3   Sources of listening difficulty

The question of reliability and the issue of construct validity present an uncomfortable dilemma for test writers and language teachers. In order to include testing formats that allow for improved face validity and broader content validity, reliability may be compromised. Specifically, if listening is to be measured in situations of actual use, situations in which intervening variables obviously come into play, reliability of measurement will be compromised. However, it is precisely the integration of information-gathering skills from spoken texts with other pragmatic skills that serves as the basis for listening development. While it is important for pedagogic reasons to identify learner problems with listening, at the same time it compromises educational principles to equate listening ability with information-gathering skill.

An unfortunate **washback effect** (a term used by Morrow, 1985) of formal testing is that classroom teaching of listening tends to be biased towards quantification of listening outcomes rather than towards the process of building reasonable interpretations. For example, teachers will often attribute any lack of understanding (i.e. poor test performance) to language variables, to a lack of knowledge of vocabulary and grammar. As Brown (1986) points out, although lack of linguistic knowledge is often a key factor in listening problems, difficulties can also arise from procedural and pragmatic sources. The listener may not know which aspects of a situation are relevant to interpreting current utterances or to how to respond (Figure 7.3).

language problem:	non-understanding of linguistic items due to phonotactic, syntactic, or lexical decoding problems
inferential problem:	inappropriate or inefficient strategy selection; inappropriate activation of background or contextual knowledge
procedural problem:	not knowing what to do, not knowing what kind of response is expected

FIGURE 7.3   Listener problems during a test

7.4   Assessment of listening ability in standardized testing

Language teachers and programme administrators must be cognizant of the important role of formal, norm-referenced testing, as language learners are often evaluated on proficiency tests, which do emphasize correctness. One aspect of instruction in listening is, arguably, instruction aimed at helping students develop the linguistic and procedural skills necessary to perform well on the formal language-testing tasks. This section reviews the listening specifications of some major standardized proficiency tests. Presumably, an awareness of these types of specifications for any test will improve a test-taker's performance.

7.4.1   Test specifications: listener role

The first specification to be noted about a listening test is that it must formalize the listener's role as respondent to an utterance, as an addressee (as in an interview), as audience member (as in a simulated lecture), as an overhearer/bystander (as in a recorded conversation), or as a judge (as in a single-utterance evaluation). Many language tests ask test-takers to switch back and forth between roles, and to imagine they are in certain roles as they take the test. This role switching may be a skill in itself, independent of the transactional and interactional listening abilities the tester is seeking to assess; clearly, a misunderstanding of roles can lead to a poorer than normal task performance by the test-taker.

7.4.2   Test specifications: skill inventories

A valid criterion-referenced listening test will be aimed at identifying appropriate configurations of skills that are identifiable in targeted situations. Configurations will vary with test takers since different patterns of communicative language use will entail different combinations of skills needed (Carroll, 1981).

We have identified core enabling skills and enacting skills which underlie effective listening (see Chapter 6 for a list of sub-skills):

(1) Recognizing prominence within utterances.
(2) Formulating propositional sense for a speaker's utterance.
(3) Formulating a conceptual framework that links utterances together.
(4) Interpreting plausible intention(s) for the speaker in making an utterance.
(5) Utilizing representation of discourse to make appropriate response.

Any criterion-based listening test will be based on a principled sampling of enabling and enacting skills. We have identified also in our discussion those interactive skills which will come into play in collaborative settings:

(1) Probing (in an appropriate manner) for more information if current understanding is not adequate for task.
(2) Checking understanding, if current understanding does not meet task criteria.
(3) Identifying as specifically as possible causes of non-understanding.

Criterion-based listening tests which are conducted in interactive contexts should provide for measurement of these skills as well as specific information-gathering.

7.4.3 Test specifications: item and response format

This section categorizes aspects of listening ability that may be tapped in specific testing formats. Ability to take a test involving spoken input is in part language ability and in part procedural ability. Language ability is probed in the interpretation of the **input texts** and **test item stems**, whereas procedural ability is reflected in interpreting and executing the **test response options**. The understanding that the listener is expected to achieve is then induced by the testing task: the test-taker must interpret the language in the test stem in relation to the response options. It is this induction that constitutes the test-taker's performance (Fredericksen, 1972).

Stem types in any listening test will include spoken or taped **presentation of the language data** as:

(1) series of words;
(2) isolated words and phrases;
(3) isolated utterances, usually a series of sentences spoken by one speaker;
(4) connected dialogue by two or more speakers;

(5) connected monologue.

The spoken data may be accompanied by visual input:

(a) text illustrations or photographs (e.g. a picture of a room with people in it);

(b) video tape (e.g. a video sequence in which people enter a room);

(c) written text or written symbols (e.g. a printed sentence: *There are some people in a room.*).

These are the characteristics of the test input and test item stems. Response option types may be usefully categorized by the **skill operation** required of the test-taker. These include the following:

(1) Placement of marker on part of the written form of the utterance (e.g. reading and listening to the pronunciation of the word 'light' and circling this word rather than 'right'). This involves perception skills and a transcoding skill. (Refer to Figure 6.1 for a listing of skills.)

(2) Gap filling, completion of an utterance or set of utterances (e.g. providing the next likely part of a dialogue, as in:

> Test taker hears 'Why isn't Sue here?' (accompanied by a picture of a woman caught in a traffic jam.)
> Test taker writes: _____.

This involves the skill of formulating a propositional sense for an utterance. (The item obviously involves other language skills as well, such as lexical retrieval and written expression.)

(3) Multiple choice, selecting a visual representation (e.g. choosing a picture that represents what a speaker is describing, such as, a two-picture sequence of a person turning off a light vs. taking out a light bulb.)

> Test taker hears: 'He's turning off the light'.

This type of item involves identifying word forms.

(4) Information transfer, producing a verbal representation or response; e.g. repeating what is heard in whole, or filling in gapped parts, as in:

> She's turning on the _____.

This kind of item requires the test-taker to transcode information.

(5) Answering questions or evaluating statements about what was heard (e.g. after hearing a short description of a person, the test-taker is presented some statements and is asked to indicate 'true' or 'false'.) This type of item involves the skills of utilizing representations of discourse to make appropriate responses.

(6)   Directive response (e.g. the test-taker must perform actions indicated by the speaker; perhaps paper-and-pencil responses, such as drawing a continuous arrow to indicate a route on a map given by the speaker). This type of item involves formulating a propositional sense for a speaker's utterance and formulating a conceptual framework that links utterances together.

(7)   Controlled note-taking (for example, completing a table or chart while listening to a lecture). This type of item also involves the skills of utilizing representations of discourse to make appropriate responses (specifically, reducing and transcoding information).

(8)   Form filling (for example, filling out a change-of-address form for someone while the person tells you the information to write down). This type of item involves formulating a propositional sense for a speaker's utterance and formulating a conceptual framework that links utterances together. Transcoding skills are also required.

(9)   Labelling or completing diagrams, tables, charts, graphs, maps, or illustrations while listening to a passage (Appendix 7A, at the end of this chapter, provides an example). As with previous items, this type involves the skills of utilizing representations of discourse to make appropriate responses (specifically, reducing and transcoding information).

(10)   Matching items, objects, and attributes. Providing selected information about the input (e.g. The test-taker hears a set of expressions and be asked to identify the setting — say, a bank, a post office, a department store — when and where these expressions might be heard). This type of item may involve interpreting plausible intentions for the speakers in making utterances, as well as formulating a conceptual framework that links utterances together. (Appendix 7B provides an example of matching in an academic listening context.)

(11)   Sorting events, names, objects in order (e.g. the test-taker hears a narrative and is asked to place pictures depicting events in the story in correct order). This type of item involves utilizing representations of discourse to make appropriate responses.

(12)   Summary writing (e.g. the test-taker hears a story or exposition and is asked to write down the main points). This type of item also involves utilizing representations of discourse to make appropriate responses.

The reason for listing these specifications is not to encourage variety of item types in listening assessment, but to show how input stem and response option specifications may be selected from specifications of targeted skills and targeted content. From the perspective of content validity, an optimal relationship between the item stem and response option will be one in which the test-taker's response is an authentic response for the listening input. (See Chapter 6 for a discussion of authenticity.)

7.5   Criteria for assessment validity

This chapter has attempted to show how the need for reliability in assessment must be balanced with the need for content and construct validity. Figure 7.4 provides a summary of criteria for validity. While all criteria for validity may not be met in every assessment, test writers can achieve greater validity by carefully considering specifications for tests at the outset. A checklist of specifications is given in Figure 7.5.

---

(1) Items should be in contexts similar to those experienced in the target settings; language used should reflect natural conditions of use.

(2) The test-taker should have the opportunity to utilize contextual knowledge in making sense of the items and response tasks.

(3) Testing tasks should reasonably reflect activities in the target situations; the focus of items should generally be on meaning rather than on form.

(4) Test-taker should have opportunity for a range of reasonable responses, rather than a single correct response. (Responses need to be scored on an entropy model of acceptability, rather than on a dichotomous scale.)

FIGURE 7.4 General criteria for validity

Test content (input)
   topics and themes to be included
   text types to be included (narrative, descriptive, etc.)
   text units to be used (phrases, singles utterances, dialogues, monologues, of what length)
   mode of input (audio, video, live)
   varieties of English to be used
   scripted or unscripted

Test tasks
   which listening skills are to be focal in the tasks?

Other skills
   what other linguistic skills are required?
   what listener roles will the test taker adopt?
   what non-linguistic skills are required to fulfil these roles?

FIGURE 7.5 Checklist of specifications for testing listening

7.6 Characterizing listening ability

Useful evaluations of a learner's listening ability must be criterion-referenced. This section presents a framework from which criterion-referenced bands can be written.

Competent listener
- able to understand all styles of speech that are intelligible to well-educated native listeners in the target community and able to seek clarification smoothly when speech is unintelligible;
- able to understand abstract concepts expressed orally;
- able to note areas where own knowledge is lacking to achieve an acceptable understanding and to note where speaker is vague or inconsistent;
- able to understand and display appropriate listener responses in a wide range of social and specialized contexts in the target culture setting;
- able to adopt an appropriate risk strategy to respond to task demands.

Listener of modest ability
- able to understand most styles of speech that are intelligible to well-educated native listeners in the target community and attempts to seek clarification when speech is unintelligible, although attempts are not always successful or appropriate;
- able to understand some abstract concepts expressed orally, but often requires repetition or re-explanation;
- able to note areas where own knowledge is lacking to achieve an acceptable understanding and to note where speaker is vague or inconsistent, but occasionally is confused about the source of difficulty in understanding;
- able to understand enough of the linguistic/pragmatic input to infer the gist of the communicative event; displays listener responses in a wide range of social and specialized contexts in the target culture setting, but often not appropriately;
- able to adopt an appropriate risk strategy to respond to task demands but often adopts an ineffective strategy which detracts from successful listening.

Listener of limited ability
- able to understand limited styles of speech that are intelligible to well-educated native listeners in the target community and is most often not successful or appropriate in attempts to seek clarification when speech is unintelligible;
- not able to understand unfamiliar abstract concepts expressed in the TL without considerable non-linguistic support; usually requires repetition or re-explanation or multiple clarification exchanges;
- usually not able to note areas where own knowledge is lacking to

achieve an acceptable understanding and to note where speaker is vague or inconsistent, often expresses confusion about the source of difficulty in understanding;
- usually not able to understand enough of the linguistic/pragmatic input to infer the gist of the communicative event, displays limited range of listener responses;
- usually does not adopt an appropriate risk strategy to respond to task demands, most often opts for a high-risk strategy which detracts from successful listening.

FIGURE 7.6 Classification of listener ability

The reader is invited to compare this scale with other proficiency scales. Two examples of norm-referenced scales (the Interagency Language Roundtable Language Skill Level Descriptions and the ACTFL Provisional Proficiency Guidelines) are provided in Appendix 7D and Appendix 7E.

7.7 Discussion questions and projects

1. Assessing listening ability

Savignon (1987), and others advocating communicative language teaching, propose that language educators shift from an orientation of 'we will teach only what we can test' to finding ways to evaluate those skills that are important for learners to develop. Do you support this view? How do considerations of reliability figure into your view?

What techniques do you use for assessment of listening ability (or what techniques have language teachers in classes in which you were a learner used)? What effect does the form of assessment commonly used have on the type of instruction used?

2. Items on tests

Consider the following items found on standardized tests. What are the test specifications that are being used by the test writer?

(a) (i) [The test-taker hears: 'Are you busy?' and must choose from possible written completions.]
(A) Yes, I am.   (B) Yes, you are.   (C) Yes, they are.

(ii) [The test-taker hears: 'John came on time in spite of the rain' and must choose from possible written paraphrases.]
(A) John came late because of the rain.

(B) John wasn't late even though it rained.

(C) John came after the rain had stopped.

(b) (i) [The test-taker hears: 'Did you see the new teachers?' and must identify, given two written alternatives, the item that was spoken.]

Did you see the new (T-shirts/teachers)?

(ii) The test-taker hears: 'The guards were against us' and must identify, given two written alternatives, the item that was spoken.]

The (gods/guards) were against us.

(c) [The test-taker hears:

Woman: Would you like to go see a film with us tonight?
Man: It's nice of you to ask, but I have to study for an exam.

The test-taker then has to select the intended meaning of the speaker, which is presumably to turn down the invitation (politely, by offering a reason).]

(A) The man will go to see a film tonight.

(B) The man can't go to see a film tonight.

(C) The man will see a film after the exam.

(D) The man will study for the exam after the film.

3. Linguistic inferences in test items

Item stem and response options can be considered in terms of linguistic inference. Freedle and Fellbaum (1987) have analysed the type of inferencing skills that are required on the Test of English as a Foreign Language. They identify the following:

matching/discrimination of similar pairs of lexical items
(e.g. stem includes: *thick*; incorrect response options include: *sick*.)

recognition of homonymity
(e.g. stem includes: *foot the bill*; incorrect response options include: *hurt his foot*.)

recognition of synonymity of utterances
(e.g. stem includes: *She was wrong*; correct response option is: *Her answer was incorrect*.)

recognition of morphological similarity
(e.g. stem includes: *John is going to enter the building*; correct response option is: *John is at the entrance of the building*.)

judgement of case matching and case relationships
(e.g. stem includes: *Rose went home*; correct response option is: *She went home.* = case matching of *Rose* and *she.*)

lexical inference
(e.g. stem includes: *somebody pressed the doorbell*; correct response option is: *somebody rang the doorbell*)

suprasentential/logical inference
(e.g. stem includes: *She cut her finger*; correct response option is: *She cut part of her hand because of carelessness.*)

Go through several items on a TOEFL listening tests.(Appendix 7C provides a sample of a TOEFL listening test.) Can you identify in each item which of these processes are required of the test taker?

4. Proficiency testing

Obtain a copy of a listening test (with accompanying tapes if any) that you have used as a teacher or have taken as a learner. Or obtain a copy of one of the published tests listed in Figure 7.7. (Alderson, Krahnke and Stansfield, 1987, provides addresses, as well as detailed information on these tests, among others.) Go through the test and make notes regarding the item stems, the response types, and the skill(s) you think you are using to respond to each item.

When you have finished, compile your notes. Make a list of item stem types, response types, and skills. Which are being systematically treated, which are not? Are there aspects of the test that are not dealt with in our discussion of listening tests? Does the test treat the areas of input and response that are important for learners of the target skills?

5. Achievement testing

How would you design a valid test of listening ability for a given group of learners? First, list a range of appropriate specifications of the test.

Consider these questions: What are the topic areas to be treated in the input? What functions and concepts need to be included? What kind of input (speakers, variety of English, style) is appropriate? What channels (face-to-face, audio, video, other support materials)? What listening skills are to be involved, and in what order of importance? What other linguistic and non-linguistic skills are to be involved, and to what extent in relation to listening? What item types will be used?

Interview formats

- Oral Proficiency Interview (OPI)
- Bilingual Syntax Measure (BSM)
- Ilyin Oral Interview (IOI)
- Association of Recognised Language Schools Oral Examinations in Spoken English (ARELS Oral Examination)

Written test formats

- Test of English as a Foreign Language (TOEFL)
- Cambridge First Certificate in English (FCE)
- English Language Testing Service (ELTS)
- Certificate of Proficiency in English (CPE)
- Test of English for Educational Purposes
- Comprehensive English Language Test (CELT)
- Test of English for International Communication (TOEIC)
- English Language Battery (ELBA) (University of Edinburgh)
- Michigan Test of English Language Proficiency (MTELP)
- Oxford Placement Test (OPT)
- Royal Society of Arts: Examination in the Communicative Use of English as a Foreign Language (RSA CUEFL)
- Secondary Level English Proficiency Test (SLEP)
- Short Selection Test (SST) (Department of Education, Canberra, Australia)
- Henderson-Moriarty ESL Placement Test (HELP)
- Australian Second Language Proficiency Ratings
- Basic English Skills Test (BEST)
- Basic Inventory of Natural Language (BINL)
- Listening Comprehension Picture Test (LCPT)
- Listening Comprehension Written Test (LCWT)

FIGURE 7.7 Published tests of listening ability

6. Characterizing listening skill

Refer to the band scale for characterizing listening ability in Section 7.6. Could this be used as a evaluation scale for a group of learners you are currently teaching? If not, how would it need to be revised or expanded? Could the scale best be used as a teaching tool; as a teacher reference?

Appendix 7A: Lancashire/Cheshire Listening Test

THIS PAPER MUST NOT BE SEEN BY CANDIDATES   A956-1-03(OI)

NORTH WESTERN REGIONAL ADVISORY COUNCIL FOR FURTHER EDUCATION

Incorporating

THE UNION OF LANCASHIRE AND CHESHIRE INSTITUTES

ENGLISH AS A SECOND LANGUAGE

LISTENING WITH UNDERSTANDING

Tuesday 22 March to Friday 25 March 1983   1 hour (approximately)

LECTURER'S SCRIPT

Supervisor: This test of your understanding of spoken English is in two parts. In each part, you will listen to a short talk. In both cases, you will hear the information twice. To show how much you understand, you will answer questions in your answer book. You will be told for each part when to listen and when to answer. Places are provided for making rough notes while you listen. These notes will not be marked.

Are there any questions?

Now turn to page 2 of your answer book and follow the instructions for Part One of the test as I read them.

Part One

In this part of the test, you will hear about one way we can classify herbs. As you listen, you will asked to take rough notes on page 2 so that you can label the diagrams on page 3.

You will now have one minute to study pages 2 and 3.

[Pause: 1 minute]

Ready to begin? As you listen, take notes on page 2.

Lecturer: Today I'd like to talk about herbs — they're plants with succulent stems — with soft stems. They have three main uses — culinary, medicinal and cosmetic. Do you understand that? We use them in preparing food, in making medicines and also in the preparation of scents and perfumes.

Herbs can be classified in many ways, but today I thought we'd look at their appearance. Let's look at the obvious, visible differences — differences that are easy to see just looking at them. We'll take a limited number of herbs and look at the upper part of the plant, the stem, and the flower part, the root system.

The leaves of some herbs are long, thin and spear-shaped. We'll call these $S1$ — so, long, thin, pointed leaves are $S1$. Then, leaves in the $S2$ group are broad and slightly jagged at the edges and pointed at the end. All right? $S2$ leaves are broader than $S1$, do not have smooth edges but are also pointed at the end. The third group of leaves, *S*3, can be differentiated from *S*2 by the fact that they have roundish ends — *S*3 leaves are like *S*2 leaves in that they have jagged edges and are quite broad, but, in contrast to *S*2, they have round ends.

Let us now look at the types of roots that occur. One group of herbs has thick, irregularly branching roots. These we can label *R*1 — all right? *R*1 are roots which are thick and fleshy and have thick, fleshy branches. The second group of roots, which we will call *R*2, have one main root with various, smaller side roots. So, *R*2 consists of a main root with several smaller side roots. Then, the final group — *R*3 roots are long and thin and several project from the base of the leaves — several, long, thin roots projecting from the base of the leaves make up *R*3.

Now, by putting these two features of roots and leaves together, we can make six classes of herbs — *A* to *F*.

You should now complete the table on page 2 as I give you the classification. Ready?

Class *A* consists of *S*1 plus *R*1; Class *B* consists of *S*1 plus *R*3; Class *C* consists of *S*2 and *R*1; Class *D* is *S*2 and *R*2; Class *E* is *S*3 and *R*1; Class *F* is *S*3 and *R*2.

I'll just go quickly through that again so you can check that your table is complete: *A* is *S*1 plus *R*1; *B* equals *S*1 plus *R*3; *C* equals *S*2 plus *R*1; *D* equals *S*2 plus *R*2; *E* equals *S*3 plus *R*1; *F* equals *S*3 plus *R*2.

Supervisor: All right? Now listen again to make sure your notes are complete. Remember you are to label the root types, the leaf types and the herb class — three things to look for.

[*Turn over*

Lecturer: Today I'd like to talk about herbs — they're plants with succulent stems — with soft stems. They have three main uses — culinary, medicinal and cosmetic. Do you understand that? We use them in preparing food, in making medicines and also in the preparation of scents and perfumes.

Herbs can be classified in many ways, but today I thought we'd look at their appearance. Let's look at the obvious, visible differences — differences that are easy to see just looking at them. We'll take a limited number of herbs and look at the upper part of the plant, the stem, and the flower part, the root system.

The leaves of some herbs are long, thin and spear-shaped. We'll call these $S1$ — so, long, thin, pointed leaves are $S1$. Then, leaves in the $S2$ group are broad and slightly jagged at the edges and pointed at the end. All right? $S2$ leaves are broader than $S1$, do not have smooth edges but are also pointed at the end. The third group of leaves, $S3$, can be differentiated from $S2$ by the fact that they have roundish ends — $S3$ leaves are like $S2$ leaves in that they have jagged edges and are quite broad, but, in contrast to $S2$, they have round ends.

Let us now look at the types of roots that occur. One group of herbs has thick, irregularly branching roots. These we can label $R1$ — all right? $R1$ are roots which are thick and fleshy and have thick, fleshy branches. The second group of roots, which we will call $R2$, have one main root with various, smaller side roots. So, $R2$ consists of a main root with several smaller side roots. Then, the final group — $R3$ roots are long and thin and several project from the base of the leaves — several, long, thin roots projecting from the base of the leaves makes up $R3$.

Now, by putting these two features of roots and leaves together, we can make six classes of herbs — A to F.

I'll go over the classification to check that your table on page 2 is correct: Class *A* consists of *S*1 plus *R*1; *B* is *S*1 and *R*3; *C* is *S*2 and *R*1; *D* is *S*2 and *R*2; *E* is *S*3 and *R*1; *F* is *S*3 and *R*2.

Supervisor: That is the end of the talk. You will now have four minutes to write your answers on page 3.

[Pause: 4 minutes]

That is the end of Part One of the test.

Now turn to page 4 and follow as I read the instructions for Part Two of the test.

A956-1-03

NORTH WESTERN REGIONAL ADVISORY COUNCIL FOR FURTHER EDUCATION

Incorporating

THE UNION OF LANCASHIRE AND CHESHIRE INSTITUTES

ENGLISH AS A SECOND LANGUAGE

LISTENING WITH UNDERSTANDING

Tuesday 22 March to Friday 25 March 1983   1 hour (approximately)

Surname ....

Other Names ....

Centre ....

Centre No. ....

Answer all questions

Write your answers in the spaces provided in this paper.

For the Examiner's use only	
Part 1	
Part 2	
Total	

2

Part One

In this part of the test, you will hear about one way we can classify herbs. As you listen, you will asked to take rough notes on page 2 so that you can label the diagrams on page 3.

For Rough Notes

Herb Type	Leaves	Roots
A		
B		
C		
D		
E		
F		

3

(a) Label the leaves. Write *S*1, *S*2 or *S*3 in the circles.

(b) Label the roots. Write *R*1, *R*2 or *R*3 in the triangles.

(c) Classify the herbs. Write *A, B, C, D, E* or *F* in the boxes.

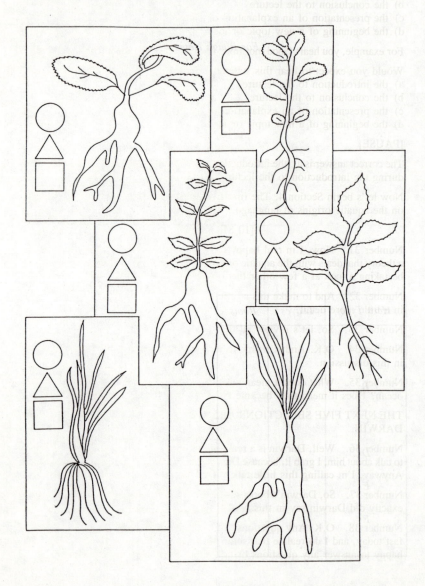

Appendix 7B: Harper Academic Listening Test
Audio Script
Section 4

Instructions: You are going to hear ten (10) short selections from the two lectures. You have to decide what part of the lecture you are listening to. The selection will come from:

a) the introduction to the lecture
b) the conclusion to the lecture
c) the presentation of an explanation or details OR
d) the beginning of a new topic or idea

For example, you hear: Good morning. Today's lecture is about Charles Darwin.

Would you expect to hear this statement during
a) the introduction to the lecture
b) the conclusion to the lecture
c) the presentation of an explanation or details OR
d) the beginning of a new topic or idea?

[PAUSE]

The correct answer is a), the introduction. You would expect to hear this selection during the introduction to the lecture.

Now let's begin Section 4. The first five selections are taken from the lecture on the aquatic origins of language.

[10 SECONDS]

Number 31.   Now, I'm real happy to be here today. We're going to discuss a theory that deals with the aquatic origins of language. And along the way we'll be taking a look at a few other theories.

Number 32.   And to make this a little clearer, I'd like to go into this business in a little more detail.

Number 33.   So, let's review all that.

Number 34.   O.K. And It's time to turn now to the most important question in this discussion.

Number 35.   What does it mean when I say that pre-humans went back to the ocean? Does it mean they became fish? No, not really. It means . . .

THE NEXT FIVE SELECTIONS ARE TAKEN FROM THE LECTURE ON DARWIN.

Number 36.   Well, Darwin is a real hero of mine, so any time I get the chance to talk about him, I grab it, because Darwin is a character who really is fascinating. Anyway, I'm calling this little talk, "Darwin, an Unlikely Revolutionary."

Number 37.   So, Darwin's book was called "The Origin of Species". But what exactly did Darwin say in this book?

Number 38.   O.K. Any questions? I went through an awful lot of stuff pretty fast today, and I do realize that some of this was unfamiliar to you. So I'd be happy to answer any questions or talk about anything that isn't clear.

Number 39. Right. We've seen that certain characteristics of Darwin's personality helped him to break with tradition. And I think there are a few small things I can point to which, ah, exemplify these characteristics pretty well.

Number 40. O.K. So much for Darwin's background. Now let's take a look at what got Darwin started on his career.

THAT IS THE END OF SECTION 4.

Student's Test Sheet
Section 4

Instructions: You are going to hear ten (10) short selections from the two lectures. You have to decide what part of the lecture you are listening to. The selection will come from:

a) the introduction to the lecture
b) the conclusion to the lecture
c) the presentation of an explanation or details OR
d) the beginning of a new topic or idea

For example, you hear: Good morning. Today's lecture is about Charles Darwin.

Would you expect to hear this statement during
a) the introduction to the lecture
b) the conclusion to the lecture
c) the presentation of an explanation or details OR
d) the beginning of a new topic or idea?

The correct answer is a), the introduction. You would expect to hear this selection during the introduction to the lecture.

Now let's begin Section 4. The first five selections are taken from the lecture on the aquatic origins of language.

31. a) the introduction to the lecture
     b) the conclusion to the lecture
     c) the presentation of an explanation or details
     d) the beginning of a new topic or idea

32. a) the introduction to the lecture
     b) the conclusion to the lecture
     c) the presentation of an explanation or details
     d) the beginning of a new topic or idea

33. a) the introduction to the lecture
     b) the conclusion to the lecture
     c) the presentation of an explanation or details
     d) the beginning of a new topic or idea

34. a) the introduction to the lecture
     b) the conclusion to the lecture
     c) the presentation of an explanation or details
     d) the beginning of a new topic or idea

35. a) the introduction to the lecture
     b) the conclusion to the lecture
     c) the presentation of an explanation or details
     d) the beginning of a new topic or idea

THE NEXT FIVE SELECTIONS ARE TAKEN FROM THE LECTURE ON DARWIN.

36. a) the introduction to the lecture
     b) the conclusion to the lecture
     c) the presentation of an explanation or details
     d) the beginning of a new topic or idea

37. a) the introduction to the lecture
     b) the conclusion to the lecture
     c) the presentation of an explanation or details
     d) the beginning of a new topic or idea

38. a) the introduction to the lecture
     b) the conclusion to the lecture
     c) the presentation of an explanation or details
     d) the beginning of a new topic or idea

39. a) the introduction to the lecture
     b) the conclusion to the lecture
     c) the presentation of an explanation or details
     d) the beginning of a new topic or idea

40. a) the introduction to the lecture
     b) the conclusion to the lecture
     c) the presentation of an explanation or details
     d) the beginning of a new topic or idea

Appendix 7C: TOEFL Listening Test

FORM 3FATF5

TEST OF ENGLISH AS A FOREIGN LANGUAGE
SCRIPT FOR THE LISTENING COMPREHENSION SECTION

SCRIPT

(MA) In a moment, you are going to hear an introductory statement by the three people who recorded this test. The purpose of this introduction is to give the proctor an opportunity to adjust the recording equipment or make changes in your seating arrangement before the actual test begins. Now listen carefully to the statement by each of the speakers whom you will hear on the test.

(Spoken in turn by MB, W, and MA) Flight number 53 to Paris will depart from gate six at 9:30 p.m. Will all passengers holding tickets kindly proceed to gate six at this time. Thank you. (5 second pause).

Now open your test book. Read the directions in your test book as you listen to the directions on the recording. (8 seconds)

LISTENING COMPREHENSION

In this section of the test, you will have an opportunity to demonstrate your ability to understand spoken English. There are three parts to this section, with special directions for each part.

*Part A

Directions: For each question in Part A, you will hear a short statement. The statements will be spoken just one time. They will not be written out for you, and you must listen carefully to understand what the speaker says.

After you hear a statement, read the four sentences in your test book, marked (A), (B), (C), and (D), and decide which one is closest in meaning to the statement you heard. Then, on your answer sheet, find the number of the question and blacken the space that corresponds to the letter of the answer you have chosen so that the letter inside the oval cannot be seen.

Look at Example I.

You will hear: (W)   John is a better student than his brother James.

You will read: (A) John does better in his studies than James.
                      (B) James is bigger than his brother John.
                      (C) John has only one brother.
                      (D) The teacher likes James better than John.

Sentence (A), "John does better in his studies than James," means most nearly the same as the statement "John is a better student than his brother James." Therefore, you should choose answer (A).

Look at Example II.

You will hear: (MB)   The truck traffic on this highway is so heavy I can barely see where I'm going.

You will read: (A) The traffic isn't bad today.
                      (B) The trucks weigh a lot.
                      (C) There are a lot of trucks on the highway.
                      (D) The highway has been closed to heavy trucks.

Sentence (C), "There are a lot of trucks on the highway," is closest in meaning to the sentence "The truck traffic on this highway is so heavy I can barely see where I'm going." Therefore, you should choose answer (C).

Now let us begin Part A with question number one.

*Unless otherwise noted, all directions will be read by (MA).

1. (MA)   After class, go straight to the post office. (12 seconds)
2. (MB)   Geometry is hard for me, but algebra is harder. (12 seconds)
3. (MA)   Greg thought he could do it himself. (12 seconds)
4. (W)   No sooner had he finished washing his car than it started to rain. (12 seconds)
5. (MB)   Cooking is not allowed in this dormitory. (12 seconds)
6. (MB)   You'd better call Margaret before it gets too late. (12 seconds)
7. (W)   He works in the library only at night. (12 seconds)
8. (MA)   How about joining us for dinner? (12 seconds)
9. (MB)   Jerry hates washing and ironing his own clothes. (12 seconds)
10. (MA) Debbie wrote a check for her son's doctor bill. (12 seconds)
11. (W)   Today is Thursday and the swimming pool is supposed to open the day after tomorrow. (12 seconds)
12. (MB) I got my passport photo taken at Nelson Studios. (12 seconds)
13. (W)   I was told that you know a lot about this museum. (12 seconds)
14. (MA) Linda's performance wasn't what I'd expected. (12 seconds)

Go on to the next page. (8 seconds)

15. (W)   If Dorothy helped you, you'd finish in no time. (12 seconds)
16. (MB) I just ran out of supplies. (12 seconds)
17. (W)   This seminar is fascinating, don't you think? (12 seconds)
18. (MB) She didn't sell her old record player after all. (12 seconds)
19. (W)   The encyclopedias were out of order. (12 seconds)
20. (W)   Our group broke up at two. (12 seconds)

This is the end of Part A. Now look at the directions for Part B as they are read to you.

Part B

Directions: In Part B you will hear short conversations between two speakers. At the end of each conversation, a third voice will ask a question about what was said. The questions will be spoken just one time. After you hear a conversation and the question about it, read the four possible answers in your test book and decide which one is the best answer to the question you heard. Then, on your answer sheet, find the number of the question and blacken the space that corresponds to the letter of the answer you have chosen.

Look at Example I.

You will hear: (MB) Is there any assignment for next Tuesday?

(W) Nothing to read or write. But we're supposed to listen to a radio
program and be ready to talk about it in class.

(MA) What have the students been asked to do before Tuesday?

You will read: (A) Read a book.
(B) Write a composition.
(C) Talk about a problem.
(D) Listen to the radio.

From the conversation you know that the assignment is to listen to a radio program and be ready to talk about it. The best answer, then, is (D), "Listen to the radio." Therefore, you should choose answer (D).

Now let us begin Part B with question twenty-one.

21. (MB) Good morning, may I help you?

(W) Yes. I'd like to cash these traveler's checks first and then open a savings account.

(MA) Where does this conversation probably take place? (12 seconds)

22. (W) We really must go to the new movie in town.

(MB) Let's eat first.

(MA) What does the man want to do? (12 seconds)

23. (MB) I think it's starting to snow.

(W) Starting to snow! The ground's already covered!

(MA) What does the woman mean? (12 seconds)

24. (W) John seems to have lost a lot of weight recently.

(MA) Yes, he's been training hard with the soccer team.

(MB) What has John been doing? (12 seconds)

25. (W) How do you find your new apartment?

(MB) Well, it's quite nice, really, although I'm having a hard time getting used to such a big building.

(MA) What is the man's problem? (12 seconds)

26. (MA) Have you ever put one of these together before?

(MB) No, never, but I think if we carry out these instructions exactly, we won't have any trouble.

(W) What is it important for them to do? (12 seconds)

27. (MB) The front tire is flat and the seat needs to be raised.

(W) Why not take it to Mr. Smith?

(MA) What kind of work does Mr. Smith probably do? (12 seconds)

28. (MA) I haven't decided which color to paint my room—white or yellow.

(W) Isn't easy to choose, is it?

(MB) What does the woman mean? (12 seconds)

29. (MB) If you'd like to take the package with you, Miss, it won't take long to wrap.

(W) There's no rush. Could you please have it delivered this week?

(MA) What does the woman mean? (12 seconds)

30. (W)   The map shows that this street goes downtown.

    (MB)   Yes, but what we want to know is how to get to the park.

    (MA)   What does the man mean? (12 seconds)

31. (MA)   My typing isn't dark enough and the paper doesn't look good.

    (W)   Why not change the typewriter ribbon and see if that helps?

    (MB)   What does the woman advise the man to do? (12 seconds)

32. (W)   Didn't you tell Tom about the meeting?

    (MB)   Whatever I say to him goes in one ear and out the other.

    (MA)   What does the man mean? (12 seconds)

33. (W)   You look like you have your hands full. Do you need some help carrying those boxes?

    (MA)   I sure do!

    (MB)   What will the woman do? (12 seconds)

34. (W)   Are you coming with us?

    (MB)   No, I have to catch up on my zoology assignments.

    (MA)   What does the man mean? (12 seconds)

35. (MA)   I heard that the newspaper gave that book a terrible review.

    (W)   It depends on which newspaper you read. (pronounce "reed")

    (MB)   What does the woman mean? (12 seconds)

This is the end of Part B. Go on to the next page. (8 seconds) Now look at the directions for Part C as they are read to you.

Part C

Directions: In this part of the test, you will hear several short talks and conversations. After each talk or conversation, you will be asked some questions. The talks and questions will be spoken just one time. They will not be written out for you, so you will have to listen carefully to understand what the speaker says.

After you hear a question, read the four possible answers in your test book and decide which one is the best answer to the question you heard. Then, on your answer sheet, find the number of the question and blacken the space that corresponds to the letter of the answer you have chosen.

Listen to this sample talk.

    You will hear: (W)   Ellis Island is closed now—to all but the tourists, that is. This island, in New
                          York harbor, was once one of the busiest places in America. It was the first
                          stop for all immigrants arriving by ship from Europe, Africa and western
                          Asia. Normally, immigrants came to Ellis Island at the rate of 5,000 a day,
                          but at times twice that many would land in a single day. Most were processed
                          through and ferried to the mainland on the same day. A total of 15 million
                          people came to America by way of Ellis Island. With the advent of air travel,
                          the island fell into disuse. Today it serves only as a reminder to tourists of the
                          heritage of modern America.

Now look at the following example.

    You will hear: (MB)   How did people generally arrive at Ellis Island?

    You will read: (A) By plane.
                          (B) By ship.
                          (C) By train.
                          (D) By bus.

The best answer to the question "How did people generally arrive at Ellis Island?" is (B), "By ship." Therefore, you should choose answer (B).

Now look at the next example.

You will hear: (MB) <u>Who visits Ellis Island today?</u>

You will read: (A) New immigrants.
                     (B) International traders.
                     (C) Fishermen.
                     (D) Tourists.

The best answer to the question "Who visits Ellis Island today?" is (D), "Tourists." Therefore, you should choose answer (D).

Now let us begin Part C with question number thirty-six.

(MA) <u>Questions 36–41</u> refer to the following lecture.

(W)   Good morning, students. I hope you have been able to read the two books about speech and hearing problems that I put in the library. Today's lecture deals with the presence of the unusually large deaf population that existed on the Massachusetts island of Martha's Vineyard for about three centuries. From the settlement of the island in the 1640's to the twentieth century, the people there, who were descended from only twenty-five or thirty original families, married mainly other residents of the island. They formed a highly inbred group, producing an excellent example of the genetic patterns for the inheritance of deafness. Indeed, in the late 1800's, one out of every twenty-five people in one village on the island was born deaf, and the island as a whole had a deafness rate at least seventeen times greater than that of the rest of the United States. Even Alexander Graham Bell, the inventor of the telephone and a prominent researcher into hearing loss, visited Martha's Vineyard to study the population, but because the principles of genetics and inheritance were still unknown, he was not able to explain the <u>patterns</u> of deafness, and why a deaf parent did not always have deaf children. In the twentieth century, the local population has mixed with people off the island, and the rate of deafness has fallen.

36. (MB) Where does this talk take place? (12 seconds)

37. (MB) What is unusual about the island of Martha's Vineyard? (12 seconds)

38. (MB) Why were so many people there deaf? (12 seconds)

39. (MB) The island's rate of deafness was how many times greater than that of the rest of the United States? (12 seconds)

40. (MB) What did Alexander Graham Bell hope to do when he went to the island? (12 seconds)

41. (MB) According to the talk, how has the island changed in the twentieth century? (12 seconds)

(MA) <u>Questions 42–46</u> refer to the following dialogue.

(MB)   Have you ever visited a redwood forest? I recently had a chance to go to Muir Woods National Monument north of San Francisco.

(W)   I've never seen a redwood tree. I really can't imagine how big they are.

(MB)   The coastal redwoods are the tallest living things; some are more than three hundred fifty feet high. But, none of the trees in Muir Woods is <u>that</u> tall. You have to go further north in California to see the tallest trees.

(W)   You said that Muir Woods is near San Francisco? I guess it must be quite a tourist attraction.

(MB)   Yes. It's less than an hour's drive away, so it's easy to get to.

(W)   I've heard that many redwood trees are thousands of years old. Are the ones in Muir Woods that old?

(MB)   The oldest documented age for a coastal redwood is more than two thousand years. The trees in Muir Woods are four hundred to eight hundred years old.

(W)   Why have they survived so long?

(MB)   They have remarkable resistance to forest fires. Their tough, thick bark protects the trees during a fire. The coastal redwoods also like a damp, foggy climate.

(W)   Then, since Muir Woods is near foggy San Francisco, it must be ideal for the trees' survival. I can't wait to

go there and see them!

42. (MA) What is the main subject of this conversation? (12 seconds)

43. (MA) Where can the tallest trees be found? (12 seconds)

44. (MA) Why do many tourists visit Muir Woods rather than other redwood forests? (12 seconds)

45. (MA) Approximately what is the oldest documented age for a redwood tree? (12 seconds)

46. (MA) What has contributed most to the redwoods' survival? (12 seconds)

(MA) Questions 47-50 are based on the following announcement.

(MB)   May I have your attention please? We will be closing in a few minutes. Please return reference books

to their shelves. People who wish to check out reserve books for overnight use may do so now.

47. (W)   For whom is the announcement primarily intended? (12 seconds)

48. (W)   When will the building be closed? (12 seconds)

49. (W)   What does the man ask the people to do? (12 seconds)

50. (W)   What does the man say about reserve books? (12 seconds)

(MA) Stop work on Section 1.

End of Recording.

Print your
full name here _____
              (last)   (first)   (middle)

FORM 3FATF5

TEST OF ENGLISH AS
A FOREIGN LANGUAGE

Read the directions on the back cover.

**Do not break the seals
until you are told to do so.**

This test book was used at the May 14, 1983,
TOEFL administration. It is distributed by the
TOEFL program office only to examinees who
took the test on May 14, 1983.

UNAUTHORIZED REPRODUCTION IS PROHIBITED.

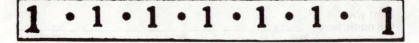

SECTION I

LISTENING COMPREHENSION

In this section of the test, you will have an opportunity to demonstrate your ability to
understand spoken English. There are three parts to this section, with special directions for
each part.

Part A

Directions: For each question in Part A, you will hear a short statement. The statements
will be spoken just one time. They will not be written out for you, and you must listen
carefully to understand what the speaker says.

After you hear a statement, read the four sentences in your test book, marked (A), (B),
(C), and (D), and decide which one is closest in meaning to the statement you heard.
Then, on your answer sheet, find the number of the question and blacken the space that
corresponds to the letter of the answer you have chosen so that the letter inside the oval
cannot be seen.

Example I	Sample Answer
You will hear:	● Ⓑ Ⓒ Ⓓ

You will read: (A) John does better in his
                      studies than James.
                (B) James is bigger than his
                      brother John.
                (C) John has only one brother.
                (D) The teacher likes James
                      better than John.

Sentence (A), "John does better in his studies than James," means most nearly the same as
the statement "John is a better student than his brother James." Therefore, you should
choose answer (A).

Example II	Sample Answer
You will hear:	Ⓐ Ⓑ ● Ⓓ

You will read: (A) The traffic isn't bad today.
                (B) The trucks weigh a lot.
                (C) There are a lot of trucks on
                      the highway.
                (D) The highway has been
                      closed to heavy trucks.

Sentence (C), "There are a lot of trucks on the highway," is closest in meaning to the sentence
"The truck traffic on this highway is so heavy I can barely see where I'm going." Therefore,
you should choose answer (C).

1. (A) Go directly to the post office
         when class is over.
    (B) Let's first straighten up the
         classroom and then go to the
         post office.
    (C) That's the most direct way to the
         post office from our class.
    (D) The post office is straight ahead
         of the classroom building.

2. (A) I don't think that algebra is
         hard.
    (B) I like algebra better than
         geometry.
    (C) Geometry isn't difficult for me.
    (D) Geometry is easier for me than
         algebra.

GO ON TO THE NEXT PAGE

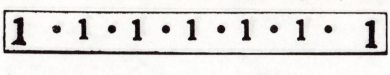

3. (A) Greg believed he could do it
    alone.
   (B) Greg thought he'd cut himself.
   (C) Greg thought he was selfish.
   (D) Greg alone believed it could
    be done.

4. (A) After it rained, he washed
    his car.
   (B) He was unable to wash his car
    because it was raining.
   (C) It began to rain right after he
    washed his car.
   (D) He had to finish washing his car
    in the rain.

5. (A) Don't make noise in the kitchen.
   (B) You may not cook here.
   (C) They were quiet when they ate.
   (D) These are homemade cookies.

6. (A) You should call Margaret soon.
   (B) Margaret will be better later on.
   (C) It's too late to call on Margaret
    now.
   (D) Margaret is the best person to
    tell.

7. (A) He never walks to the library at
    night.
   (B) There is only one librarian here
    at night.
   (C) The library is the only place to
    study.
   (D) He never works in the library in
    the daytime.

8. (A) How was your dinner?
   (B) Please have dinner with us.
   (C) We had dinner together.
   (D) Will there be four of us for
    dinner?

9. (A) Jerry dislikes the clothes he has.
   (B) Jerry doesn't like doing his
    laundry.
   (C) Jerry hates to take showers.
   (D) Jerry's clothes don't need
    ironing.

10. (A) Debbie checked with her son's
    doctor.
    (B) Debbie sent her son for a
    checkup.
    (C) Debbie paid her son's doctor.
    (D) Debbie wrote a note to the
    doctor's son.

11. (A) The pool was scheduled to open
    on Tuesday.
    (B) The pool is opening today.
    (C) The pool will open tomorrow.
    (D) The pool should be open on
    Saturday.

12. (A) Nelson Studios took the picture
    for my passport.
    (B) I studied the photograph of the
    port.
    (C) I took my passport to the
    studios.
    (D) I pass by Nelson Studios on my
    way to work.

13. (A) I told you to see a lot of
    museums.
    (B) You've taught me a great deal
    here.
    (C) People say that you know this
    place well.
    (D) Many museums are like this one,
    you know.

14. (A) I'd expected Linda to give a
    performance.
    (B) Linda hadn't been expecting to
    perform.
    (C) I'd expected Linda to do things
    differently.
    (D) Linda had expected me to be
    there.

GO ON TO THE NEXT PAGE ▶

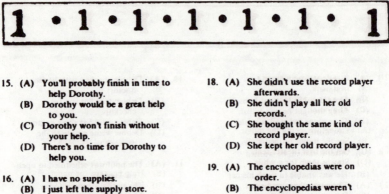

15. (A) You'll probably finish in time to help Dorothy.
    (B) Dorothy would be a great help to you.
    (C) Dorothy won't finish without your help.
    (D) There's no time for Dorothy to help you.

16. (A) I have no supplies.
    (B) I just left the supply store.
    (C) I just found a supply.
    (D) I went out to get supplies.

17. (A) You don't think the seminar is fascinating, do you?
    (B) The seminar will continue while we are eating.
    (C) I find the seminar extremely interesting.
    (D) The dissemination of information is fast, isn't it?

18. (A) She didn't use the record player afterwards.
    (B) She didn't play all her old records.
    (C) She bought the same kind of record player.
    (D) She kept her old record player.

19. (A) The encyclopedias were on order.
    (B) The encyclopedias weren't checked out.
    (C) The encyclopedias weren't any good.
    (D) The encyclopedias were improperly arranged.

20. (A) We broke two cups.
    (B) We left at two o'clock.
    (C) We divided into two groups.
    (D) We met two people.

Part B

Directions: In Part B you will hear short conversations between two speakers. At the end of each conversation, a third voice will ask a question about what was said. The question will be spoken just one time. After you hear a conversation and the question about it, read the four possible answers in your test book and decide which one is the best answer to the question you heard. Then, on your answer sheet, find the number of the question and blacken the space that corresponds to the letter of the answer you have chosen.

Example I   Sample Answer

You will hear: Ⓐ Ⓑ Ⓒ ●

You will read: (A) Read a book.
                   (B) Write a composition.
                   (C) Talk about a problem.
                   (D) Listen to the radio.

From the conversation you know that the assignment is to listen to a radio program and be ready to talk about it. The best answer, then, is (D), "Listen to the radio." Therefore, you should choose answer (D).

GO ON TO THE NEXT PAGE

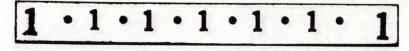

21. (A) In a department store.
    (B) In a bank.
    (C) At a tourist bureau.
    (D) At a hotel.

22. (A) Eat before seeing the movie.
    (B) See the movie immediately.
    (C) Get the first theater seat.
    (D) Stay in town for a while.

23. (A) The winter has just begun.
    (B) Once it starts, it'll snow a lot.
    (C) They're ready for the snow.
    (D) It has been snowing for some
        time.

24. (A) Traveling a lot.
    (B) Getting a lot of exercise.
    (C) Working too hard.
    (D) Waiting for the train.

25. (A) He can't find his new building.
    (B) He had a bigger apartment
        before.
    (C) He's not accustomed to the large
        building.
    (D) He's having a hard time finding
        an apartment.

26. (A) Find the trouble.
    (B) Carry the parts outside.
    (C) Practice working together.
    (D) Follow the directions.

27. (A) He fixes bicycles.
    (B) He raises sheep.
    (C) He sells chairs.
    (D) He's a gardener.

28. (A) It doesn't matter which color the
        man chooses.
    (B) It's a difficult decision.
    (C) She doesn't like either color.
    (D) The man should choose a
        different room.

29. (A) She'd like the store to send it
        to her.
    (B) It will arrive next week.
    (C) It must be wrapped quickly.
    (D) She'll take it with her to save
        trouble.

30. (A) They want to go downtown.
    (B) He wants to go to the park, but
        she doesn't.
    (C) He doesn't know where to park
        the car.
    (D) He wants to find out the
        location of the park.

31. (A) Try a new ribbon.
    (B) Help her type the paper.
    (C) Get another typewriter.
    (D) Change the paper.

32. (A) Tom is unable to hear well.
    (B) Tom didn't say anything at the
        meeting.
    (C) Tom doesn't listen to him.
    (D) Tom went out before the
        meeting was over.

33. (A) Help fill up the boxes.
    (B) Take some of the boxes.
    (C) Look for something else.
    (D) Make sure her hands are clean.

34. (A) He wants the others to follow
        him.
    (B) He must study the animals he
        caught.
    (C) He will catch up with them later.
    (D) He is behind in his schoolwork.

35. (A) You should believe everything
        you read.
    (B) She thinks the book is excellent.
    (C) She wonders which newspaper
        he reads.
    (D) Reaction to the book has been
        varied.

GO ON TO THE NEXT PAGE

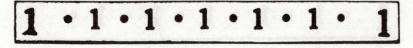

Part C

Directions: In this part of the test, you will hear several short talks and conversations. After each talk or conversation, you will be asked some questions. The talks and questions will be spoken just one time. They will not be written out for you, so you will have to listen carefully to understand what the speaker says.

After you hear a question, read the four possible answers in your test book and decide which one is the best answer to the question you heard. Then, on your answer sheet, find the number of the question and blacken the space that corresponds to the letter of the answer you have chosen.

Listen to this sample talk.

You will hear:

Now look at the following example.

You will hear:

You will read: (A) By plane.
                 (B) By ship.
                 (C) By train.
                 (D) By bus.

Sample Answer

Ⓐ ● Ⓒ Ⓓ

The best answer to the question "How did people generally arrive at Ellis Island?" is (B), "By ship." Therefore, you should choose answer (B).

Now look at the next example.

You will hear:

You will read: (A) New immigrants.
                 (B) International traders.
                 (C) Fishermen.
                 (D) Tourists.

Sample Answer

Ⓐ Ⓑ Ⓒ ●

The best answer to the question "Who visits Ellis Island today?" is (D), "Tourists." Therefore, you should choose answer (D).

36. (A) At a telephone laboratory.
    (B) At the library.
    (C) On Martha's Vineyard.
    (D) In a lecture hall.

37. (A) It was settled more than
         300 years ago.
    (B) Alexander Graham Bell visited
         there.
    (C) A large number of its residents
         were deaf.
    (D) Each family living there had
         many children.

38. (A) They inherited deafness.
    (B) An epidemic struck the island.
    (C) The climate caused hearing loss.
    (D) It was an unlucky place.

39. (A) Two.
    (B) Seventeen.
    (C) Twenty-five.
    (D) Forty.

GO ON TO THE NEXT PAGE

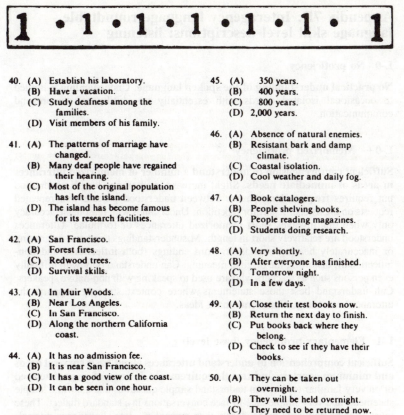

1 · 1 · 1 · 1 · 1 · 1 · 1

40. (A) Establish his laboratory.
    (B) Have a vacation.
    (C) Study deafness among the families.
    (D) Visit members of his family.

41. (A) The patterns of marriage have changed.
    (B) Many deaf people have regained their hearing.
    (C) Most of the original population has left the island.
    (D) The island has become famous for its research facilities.

42. (A) San Francisco.
    (B) Forest fires.
    (C) Redwood trees.
    (D) Survival skills.

43. (A) In Muir Woods.
    (B) Near Los Angeles.
    (C) In San Francisco.
    (D) Along the northern California coast.

44. (A) It has no admission fee.
    (B) It is near San Francisco.
    (C) It has a good view of the coast.
    (D) It can be seen in one hour.

45. (A) 350 years.
    (B) 400 years.
    (C) 800 years.
    (D) 2,000 years.

46. (A) Absence of natural enemies.
    (B) Resistant bark and damp climate.
    (C) Coastal isolation.
    (D) Cool weather and daily fog.

47. (A) Book catalogers.
    (B) People shelving books.
    (C) People reading magazines.
    (D) Students doing research.

48. (A) Very shortly.
    (B) After everyone has finished.
    (C) Tomorrow night.
    (D) In a few days.

49. (A) Close their test books now.
    (B) Return the next day to finish.
    (C) Put books back where they belong.
    (D) Check to see if they have their books.

50. (A) They can be taken out overnight.
    (B) They will be held overnight.
    (C) They need to be returned now.
    (D) They are on a special shelf.

THIS IS THE END OF THE LISTENING COMPREHENSION SECTION OF THE TEST.

**THE NEXT PART OF THE TEST IS SECTION 2. TURN TO THE
DIRECTIONS FOR SECTION 2 IN YOUR TEST BOOK,
READ THEM, AND BEGIN WORK.
DO NOT READ OR WORK ON ANY OTHER SECTION OF THE TEST.**

STOP STOP STOP **STOP** STOP STOP STOP

Appendix 7D: Interagency language roundtable language skill level descriptions: listening

L-0   No proficiency

No practical understanding of the spoken language. Understanding is limited to occasional isolated words with essentially no abililty to comprehend communication.

L-0+   Memorized proficiency

Sufficient comprehension to understand a number of memorized utterances in areas of immediate needs. Slight increase in utterance length understood but requires frequent long pauses between understood phrases and repeated requests on the listener's part for repetition. Understands with reasonable accuracy only when this involves short memorized utterances or formulae. Utterances understood are relatively short in length. Misunderstandings arise due to ignoring or inaccurately hearing sounds or word endings (both inflectional and non-inflectional), distorting the original meaning. Can understand only with difficulty even persons such as teachers who are used to speaking with non-native speakers. Can understand best those statements where context strongly supports the utterance's meaning. Gets some main ideas.

L-1   Elementary proficiency (base level)

Sufficient comprehension to understand utterances about basic survival needs and minimum courtesy and travel requirements. In areas of immediate need or on very familiar topics, can understand simple questions and answers, simple statements and very simple face-to-face conversations in a standard dialect. These must often be delivered more clearly than normal at a rate slower than normal, with frequent repetitions or paraphrase (that is, by a native used to dealing with foreigners). Once learned, these sentences can be varied for similar level vocabulary and grammar and still be understood. In the majority of utterances, misunderstandings arise due to overlooked or misunderstood syntax and other grammatical clues. Comprehension vocabulary inadequate to understand anything but the most elementary needs. Strong interferences from the candidate's native language occurs. Little precision in the information understood owing to tentative state of passive grammar and lack of vocabulary. Comprehension areas include basic needs such as: meals, lodging, transportation, time and simple directions (including both route instructions and orders from customs officials, policemen, etc.). Understands main ideas.

L-1+   Elementary proficiency (higher level)

Sufficient comprehension to understand short conversations about all survival needs and limited social demands. Developing flexibility evident in understanding into a range of circumstances beyond immediate survival needs. Shows spontaneity in understanding by speed, although consistency of understanding uneven. Limited vocabulary range necessitates repetition for understanding. Understands commoner time forms and most question forms, some word order patterns but miscommunication still occurs with more complex patterns. Cannot sustain understanding of coherent structures in longer utterances or in unfamiliar situations. Understanding of descriptions and the giving of precise information is limited. Aware of basic cohesive features, e.g., pronouns, verb inflections, but many are unreliably understood, especially if less immediate in reference. Understanding is largely limited to a series of short, discrete utterances. Still has to ask for utterances to be repeated. Some ability to understand the facts.

L-2 Limited working proficiency (base level)

Sufficient comprehension to understand conversations on routine social demands and limited job requirements. Able to understand face-to-face speech in a standard dialect, delivered at a normal rate with some repetition and rewording, by a native speaker not used to dealing with foreigners, about everyday topics, common personal and family news, well-known current events, and routine office matters through descriptions and narration about current, past and future events; can follow essential points of discussion or speech at an elementary level on topics in his/her special professional field. Only understands occasional words and phrases of statements made in unfavorable conditions, for example through loudspeakers outdoors. Understands factual content. Native language causes less interference in listening comprehension. Able to understand the facts, i.e., the lines but not between or beyond the lines.

L-2+ Limited working proficiency (higher level)

Sufficient comprehension to understand most routine social demands and most conversations on work requirements as well as some discussions on concrete topics related to particular interests and special fields of competence. Often shows remarkable ability and ease of understanding, but under tension or pressure may break down. Candidate may display weakness or deficiency due to inadequate vocabulary base or less than secure knowledge of grammar and syntax. Normally understands general vocabulary with some hesitant understanding of everyday vocabulary still evident. Can sometimes detect emotional overtones. Some ability to understand between the lines (i.e., to grasp inferences).

L-3 General professional proficiency (base level)

Able to understand the essentials of all speech in a standard dialect including technical discussions within a special field. Has effective understanding of face-to-face speech, delivered with normal clarity and speed in a standard dialect, on general topics and areas of special interest; understands hypothesizing and supported opinions. Has broad enough vocabulary that rarely has to ask for paraphrasing or explanation. Can follow accurately the essentials of conversations between educated native speakers, reasonably clear telephone calls, radio broadcasts, news stories similar to wire service reports, oral reports, some oral technical reports and public addresses on non-technical subjects; can understand without difficulty all forms of standard speech concerning a special professional field. Does not understand native speakers if they speak very quickly or use some slang or dialect. Can often detect emotional overtones. Can understand between the lines (i.e., grasp inferences).

L-3+   General professional proficiency (higher level)

Comprehends most of the content and intent of a variety of forms and styles of speech pertinent to professional needs, as well as general topics and social conversation. Ability to comprehend many sociolinguistic and cultural references. However, may miss some subtleties and nuances. Increased ability to comprehend unusually complex structures in lengthy utterances and to comprehend many distinctions in language tailored for different audiences. Increased ability to understand native speakers talking quickly, using non-standard dialect or slang; however, comprehension not complete. Some ability to understand "beyond the lines" in addition to strong ability to understand "between the lines".

L-4   Advanced professional proficiency (base level)

Able to understand all forms and styles of speech pertinent to professional needs. Able to understand fully all speech with extensive and precise vocabulary, subtleties and nuances in all standard dialects on any subject relevant to professional needs within the range of his/her experience, including social conversations; all intelligible broadcasts and telephone calls; and many kinds of technical discussions and discourse. Understands language specifically tailored (including persuasion, representation, counseling, and negotiating) to different audiences. Able to understand the essentials of speech in some non-standard dialects. Has difficulty in understanding extreme dialect and slang, also in understanding speech in unfavorable conditions, for example through bad loudspeakers out doors. Understands "beyond the lines" all forms of the language directed to the general listener, (i.e., able to develop and analyze the argumentation presented).

L-4+   Advanced professional proficiency (higher level)

Increased ability to understand extremely difficult and abstract speech as well as ability to understand all forms and styles of speech pertinent to professional needs, including social conversations. Increased ability to comprehend native speakers using extreme non-standard dialects and slang as well as to understand speech in unfavorable conditions. Strong sensitivity to sociolinguistic and cultural references. Accuracy is close to that of the well-educated native listener but still not equivalent.

L-5   Functionally native proficiency

Comprehension equivalent to that of the well-educated native listener. Able to understand fully all forms and styles of speech intelligible to the well-educated native listener, including a number of regional and illiterate dialects, highly colloquial speech and conversations and discourse distorted by marked interferences from other noise. Able to understand how natives think as they create discourse. Able to understand extremely difficult and abstract speech.

Appendix 7E: The ACTFL Proficiency Guidelines, 1986

Generic Descriptions—Listening

These guidelines assume that all listening tasks take place in an authentic environment at a normal rate of speech using standard or near-standard norms.

Novice
The Novice level is characterized by an ability to recognize learned material and isolated words and phrases when strongly supported by context.

Novice-Low
Understanding is limited to occasional isolated words, such as cognates, borrowed words, and high-frequency social conventions. Essentially no ability to comprehend even short utterances.

Novice-Mid
Able to understand some short, learned utterances, particularly where context strongly supports understanding and speech is clearly audible. Comprehends some words and phrases from simple questions, statements, high-frequency commands, and courtesy formulae about topics that refer to basic personal information or the immediate physical setting. The listener requires long pauses for assimilation and periodically requests repetition and/or a slower rate of speech.

Novice-High
Able to understand short, learned utterances and some sentence-length utterances, particularly where context strongly supports understanding and speech is clearly audible. Comprehends words and phrases from simple questions, statements, high-frequency commands, and courtesy formulae. May require repetition, rephrasing and/or a slowed rate of speech for comprehension.

Intermediate
The Intermediate level is characterized by an ability to understand main ideas and some facts from interactive exchanges and simple connected aural texts.

Intermediate-Low
Able to understand sentence-length utterances which consist of recombinations of learned elements in a limited number of content areas, particularly if strongly supported by the situational context. Content refers to basic personal background and needs, social conventions, and routine tasks, such as getting meals and receiving simple instructions and directions. Listening tasks pertain primarily to spontaneous face-to-face conversations. Understanding is often uneven; repetition and rewording may be necessary. Misunderstandings in both main ideas and details arise frequently.

Intermediate-Mid
Able to understand sentence-length utterances which consist of recombinations of learned utterances on a variety of topics. Content continues to refer primarily to basic personal

background and needs, social conventions, and somewhat more complex tasks, such as lodging, transportation, and shopping. Additional content areas include some personal interests and activities, and a greater diversity of instructions and directions. Listening tasks not only pertain to spontaneous face-to-face conversations but also to short routine telephone conversations and some deliberate speech, such as simple announcements and reports over the media. Understanding continues to be uneven.

Intermediate-High	Able to sustain understanding over longer stretches of connected discourse on a number of topics pertaining to different times and places; however, understanding is inconsistent due to failure to grasp main ideas and/or details. Thus, while topics do not differ significantly from those of an Advanced-level listener, comprehension is less in quantity and poorer in quality.
Advanced	The Advanced level is characterised by an ability to understand main ideas and most details of connected discourse on a variety of topics beyond the immediacy of the situation, including some topics where comprehension is complicated due to an unexpected sequence of events.
Advanced	Able to understand main ideas and most details of connected discourse on a variety of topics beyond the immediacy of the situation. Comprehension may be uneven due to a variety of linguistic and extralinguistic factors, among which topic familiarity is very prominent. These texts frequently involve description and narration in different time frames or aspects, such as present, nonpast, habitual, or imperfective. Texts may include interviews, short lectures on familiar topics, and news items and reports primarily dealing with factual information. Listener is aware of cohesive devices but may not be able to use them to follow the sequence of thought in an oral text.
Advance-Plus	Able to understand the main ideas of most speech in a standard dialect; however, the listener may not be able to sustain comprehension in extended discourse which is propositionally and linguistically complex. Listener shows an emerging awareness of culturally implied meanings beyond the surface meanings of the text but may fail to grasp sociocultural nuances of the message.
Superior	The Superior level is characterized by an ability to understand concrete and abstract topics in extended discourse offered by speakers using native-like discourse strategies.
Superior	Able to understand the main ideas of all speech in a standard dialect, including technical discussion in a field of specialization. Can follow the essentials of extended discourse which is propositionally and linguistically

complex, as in academic/professional settings, in lectures, speeches, and reports. Listener shows some appreciation of aesthetic norms of target language, of idioms, colloquialisms, and register shifting. Able to make inferences within the cultural framework of the target language. Understanding is aided by an awareness of the underlying organizational structure of the oral text and includes sensitivity for its social and cultural references and its affective overtones. Rarely misunderstands but may not understand excessively rapid, highly colloquial speech or speech that has strong cultural references.

Distinguished   The Distinguished level is characterized by an ability to understand accurately most linguistic styles and forms from within the cultural framework of the language.

Distinguished   Able to understand all forms and styles of speech pertinent to personal, social, and professional needs tailored to different audiences. Shows strong sensitivity to social and cultural references and aesthetic norms by processing language from within the cultural framework. Texts include theatre plays, screen productions, editorials, symposia, academic debates, public policy statements, literary readings, and most jokes and puns. May have difficulty with some dialects and slang.

Notes

1. Estimates on closed measures are amenable to higher reliability in two respects. First, fluctuations in the test-taker's reading, writing, and speaking ability will not be reflected in these tasks. For example, a non-verbal indication of signal detection (e.g. 'yes, I heard (A)' vs 'no, I didn't hear (A)') is not affected by a test-taker's reading or writing ability, whereas a written completion item is affected by this 'extra' linguistic ability. Second, with closed measures, the listening input can be adjusted to fit test-takers' abilities and thus produce an appropriate range of scores. For example, since range of correct vs. incorrect responses on any item among a group of test-takers influences test reliability, the test writer can adjust the input (based on results of pre-testing) to increase the probability that an item will discriminate among test-takers for a chosen response type, say, signal detection.

8   Listening in a language curriculum

8.0   Introduction: approaches to curriculum design

This chapter considers more fully the place of listening in a language curriculum, building upon the ideas concerning development of listening ability addressed in Chapter 6. In order to do this, the chapter begins by examining the role of a syllabus in a language curriculum. Attention then turns to the place of listening in what is referred to as a task-based approach to syllabus design. (The term **curriculum** will be used to refer to planning of content, methodology, and means of evaluation in a language course or language programme; the term **syllabus** will be used to refer to the scope and sequencing of the content of the course.)

Examples are provided of how task-based learning projects entail listening (and other macro-skill) development and it is shown how activities involving listening inputs can be appropriately graded. Ways will also be suggested in which specific practices for listening development can be used in the language classroom to support task-based learning. In addition, consideration is given to the issues of self-direction in developing listening ability and instructor skill in listening to language learners.

8.1   Syllabus type

A first distinction in curriculum design is that between language 'products' and learner 'processes' as the appropriate orientation towards the curriculum. This distinction is a useful starting point for discussing what formal instruction might do towards developing learner ability with a second language. In a product-oriented view of syllabus design, language skills are treated as 'channels' through which content can be processed. Skills are to be developed in order to enable learners to acquire language 'products' — words, grammatical rules, facts, and concepts — more efficiently.

In a **product orientation** to a syllabus, linguistic items (i.e. vocabulary expressions and grammatical structures) or discrete socio-functional behaviours (such as greeting someone and responding to greetings) are identified as the primary targets which the learners are to come to use or recognize. These language targets are usually drawn systematically (and in an *a priori* fashion) from an inventory of linguistic items (such as a grammar of English) or from a taxonomy of sociolinguistic behaviours used by native speakers of the language, such as the Threshold list of language functions (cf. van Ek and Alexander, 1980; Wilkins, 1976).

Product-oriented syllabuses have the advantage of providing thorough *a priori* descriptions of content in some domain (syntactic or phonological structures, for example). This is an advantage for teachers who want to know in advance what they are going to teach, and for learners who want to know what they are supposed to learn (or should have learned). This apparent advantage of product syllabuses, however, is the very source of much criticism that has been levelled against them. Instructors who use product syllabuses may tend to overlook the actual learnability of items that are sequenced; items in the syllabus are assumed to be easy or difficult on the basis of their position in the hierarchy description alone (Nunan, 1988; Long and Crookes, 1987). Within product syllabuses, language macro-skills are thought of as means through which prescribed items are presented, practised, and learned. Listening, specifically, can be viewed as a processing channel through which language products are presented to the learner.

In **process-oriented** syllabuses, language development is viewed as progressive gains in skills for handling information and strategies for handling interactions and procedures, with macro-level skills (such as listening) viewed as supportive of the outcomes of learning tasks (Nunan, 1988, 1989). In a process-oriented syllabus, the focus of instruction is shifted from a grading of products to be mastered to a grading of procedures and tasks which will involve learners in successive encounters with language. Adequate process-oriented syllabuses are concerned with the quantity and quality of language input to learners as well as with the degree of learner language output. However, the focus of grading in a process-oriented syllabus is based not primarily on notions of linguistic difficulty in input or output of a pedagogic task (nor on the real-world task on which it is based), but on the converging psycholinguistic and social demands of language use that the classroom task entails for the learners.

> Difficulty here [in a process type syllabus] . . . does not mean difficult in terms of the linguistic demands of . . . a target task . . . which motivated selection of a pedagogic task. Rather, it refers to the difficulty of pedagogical tasks in such aspects as the number of steps involved in

their execution, the number of parties involved, the assumptions they make about presupposed knowledge, the intellectual challenge they pose, their location (or not) in displaced time and space, and so on.

(from Long, 1985, p. 93)

In a process-oriented view of learning, 'problems' (activities requiring heuristic outcomes) are presented to learners; solving these problems requires development of language skills or leads to the acquisition of language skills. In this way, skill development is inherent in a process-oriented approach to syllabus design. In a process-oriented approach, the instructor must be equipped with methods for assisting development of language macro-skills; generally this is done only in the larger context of a problem-solving task. Language skill is a means to participate in a purposeful task.

Another way of stating the relationship (between skill development and syllabus) is that in a process-oriented syllabus, language skills (such as listening skills) and content can be linked in a curricular cycle. In this cycle, texts are used as starting points or as necessary sources of information needed for a task (as they often are in 'real-life' tasks), skills support interpretation of texts in the task context, language is understood in the context of a task, and appropriately graded and linked tasks constitute the syllabus (content) of the language course (Long, 1985; Long and Crookes, 1987).

8.2 Grading

Instruction of any complex skill involves **grading** (estimation of performance difficulty experienced by the learner with any activity) and **sequencing** (estimation of appropriate order of presentation, practice, and assessment). Grading of activities for listening-skill development is best done within overall language-task grading; grading of listening tasks within larger learning projects can be achieved through manipulation of support in task variables (input, role/setting, procedures, outcomes, feedback) outlined in Chapter 6.

Anderson and Lynch (1988) provide a useful visualization of grading as a set of slide controls (as on the control panel of a recording studio). Using this metaphor, we can imagine the learner's experience of difficulty with a language text as a function of how near the maximum each of these controls is set (Figure 8.1).

The control for language forms can be said to include variations of speaker style (which might be unfamiliar or distracting to the listener) and the degree of clarity of the speaker. The control for content can be

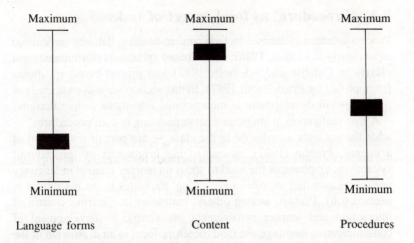

FIGURE 8.1   A prototype for grading: adjusting factors of difficulty
(adapted from Anderson and Lynch, 1988)

said to include the density of information points, the consistency of information, and the cognitive challenge of the text information for the learners. The control for procedures can be said to include how much production is required in a response and how many (how few) choices the listener has in responding (Anderson and Lynch, 1988).

Using the notion of controls for difficulty, we can then predict problems that learners might experience in different aspects of the task. These aspects might be linguistic, inferential, or procedural, as noted in Chapter 7:

linguistic aspect: non-understanding of linguistic items due to phonotactic, syntactic, or lexical decoding problems

inferential aspect: inappropriate or inefficient strategy selection; inappropriate activation of background or contextual knowledge

procedural aspect: not knowing what to do, not knowing what kind of response is expected

In a process-oriented approach, we can estimate learner difficulty with a listening text, but rather than adjust the text (input), we would adjust the task variables that make the input more usable to the learner in terms of the overall task goal.

8.3 'Procedure' as focal aspect of tasks

Process-oriented syllabuses include content-based syllabuses (articulated most clearly in Mohan, 1986), theme-based syllabuses (formulated most clearly in Candlin and Edelhoff, 1982) and project-based syllabuses (exemplified by Fried-Booth,1987). In this section we will examine how listening-skill development is incorporated into these course designs.

A first realization in language-course planning is that 'procedures' — what the students actually do in the class — are part of the content of a course. Prabhu (1987), as one of the originators of 'procedural' syllabuses, emphasizes the need to focus on learner control in language use (corresponding to 'role' and 'setting' variables in the discussion in Section 6.6). Prabhu, among others, maintains that learner control of interaction and learner involvement are central to development of communicative language use (and therefore focal to an evaluation of the utility of classroom instruction in second-language acquisition). Prabhu cites three types of task as being central to the approach: information-gap tasks, opinion-gap tasks, and reasoning-gap tasks.

Information-gap tasks are goal-directed activities in which the interlocutors do not share the same information, but must converge upon solutions to a problem given the information they have collectively. Information sharing becomes the basis of the learning activity. (See Appendix 8A for an example of an information gap of the type commonly found in ESL/EFL materials.)

Opinion-gap tasks are goal-directed activities in which the interlocutors are to clarify their opinions (or 'values') on a topic in order to convince someone or to reach a consensus or compromise. An example of an opinion-gap activity is having learners state, justify, and revise their opinions (and optionally seek to reach a consensus of opinion) of characters in 'character dilemma stories' (such as the legendary 'Alligator River Story'). (Information about the story to be presented to learners is, of course, necessarily presented through listening or reading texts.)

Reasoning-gap tasks are activities in which learners are presented the same body of information, and are required to reason toward solutions, positions, or verdicts. One example is having learners review legal cases (such as those presented in case notes for law students; see Goldenberg *et al.*, 1981, for examples) and present positions to support the prosecution or the defence. Another example is having learners generate solutions to 'lateral thinking' problems or generate alternate treatments of ideas and proposals (see the CORT materials of deBono, 1986, for an original paradigm). In this type of reasoning-gap activity, the 'gap' of reasoning is a collaborative one rather than a conflicting one. Again, input texts in a listening or reading mode are required for the task.

8.3.1   Learner strategies in information-gap tasks

Aside from whatever spoken input gap tasks require, these tasks can be thought of as leading to collaborative discourse and thus calling for the discourse listening skills outlined in Chapter 4. Convergent tasks are particularly useful for developing these skills since the interlocutors have a mutual commitment to repair trouble spots in the discourse.

Pica *et al.* (1987) point out that the focus of interactive listening practice should be not on what learners understand but on **how learners come to understand language they do not initially understand**. Learners engaging in information-gap (or opinion-gap or reasoning-gap) tasks need to employ strategies for seeking and providing clarification and for checking and confirming their understanding. The participants' use of clarification strategies is to a large extent shaped by whether the task is a one-way gap task (in which one interlocutor is in control of the necessary information to complete the task) or a two-way gap task (in which both interlocutors have complementary information to be negotiated). Two-way information gaps allow for a balance of listener roles and options for negotiation.

Consider the following example of discourse that takes place during an information-gap task, in which A is a speaker (here, a native speaker of English) giving directions to a listener B (a non-native speaker of English) in order that they both arrive at the same arrangement of objects on a felt board.

(1) A: And right on the roof of the truck, place the duck + the duck
(2) B: I to take it? Dog?
(3) A: Duck.
(4) B: Duck.
(5) A: It's yellow and it's a small animal. It has two feet.
(6) B: I put where it?
(7) A: You take the duck and put it on top of the truck + do you see the duck?
(8) B: Duck?
(9) A: Yeah + quack quack quack. That one. The one that makes that sound.
(10) B: Ah yes. I see in the + in the head of him.
(11) A: OK + see?
(12) B: Put what?
(13) A: OK + put him on top of the truck.

(14) B: Truck?
(15) A: The bus+ where the boy is.
(16) B: Ah yes.
(from Pica, Young, and Doughty 1987, p. 740)

This segment, in which the speakers finally transact one bit of information, is marked by a density of clarification oriented moves — **confirmation checks** (Turns 2, 8, 14) and **clarification requests** (Turns 6, 12), which are usually made by the listener, and **comprehension checks** (Turns 7, 11), which are usually made by the speaker.

In any segment of collaborative discourse, the speaker and listener can adopt this type of 'low risk' orientation towards the discourse transaction. Low-risk strategies are those associated with the 'success principle' (Brown *et al.*, 1985), in which the listener wants to be assured that the understanding arrived at is as close as possible to a targeted understanding.

High-risk strategies, on the other hand, are those associated with the parsimony principle' (Brown and Yule, 1983), in which the listener assumes that new information requires no change or minimal change from current knowledge. A listener utilizing the parsimony principle is then less likely to look for and less likely to query discrepancies between information in the speaker's contribution and what is already known.

If we look at strategies of interlocutors involved in collaborative tasks, we can note how each adopts a relative 'risk' in trying to understand a partner's contributions.

A high-risk strategy for the hearer entails the following:
(1) Assume maximal identity of information — e.g. assume a mentioned entity is the one you have in mind (in focus).
(2) When detail is lacking, e.g. in specifying an entity or relationship, use a best-guess tactic.
(3) Assume your information is secure and ignore incompatible information (e.g. refuse to incorporate extra information that does not make sense).
(4) Only process speaker's turn in terms of what you know — don't request additional information, give minimal feedback so that speaker doesn't give additional information.

A low-risk strategy for the hearer entails the following:
(1) Check that all entities are unambiguously identified (e.g. by name and by location).
(2) Require exact specification of descriptions.
(3) Check that the speaker knows what you understand.
(4) If necessary, recapitulate your movements.
(5) Do not make any new interpretation until you are sure you have the required information.

(6) Move minimally away from current focus.
(7) Be prepared for your partner's understanding to be different from your own.
(8) Constantly test speaker's representation.
(9) Remind speaker of your goals.
(based on Brown *et al.*, 1985, p. 25)

The following is an example of interlocutors using a 'high risk' strategy. (see Appendix 8A at the end of this chapter).

(T1)   A: just go + start from the bottom
(T2)   B: whereabout
(T3)   A: go up + Palm Beach
(T4)   B: right
(T5)   A: then you just + go down to the waterfall
(T6)   B: right
(T7)   A: and up
(T8)   B: right
(T9)   A: the hill + + and over the bridge + +
(T10) B: I've not got a bridge
(T11) A: and keep going up and you reach the top
(from Brown *et al.*, 1985, p. 23)

B assumes that the information in A's Turns 5 and 7 is consistent with the information B has (even though this is not the case). By Turn 9, B realizes something is going wrong and attempts to initiate a repair ('I've not got a bridge'), but A overrides this attempt to repair the conversation and continues giving directions.

Let us compare this extract with one in which the listener clearly adopts a low-risk strategy.

A: directly above that cactus you have a crashed plane
B: ah right + erm + oh yes + I have a crashed plane marked here + can I check this + my crashed plane is above my cacti — — so we both have a crashed plane and it's just above the imaginary horizontal...
(from Brown *et al.*, 1985, p. 24)

Here the listener seems to depend too heavily on a low-risk strategy. As cases such as this demonstrate, enactment of a low-risk strategy makes the discourse slow down and assume occasionally absurd dimensions. Thus, while a low-risk orientation is often required, it is often inappropriate and unnecessary to maintain a low-risk strategy throughout an entire discourse. A balance of low- and high-risk strategies at appropriate points in the discourse is the aim.

Process syllabuses require interaction of the kind illustrated in this section. Instruction in a process syllabus involves demonstration of strategies and encouragement of strategy development (such as adopting an appropriate 'risk strategy'). Other strategies are listed in Section 6.3.

(See also Wenden and Rubin, 1987, for discussion of development of learner strategies in classroom settings.)

8.3.2   Interactive listening: developing appropriate responses

In addition to problems involved in transfer and negotiation information, L2 learners will often experience problems understanding how to signal non-understanding without losing face, and in general, how to respond appropriately. Part of listening instruction therefore involves seeing that learners are aware of differences in cultural styles of listener feedback, and options for providing such feedback.

It is important for learners to become aware of a range of 'listenership cues' (e.g. sighing, smiling, laughing, frowning, shaking one's head, verbal and non-verbal back-channelling), especially those that are normally not displayed by listeners in their own culture. Learners should realize that use of unexpected signs (or the absence of such signs where expected) may lead to conversational difficulties in speaker–listener monitoring of the state of the talk.

Many situations require listener response of an affective nature. Ginsberg (1986), for example, has noted how listeners in friendly conversations display their acceptance of conversation topics through affective responses. Ginsberg constructs ten categories of listener feedback:

(1)   *empathetic* (e.g. 'Oh, I'm sorry to . . .');
(2)   *expository feedback* (e.g. 'I think it's . . .');
(3)   *interrogative* (e.g. 'What do you mean by . . .?');
(4)   *self-disclosure* (e.g. 'Yes, I sometimes . . .');
(5)   *suggestion* (e.g. 'Why don't you just . . .');
(6)   *positive evaluation* (e.g. 'That was a good . . .');
(7)   *criticism* (e.g. 'I think you're missing the point . . .');
(8)   *joking* (e.g. 'Yes, well at least . . .');
(9)   *reactive* (e.g. 'Oh, no!');
(10) *completions* (.e.g. S: 'So I decided to do it . . .'; L: . . . 'yourself?').
(based on Ginsberg, 1986, p. 358)

Awareness of listener options and strategies can increase a learner's effectiveness and ease in participating in information-gap, opinion-gap, and reasoning-gap tasks.

8.4   Content as input for tasks

Content-based approaches to language learning are often based on written support text, or texts in various media (see Candlin and Edelhoff, 1982, for an explanation); often the content-based syllabus is based on well-defined subject areas (such as Greek mythology, Russian history, the American government, geometry).

A marked advantage of content approaches is that classroom tasks can be sequentially and thematically connected. The outcomes of one class serve as input to the next class. Listening exercises, when they are required, will be contextualized, a critical factor in 'real-life' listening (Ur, 1984). A practical drawback of content-based approaches is that language learners may not be grouped according to content-area interests. Moreover, many learners may not understand why they are being asked to study content (say history or politics) in an ESL or EFL course. (See Nunan, 1988, for a discussion of this particular 'negotiation problem'.)

A suitable middle ground for language teaching, one which draws upon the strengths of a content-based approach and builds upon learner needs to develop skills and expectations of identifying language 'products' in their learning, is a **project-based approach**. Project-based learning allows for a 'layered' approach to developing language skills. Yalden (1987) suggests that beyond the beginning stages of language learning (or beginning stages of re-learning language as a system of spoken interaction for those who have had meaningful exposure only to the written language), once learners are beginning to use language skills effectively, a 'layered' approach to developing language skills is preferable. In a layered approach, steps in a project (a principled sequence of tasks leading to a tangible outcome) are planned on the basis of the skills that the learners most need to develop (Fried-Booth, 1987).

Let us consider how this is done. In a project for secondary school learners on 'world food shortage', informational input may be provided from listening texts (interviews, lectures, video documentaries) for learners who need to develop listening skills. Learners will need to draw upon and develop listening skills in order to complete a given project stage (for example, preparing a report on agriculture in a particular country). When listening skills are needed in a project (e.g. in gathering information from a video film or through an interview), the instructor must plan how to manipulate task-support variables (outlined in Chapter 6) in order to make the information accessible. Instructors will identify stages in which listening skills and strategies are needed (see Section 6.2 for a sketch list of strategies). See Appendix 8B for a graphic used in planning the stages of a project and Appendix 8C for a sample project design.

8.5 Specific instruction in listening skills

This section presents examples of the types of instruction that might occur at various stages in the context of a project.

8.5.1   Selective listening: informational input to tasks

Selective-listening exercises are aimed at helping students derive specific information from texts, even when the texts themselves are well beyond the students' current level of linguistic and content knowledge.

The principles for development of selective listening exercises are:

(1) Providing information in a large enough context that allows the listeners to make inferences in part on contextual cues.

(2) Providing task support which focuses students' attention on information to be derived from the text.

(3) Assisting listeners in a pre-listening phase to predict the form that the information will take and to anticipate the cues that will precede the needed information. ('Predictive markers' is a helpful term that Tadros, 1982, uses.)

Listening activities in general should consist of a well-structured pre-listening phase which should make the context for listening explicit, clarify purposes for listening, and establish roles, procedures, and goals for listening. (See Underwood, 1989, for detailed discussion of the structure of listening activities.)

With selective listening activities, the task outcome should be 'closed', with suitably focused choices to be made by the listener (see Chapter 5 for further definition). A post-listening phase (i.e. following the first attempt at the task outcome) should allow for simple negotiation of information needed for task completion and feedback on the outcome. A more intensive study of selected language forms in the text may follow, but only after meaning of the text has been established. See Appendix 8D for an example of a selective listening task format.

8.5.2   Global listening: thematic input to tasks

Global listening exercises are aimed at helping students construct an overall sense, or gist, of a text. Well-constructed global listening exercises can be helpful in developing the ability to identify topics and transition points between topics. The principles for the development of global listening exercises are:

(1) building expectations of the topic prior to listening;

(2) providing redundant cues to the same information in the text in order that listeners will have several chances to build inferences about the topic;

(3) providing minimal task structure and allowing for rather 'open' responses (see Section 5.2 for definition of response types);

(4) evaluating the outcome in terms of reasonable interpretations that the learners arrive at rather than on pre-ordained 'correct' responses.

8.5.3   Intensive listening: 'formal' input to tasks

Intensive listening exercises are aimed at focusing learner attention on features of the language system once text meaning has been established to some extent. The principles for development of intensive listening are in many ways parallel to those in 'grammatical consciousness raising' (see Rutherford, 1987, for a discussion of this approach to teaching and learning of grammar):

(1) Drawing attention to language features in a text which affect interpretation of the text. This may be a phonological feature (e.g. segmental contrast or intonational contrast), a grammatical feature, a lexical feature, a discourse feature.
(2) Assuring that features to be focused upon are learnable by the students. (A teacher could easily identify features which the students 'missed' altogether, but these may be unlearnable at that time. Efforts to draw students' attention to these features would likely be ineffective, and possibly counter-productive.)
(3) Providing a closed outcome in which the students select which features were displayed in the text.
(4) Allowing opportunities for student questions about the feature.

There are very few examples of intensive listening exercises in published textbooks which adhere to all of these principles, although many textbooks provide practice in intensive listening before the meaning of a text has been established. (In some cases, the texts which are presented have no contextual meaning whatsoever; they are merely presented to illustrate the language feature.)

Appendix 8E provides an example of a cloze-dictation exercise focusing on grammar in question forms (questions which appeared in an earlier selective listening exercise.) Other examples would be: ordering statements in the sequence in which they were made in the text; matching utterances with the correct speaker; identifying which intonation contour was used in a particular utterance.

8.6   Self-instruction in listening

One aspect of formal language learning that is often underemphasized is **self-instruction**, 'situations in which a learner, with others or alone, is working without the direct control of the teacher' (Dickinson, 1987, p. 5). For all learners, and especially for those who experience difficulty in developing listening skills and strategies, self-instruction can play a vital complementary role to classroom instruction. Promoting effective self-instruction in listening and encouraging students simply to 'listen more' (watch more television, talk to more speakers of the target language, etc.) are quite different proposals. Simple exposure to spoken language is not sufficient to develop language skills.

Effective self-instruction for listening skills most often requires the ongoing support of a trained instructor who can guide the learner in several respects:

(1) Selecting appropriate authentic (audio or video) materials and appropriate textbook materials.
(2) Adapting pre-recorded material for self-instruction; preparing appropriate tasks to accompany recorded material.
(3) Suggesting appropriate ways to approach conversations with target language speakers (TLS) in the community.
(4) Planning realistic goals (in view of resources available, including the time the student has for self-instruction).
(5) Promoting appropriate listening strategies to deal with particular learner needs.
(6) Keeping records of recorded material used.
(7) Providing feedback on the learner's progress.

Here only a few of these items will be considered in detail; the reader is referred to Dickinson (1987) and Riley and Zoppis (1985) for detailed guidance on setting up and (perhaps more importantly) maintaining a self-instruction program.

The selection of appropriate materials in a self-instruction programme component is vital. Authentic materials (in various formats of audio and video) abound; usually a small set of high-interest materials is more useful than a large collection that includes items learners will rarely use. Generally, most programmes can afford to buy only a limited number of materials in any event and copying of audio and video tapes is not legal.

For maximal use of materials available, and in order not to intimidate learners in the start-up process, materials should be clearly indexed (duration of the programme, general theme and content, recommendations from other users, description of any accompanying task materials), and preferably be cross-referenced in an accessible database (see Riley and Zoppis, 1985). It should be accepted at the outset that most authentic recordings (i.e. those designed primarily for native-speaker audiences, such as songs, interviews, and films) that are useful for self-instruction will contain a great number of language forms that are beyond most learners' level of competence. Instructors and learners can use authentic materials effectively only when appropriate exercises (global, selective, and intensive exercises or actual listener-generated exercises) accompany the materials.

If the instructor lacks the time to develop exercises, learners can utilize a general set of 'standard questions' (see Scott *et al.*, 1984). Standard questions are those which ask the student to make some predictions about the text before listening, write a summary of each section, indicate level of interest in the material, identify areas of difficulty in the text, list several new expressions, and write a brief recommendation of the text. Standard questions like these enable the students to focus on an appropriate orientation to the text, by helping them to activate appropriate expectations and selecting relevant criteria for understanding.

The last point on the list — providing feedback on the learner's progress of self-instruction — is most important for maintaining a self-instruction programme. Without some instructor feedback, even the most highly motivated learners will tend to lose interest in structured self-instruction. Instructor guidance need not be overly time consuming, but should include regular consultation about strategies the learner uses while listening (these comments may be made through comments in each learner's 'listening journal'), the particular programmes the learner finds interesting, how well the learner is managing the tasks and standard questions, and the type of notes the learner takes while listening.

8.7 Listening to learners: a teaching skill

In Section 6.5, an outline was given of ways in which proficient speakers 'easify' language in order to make information more accessible to listeners (and the possible problems in doing this). The skill of providing appropriate interactional adjustments and text adjustments underlies effective teaching, and is especially important in assisting learners in developing listening skill. Another teaching skill, quite closely related, is the skill of listening to learners. It is appropriate in this chapter to consider not only learner strategies for listening, but also instructor strategies for listening.

Let us examine first some extracts of NS — NNS discourse which have features similar to those found in language classrooms.
sample 1

    (T1)   NS: Are you going to visit San Francisco? Or Las Vegas?
    (T2)   NNS: Yes, I went to Disneyland and Knottsberry Farm.
    (T3)   NS: Oh yeah?
(from Long, 1983)

sample 2:

(T1)   NS: ... how long do you think or how long do you want to
               wait to be able to speak and read so you can go to college?
(T2)   NNS: [silence]
(T3)   NS: What − two years? one year?
(T4)   NNS: One year?
(T5)   NS: One year? Do you think in one year you can learn to speak
               and read well enough to go to college?
(T6)   NNS: [silence]
(T7)   NS: Do you understand what I'm + what I'm going for?
(T8)   NNS: College?
(from Long, 1983)

sample 3:

(T1)   NNS: Turkey I like
(T2)   NS: Really? Where did you eat turkey? Where do you eat the
               turkey?
(T3)   NNS: ... Uhm in (university restaurant)
(T4)   NS: Here?
(T5)   NNS: Yes, sandwich
(T6)   NS: Turkey sandwiches, yeah.
(from Long, 1983)

sample 4:

(T1)   NS: gehen Sie zur Arbeit? (*do you go to work?*)
(T2)   NNS: ?isch? nee (*me? no?*)
(T3)   NS: ?was machen Sie? (*what do you do?*)
(T4)   NNS: so mit zweit kinder +klein (*so with two children, small*)
(T5)   NS: ah ja (*oh yes*)
(T6)   NNS: und e hause kuchen putzen (*and er house, cook, clean*)
(T7)   NS: ah ja (*oh yes*)
(T8)   NNS: A essen [ ] Kind kie andered Kind viel Arbeit (*eat ...
               child the other child a lot of work*)
(T9)   NS: ja ja Sie arbeiten im Haushalt (*yes yes you do housework*)

[several intervening turns on topic of children]

(T10)   NS: wie+ wie ist so ein Arbeitstag E was machen Sie zuerst
               morgens? (*what, what is your working day like? er what do
               you do first thing?*)
(T11)   NNS: zu essen was? (*eat? what?*)
(T12)   NNS: mhm. (*mhm*)
(T13)   NNS: jetz? heute? (*now? today?*)
(T14)   NS: zum Beispiel ja (*for example, yes*)
(T15)   NNS: ja ich essen wann mein Mann zuhaus na ... (*yes, I eat
               when my husband home, no*)
(from Bremer *et al.*, 1988)

In these examples the more proficient speaker is required to use some
strategy to allow the discourse to proceed when understanding problems

occur. Long (1981) notes that speakers can use discourse strategies for avoiding trouble in discourse:

(1) relinquish topic control;
(2) select salient topics;
(3) treat topics briefly;
(4) make new topics salient;
(5) check NNS's comprehension.

Long also points out tactics for repairing trouble once it has emerged in the discourse:

(6) accept unintentional topic switch;
(7) request clarification (using only referential, not display questions);
(8) confirm own comprehension;
(9) tolerate ambiguity.

In the examples cited, we can see evidence of many of these tactics.

In sample 1, there is evidence of misunderstanding of the time suggested by the NS in Turn 1. The NNS in Turn 2 responds with events in the past. Rather than 'repair' this misunderstanding, the NS treats the response in Turn 2 as a topic nomination. The understanding problem is, we might assume, recognized by the NS, but no repair is initiated, possibly because the degree of misunderstanding does not preclude some development of the talk in the anticipated direction — 'talk about travel'.

In sample 2, we see how a single misunderstanding can lead to understanding problems which are maintained over several turns. In this extract the NS attempts to treat the clarification requests by the learner as topic nominations, leading into a deepening cycle of confusion. It is difficult to unravel communication problems once they have accumulated in this fashion (at Turn 8). Most likely, the conversation can continue only through use of a conversational tactic in which the speakers accept the ambiguity of the prior several turns and continue with a more salient topic.

In sample 3, we can see how the NS tolerating ambiguity (beginning in Turn 5) allows the conversation to continue. Continuing the conversation (at Turn 6) is possible because a common frame of reference is maintained, whereas in sample 2 the two interlocutors do not apparently have the same frame of reference ('going to college'?, 'learning to read and write'?) Once an interpretive frame of reference is established, it is generally easier to work out understanding problems that occur.

In sample 4, a misunderstanding occurs in Turn 12, but because of the shared frame of reference ('daily routine'), the NS works out a feasible interpretation which is still on topic. The NS accepts an inadvertent topic switch. In sample 4, the learner most probably heard 'zuerst' (first thing) as 'zuessen' (to eat), as the reformulation in Turn

11 indicates. In doing this, the learner makes a logical link to an established frame of reference ('daily activities'). Therefore, the NS does not find it necessary to initiate a clarification exchange. The shift of topic caused by the misunderstanding does not disrupt the conversation.

The orientation towards listening that instructors need to develop is one of working toward a mutual understanding with the learner, without seizing the speaker's role and without insisting on precise formulations of all information once meaning and intention are established. The converse of this conversational orientation leads to the instructor commandeering the speaker's role and insisting on precision. Consider the following extract from a language lesson.

> T: OK where is John Martin's? Phung? John Martin's?
> S   Oh, Gawler Pla(ce)
>   Gawler Place.
> T: John Martin's?
> S: Gawler Place.
> T: Gawler Place? No.
> S: [Inaudible]
> T: Charles . . .?
> S: Charles
> T: Street
> S: Charles Street and, er Rundle Mall
> T: Rundle Mall, yeah, so it's on the . . .?
> S: on the, on the corner of, on the corner
> T: on the corner of . . .? Charles Street
> S: Charles Street
> T: and?
> S: and
> T: Rundle Mall, yeah, yeah? John Martin's is on the corner of
>   Charles Street and Rundle Mall.

(from Nunan, 1988, p.85)

This type of discourse is not uncommon in classrooms in which the instructor places a high premium on accuracy. Clearly, the instructor in this extract is not exhibiting a 'normal' listener orientation of focusing on the intended meaning of the speaker. With repeated exposure to this kind of discourse pattern, the quality of listening practice that the learners receive in many classrooms is of decreased value. (See Long and Sato, 1983, for the seminal work examining discourse patterns in L2 classrooms.)

The following extract (presumably with learners of similar level to those in the above extract) exhibits a more 'real-world' listening strategy on the part of the instructor.

> S: My mother is by bicycle. By bicycle, yes, many, many, water.

T: She had an accident?
S: In China, my mother is a teacher, my father is a teacher. Oh, she
     go finish by bicycle, er go to . . .
S: House?
S: No house, go to . . .
S: School?
S: No school. My mother.
T: Mmm.
S: Go to here mother.
T: Oh, your grandmother.
S: Grandmother. On, yes, by bicycle, by bicycle, oh, is, um, accident
     [gesture]
T: In water?
S: In water, yeah.
T: In a river?
S: River, yeah, river. Oh, yes, um, dead.
     Dead! Dead! Oh!
T: Dead? Your mother? [general consternation]
(from Nunan, 1988, p. 140)

In this case the teacher is listening for the meaning the speaker is trying
to convey and helps the speaker through the kind of prompting techniques
found in NS−NS discourse (see Chapter 4). Rather than following the
well-known classroom pattern of question−response−feedback (teacher
elicit + student respond + teacher react), the instructor allows the student
to control the information flow and inserts clarification questions only
as needed. This is the type of listening skill that is required of instructors
in order that learners come to develop discourse strategies that are useful
outside of the classroom.

8.8   Discussion questions and projects

1. Evaluating classroom material.

Select a unit from a textbook you are currently using in which listening
skills are involved. In what ways is the material consistent with the
syllabus you envisage for the course?

   Evaluate the approach of the author to the treatment of task variables
(as defined in Chapter 6 and discussed in this chapter):

- input
- roles and setting
- procedures
- outcome
- monitoring and feedback

2. 'Easification' of texts

Some listening textbooks attempt to 'easify' spoken texts, both monologues and conversational texts, during the recording process. Common techniques are including more 'redundancy' (direct repetition and rephrasing) and using more explicit cohesion markers than native speakers typically include in order to make a text more coherent for the listener.

Consider the two passage below, recorded intentionally for a language textbook (the first sample) and for a radio broadcast (the second sample) designed for second-language learners. How is the text 'easified'? Do you find that this kind of text manipulation assists learners in developing listening skills and strategies? If so, in what way? If not, why not?

Sample 1 (from Cervantes *et al.*, 1985, pp. 9–10)
[from halfway through a conversation]

R: So, she lived in Hawaii all her life?
F: Well, when her kids were in high school, all her children were in high school, she got a letter from Japan, saying that her mother was sick.
R: Oh, the letter said her mother was sick.
F: Right. Her mother was old and she wasn't very healthy and the letter said, the letter was from her brother and the letter said that he mother was dying. So, because her kids were old enough, she decided to go back to see her mother.
R: She didn't take her children?
F: No, she went back alone. And when she got back to Japan, a couple weeks after she got back, the war broke out, the second world war.
R: The second world war. So she was in Japan and her family was in Hawaii.
F: And so she was stuck in Japan, she couldn't return to Hawaii because of the war ...

Sample 2: (from Campton and Jones, 1978, pp. 72–73)
[from the middle of an episode – J = John, M = Mary, H = housewife]

J: We've come to see Miss Haverall. But is that Miss Haverall?
M: This is her house. It's the right number.
H: Are you looking for someone, dear?
M: We're looking for Miss Haverall.
H: Miss Haverall, dear?
J: Is that Miss Haverall up there at the window?
H: Yes, dear. That's Miss Haverall. That's the lady you're looking for – if you're looking for Miss Haverall.
M: She threw a bottle at us.
H: Yes, dear. She throws bottles. She throws bottles at everybody.

She keeps people away with her bottles. She never hits anybody though.

J: She's mad.
H: She's harmless.
J: She's harmless, is she?
H: She never hits anybody with her bottles ...

3. Listener difficulty

Identify a language learner you have worked with who has exhibited problems with listening. What kind of practice, including self-instruction, could you devise to help the learner? (Consider design of tasks that encourage the listener to adopt various strategies.)

4. The role of written materials

Read the three statements that follow. Which do you agree with? How would you carry out proposals for dealing with the problem each statement suggests?

(a)   'For learners who already have had considerable exposure to written English but little or no exposure to spoken English (often said of Japanese and Polish learners of English, for example), listening instruction without resort to analysis of a corresponding written script is essential.'

(b)   'For learners who are not literate in English (and possibly not literate in their native language), listening instruction is more difficult since most listening practice requires some reading.'

(c)   'Learners who have access to the transcripts of taped programs, conversations, and lectures they listen to tend to learn more about language than those who don't.' (See Lebauer, 1984.)

5. Cultural variables in listener participation

In different cultures listeners may be expected to provide particular signals which are essential to communication. For example, Ishii (1984) demonstrates that listeners in Japan employ semi-verbal signs (such as hissing sounds) as feedback to show psychological filtering of the appropriacy of information in the exchange.

Ask a group of learners from a particular cultural background to list listener behaviours. (Use of video recordings would be helpful.) Ask them to find similarities and differences between listener signals acceptable in their culture and those in a target culture.

6. Longitudinal studies

Benson (1987) conducted a study in which he recorded how a non-native speaker of English passed one course at an American university. Benson investigated, over the period of a university semester, the relative importance of this one student's preparation for class, use of listening skills and strategies in the class, preparation of assignments, studying for tests, and evolving attitudes about the instructor, subject matter, and fellow students — in short, all of those behaviours and attitudes which contributed to his eventually passing the course. Longitudinal studies like this enable the researcher to place learning activities into a large context of goals and see the relative importance of various activities and skills in achieving these goals.

What type of information is a longitudinal case study likely to provide about a learner's development?

Appendix 8A: An information-gap task

The listener, using this map, is to follow instructions from the speaker. The listener draws a line from the landing point to the mine.

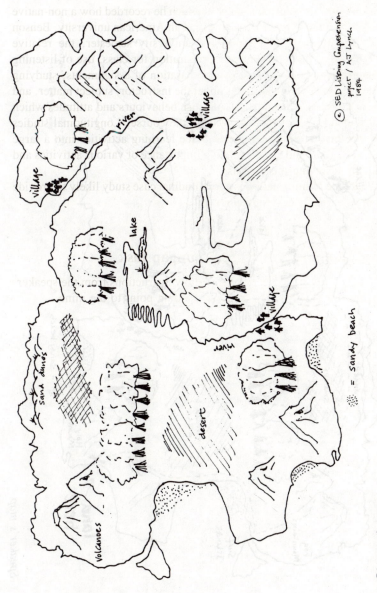

© SED Listening Comprehension project / AJ Lynch 1984

☷ = sandy beach

Listener's map

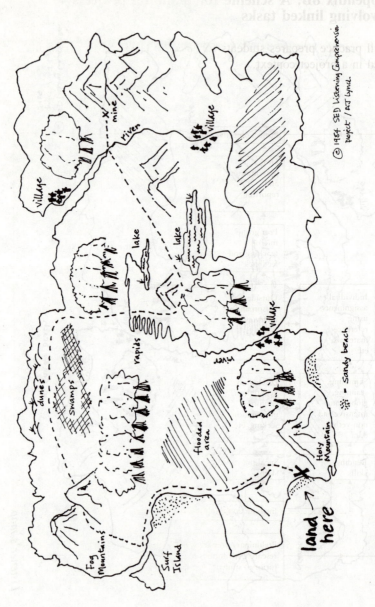

Speaker's map

Appendix 8B: A scheme for planning projects involving linked tasks

Skill practice prepares students for specific tasks. Skills are then used in a project context.

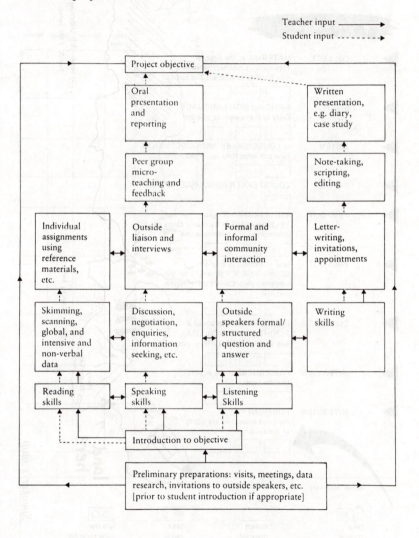

Teacher input ⟶
Student input ⇢

- Project objective
- Oral presentation and reporting
- Written presentation, e.g. diary, case study
- Peer group micro-teaching and feedback
- Note-taking, scripting, editing
- Individual assignments using reference materials, etc.
- Outside liaison and interviews
- Formal and informal community interaction
- Letter-writing, invitations, appointments
- Skimming, scanning, global, and intensive and non-verbal data
- Discussion, negotiation, enquiries, information seeking, etc.
- Outside speakers formal/ structured question and answer
- Writing skills
- Reading skills
- Speaking skills
- Listening Skills
- Introduction to objective
- Preliminary preparations: visits, meetings, data research, invitations to outside speakers, etc. [prior to student introduction if appropriate]

(from Fried-Booth, 1987)

Appendix 8C: A sample project design

'Project Airport' (Legutke, 1983) focuses on exploratory activities and interviews in an international airport. This table is used by students as they plan the project with the instructor.

Step 5: We would like to . . .		indi-vidual	partner	group	hithist
▶ . . . COLLECT	MATERIAL at the airport: Timetables, brochures, posters. Buy English newspapers and books. ▢▢▢				
▶ . . . STUDY	SIGNS and SIGN LANGUAGE. Copy as many signs as you can. ▢▢▢				
▶ . . . LISTEN	to LOUDSPEAKER ANNOUNCEMENTS. Find out what they say. Take notes. ▢▢				
▶ . . . TAPE	LOUDSPEAKER ANNOUNCEMENTS. ▢				
▶ . . . FIND OUT	how to explain in English TELEPHONING in Germany. Copy the information in a telephone box. ▢▢▢				
▶ . . . FIND OUT	how to explain in English GOING BY F V V (Frankfurter Ver-kehrsverbund). Collect information material. ▢▢▢				
▶ . . . COLLECT	information material about a FLIGHT TO LONDON, USA, . . . Ask at the BA, PAN AM, . . . counter. ▢▢▢				
▶ . . . INTERVIEW	PASSENGERS at the airport. Use the tape. ▢▢▢				
▶ . . . INTERVIEW	FOREIGNERS. Find out what they are doing at the airport. ▢▢▢				

Other activities

take photos   collect material   take notes   use the tape recorder

(from Legutke and Thiel, 1983)

Appendix 8D: Selective listening practice

Students listen to conversations consisting of several exchanges, selecting and recording (on a sheet) specific information.

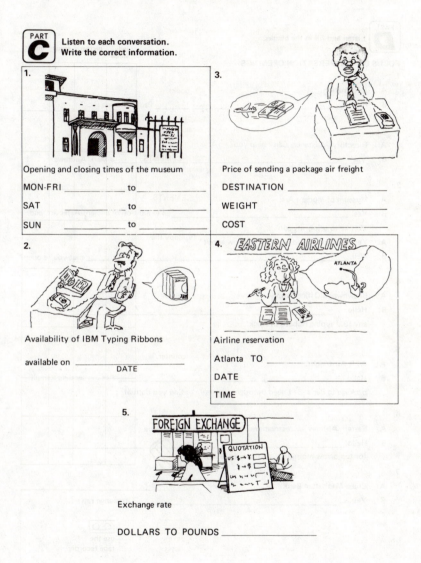

PART C Listen to each conversation.
Write the correct information.

1.

Opening and closing times of the museum

MON-FRI _____ to _____

SAT _____ to _____

SUN _____ to _____

2.

Availability of IBM Typing Ribbons

available on _____
　　　　　　　　　DATE

3.

Price of sending a package air freight

DESTINATION _____

WEIGHT _____

COST _____

4. EASTERN AIRLINES

ATLANTA

Airline reservation

Atlanta TO _____

DATE _____

TIME _____

5. FOREIGN EXCHANGE

QUOTATION

Exchange rate

DOLLARS TO POUNDS _____

(from Rost, 1986)

Appendix 8E: Intensive listening practice

Having already worked with the audio text to perform a selective or global task. students now listen again to focus on selected language forms.

PART
D   Listen and fill in the blanks.

FOCUS ON CONVERSATION OPENINGS

1.
    A: Information.
    B: Hello. _____ _____ _____ _____ _____ Paula Thomas . . .

2.
    A: Directory Assistance. Can I help you?
    B: Yes. _____ _____ _____ _____ _____ a Mark Andrews.

3.
    A: Museum of Modern Art.
    B: Yes. ____ _____ _____ _____ _____ an exhibition of ancient Aztec art, and
         I'd like to bring my son . . .
    A: Yes, sir. What would you like to know about?
    B: Well, _____ _____ _____ _____ _____ _____ that you're open?

4.
    A: Brownwood Office Supply.
    B: Hello . . . _____ _____ _____ _____ ____ _____ _____
         any IBM typing ribbons in stock . . .

5.
    A: ATR Air freight.
    B: Hello. _____ _____ _____ _____ _____ rates . . . sending a small
         package to Paris . . . I need overnight delivery . . . Can you do that? . . .

6.
    A: Eastern Airlines . . . reservations . . .   This is . . . Andrea Parks.
    B: Hello. _____ _____ _____ _____ _____
         for tomorrow morning . . . Atlanta to Miami . . .

7.
    A: Chase Manhattan Bank .
    B: Yes . . . _____ _____ _____ _____ _____ exchange rates . . .

(from Rost, 1986)

References

Abelson, R. 1981. Psychological status of the script concept. *American Psychologist*, **36**, 715—29.

Adger, C. 1986. When difference does not conflict: successful arguments between Black and Vietnamese classmates. *Text*, **6**(2), 223—238.

Adelman, C. 1981. On first hearing. In Adelman, C. (ed.) *Uttering, Muttering*. London: Grant McIntyre.

Aitchison, J. 1983. *The Articulate Mammal: An introduction to psycholinguistics*, second edition. London: Hutchinson.

Aitchison, J. 1987. *Words in the Mind*. London: Blackwell.

Alderson, J.C. 1984. Reading in a foreign language: a reading problem or a language problem? In Alderson, J. and Urquhart, A. (eds) *Reading in a Foreign Language*. London: Longman.

Alderson, J.C. and Hughes, A. (eds) 1981. *Issues in Language Testing*. London: The British Council.

Alderson, J.C. and Urquhart, A. (eds) 1984. *Reading in a Foreign Language*. London: Longman.

Alderson, J.C. and Urquhart, A. 1988. This test is unfair: I'm not an economist. In Carrell, P., Devine, J., and Eskey, D. (eds) *Interactive Approaches to Reading*. Cambridge: CUP.

Alderson, J.C., Krahnke, K. and Stansfield, C. 1987. *Review of English Language Proficiency Tests*. Washington DC: TESOL.

Allen, H.B. 1976. *A Linguistic Atlas of the Upper Midwest*. Minneapolis: University of Minnesota Press.

Allen, J. and Davies, A. 1977. *Testing and Experimental Methods*. Oxford: OUP.

Allwood, J. 1986. Some perspectives on understanding in spoken interaction. In Wetterstrom and Aberg (eds) *Logic and Abstraction*. Acta Univertatis Gothburgensis.

Anderson, A. and Lynch, T. 1988. *Listening*. Oxford: OUP.

Anderson, J.R. 1983. *The Architecture of Cognition*. Cambridge, MA: Harvard University Press.

Anderson, R.C. 1977. The notion of schemata and the educational enterprise. In Anderson, R., Spiro, R. and Montague, W. (eds) *Schooling and the Acquisition of Knowledge*. Hillsdale, NJ: Erlbaum.

Anderson, R.C., Reynolds, R.E., Schallert, D. L. and Goetz, E.T. 1977. Frameworks for comprehending discourse. *American Educational Research Journal*, **14**, 367—81.

Angell, L. and Young, S. 1981. A theoretical discussion of comprehension measurement techniques. Manuscript. Clemson University.

Aronson, E., Blaney, N., Stephan, C., Sikes, J, and Snapp, M. 1980. *The Jigsaw Classroom*. Beverly Hills, CA: Sage Press.

Asher, J. 1969. The total physical response approach to second language learning. *Modern Language Journal*, **53**, 3−17.

Asher, J. 1981. The extinction of language learning. In Winitz, H. (ed.) *The Comprehension Approach to Foreign Language Instruction*. Rowley, MA: Newbury House.

Austin, J.L. 1962. *How to do Things with Words*. Oxford: OUP.

Barnes, D. 1976. *From Communication to Curriculum*. Harmondsworth: Penguin.

Barnes, D. and Todd, F. 1981. Talk in small learning groups. In Adelman, C. (ed.) *Uttering, Muttering: Collecting, using, and reporting talk for social and educational research*. London: McIntyre.

Beattie, G. 1983. *Talk: An analysis of speech and non-verbal behavior in conversation*. Milton Keynes: Open University Press.

Beauvois, M.F. and Derouesne, J. 1980. Phonological alexia: three disassociations. *Journal of Neurology, Neurosurgery, and Psychiatry*, **42**, 1115−24.

Beebe, L. 1985. Input: choosing the right stuff. In Gass, S. and Madden, C. (eds), *Input in Second Language Acquisition*. Rowley, MA: Newbury House.

Beebe, L. (ed.) 1988. *Second Language Acquisition: Multiple perspectives*. Cambridge, MA: Newbury House.

Benson, M. 1987. An overseas student in higher education: a case study of academic learning in English as a second language. Ph.D. dissertation. Florida State University.

Berg, T. 1987. The case against accommodation: evidence from German speech error data. *Journal of Memory and Lanaguage*, **26**, 277−99.

Besse, H. 1981. The pedagogic authenticity of a text. In *The Teaching of Listening Comprehension*. London: The British Council.

Black, H. 1986. Assessment for learning. In Nuttall, D. (ed.) *Assessing Educational Achievement*. London: The Falmer Press.

Boden, D. and Bielby, D. 1986. The way it was: topical organization in elderly conversation. *Language and Communication*, **6**(1/2), 73−89.

Bond, Z. and Garnes, S. 1980. Misperceptions of fluent speech. In Cole, R. (ed.) *Perception and Production of Fluent Speech*. Hillsdale, NJ: Erlbaum.

Bower, G. 1978. Experiments on story comprehension and recall. *Discourse Processes*, **3**, 211−32.

Boyle, J. 1984. Listening comprehension − the crossroads between language and psychology. *PASAA* (Hong Kong), **14**, 1−17.

Bransford, J. and Johnson, M. 1972. Contextual prerequisites for understanding: some investigations of comprehension and recall. *Journal of Verbal Learning and Verbal Behavior*, **11**, 717−26.

Brazil, D. 1983. Intonation and discourse: some principles and procedures. *Text*, **3**(1), 39−70.

Brazil, D. 1985. *The Communicative Value of Intonation in English*. English Language Research, University of Birmingham.

Breen, M. 1987. Learner contribution to task design. In Candlin, C. and Murphy, D. (eds) *Language Learning Tasks*. New York: Prentice-Hall International.

Bregman, A. 1983. The formation of auditory systems. In Requin, J. (ed.) *Attention and Performance*. Hillsdale, NJ: Erlbaum.

Bremer, K., Broeder, P., Roberts, C., Simonot, M. and Vasseur, M. 1988. *Procedures Used to Achieve Understanding in a Second Language*. Strasbourg: European Science Foundation.

Brewer, W. 1985. The story schema: universal and culture-specific properties. In Olson, D., Torrance, N., and Hildyard, A. *Literacy, Language, and Learning*. Cambridge: CUP.

Bridges, A., Sinha, C. and Walkerdine, V. 1982. The development of comprehension. In Wells, G. (ed.) *Learning Through Interaction: The study of language development*. Cambridge: CUP.

Browman, C. 1980. Perceptual processing: evidence from slips of the ear. In Fromkin, V. (ed.) *Errors in Linguistic Performance*. New York: Prentice-Hall.

Brown, A. and Day, J. 1983. Macrorules for summarizing texts: the development of expertise. *Journal of Memory and Language*, **22**, 1–14.

Brown, George. 1978. *Lecturing and Explaining*. London: Methuen.

Brown, George and Bakhtar, M. 1983. *Styles of Lecturing*. Report. University of Nottingham.

Brown, Gillian. 1977. *Listening to Spoken English*. London: Longman.

Brown, Gillian. 1986. Investigating listening comprehension in context. *Applied Linguistics*, **3**, 284–302.

Brown, Gillian. 1987. Twenty-five years of teaching listening comprehension. *Forum*, **25**(4), 11–15.

Brown, Gillian and Yule, G. 1983a. *Discourse Analysis*. Cambridge: CUP.

Brown, Gillian, Anderson, A., Shillcock, R. and Yule, G. 1984. *Teaching Talk*. Cambridge: CUP.

Brown, Gillian, Currie, K., and Kenworthy, J. 1980. *Questions of intonation*. London: Croom Helm.

Brown, Gillian, Anderson, A., Shadbolt, N. and Lynch, A. 1985. *Report on Listening Comprehension*. Project sponsored by the Scottish Education Department (JHH/190/1). Edinburgh.

Brown, P. and Levinson, S. 1978. Universals in language usage: politeness phenomena. In Goody, E. (ed.) *Questions and Politeness: Strategies in social interaction*. Cambridge: CUP.

Burton, D. 1981. Analyzing spoken discourse. In Coulthard, M. and Montgomery, M. (eds) *Studies in Discourse Analysis*. London: RKP.

Button, G. and Casey, N. 1984. Generating topic: the use of topic initial elicitors. In Atkinson, J. and Heritage, J. (eds) *Structures of Social Action*. Cambridge: CUP.

Bygate, M. 1987. *Speaking*. Oxford: OUP.

Campton, D. and Jones, A.L. 1978. *The Missing Jewel*. London: BBC.

Candlin, C. 1981. Discoursal patterning and the equalizing of interpretive opportunity. In Smith, L. (ed.) *English for Cross-cultural Communication*. London: Macmillan.

Candlin, C. 1983. The language of unequal encounters: discoursal features in police-client interviews. Manuscript. University of Lancaster.

Candlin, C. 1987a. Beyond description to explanation in cross-cultural discourse. In Smith, L. (ed.) *Discourse Across Cultures*. New York: Prentice-Hall International.

Candlin, C. 1987b. Toward task-based language learning. In Candlin, C. and

Murphy, D. (eds) *Language Learning Tasks*. Englewood Cliffs, NJ: Prentice-Hall.

Candlin, C. and Edelhoff, C. 1982. *Challenges* (Teacher's Book). London: Longman.

Candlin, C., Kirkwood, J., and Moore, H. 1974. *Study Skills in English*. Department of Linguistics, University of Lancaster.

Carpenter, P. and Just, M. 1977. Integrative processes in comprehension. In Laberge, D. and Samuels, S. (eds) *Basic Processes in Reading: Perception and comprehension*. Hillsdale, NJ: Erlbaum.

Carrell, P. 1988. Interactive text processing: implications for ESL/second language reading classrooms. In Carrell, P., Devine, J. and Eskey, D. (eds) *Interactive Approaches to Reading*. Cambridge: CUP.

Carroll, B. 1981. *Testing Communicative Performance*. Oxford: Pergamon.

Carroll, J.B. 1972. Stalking the wayward factors: review of Guilford and Hepford's *Analysis of Intelligence*. *Contemporary Psychology*, **17**, 321−4.

Cervantes, R. Noji, F. and Mukai, M. 1985. *Developing Listening Comprehension: People talking about people*. Tokyo: Eichosha Shinsha.

Chafe, W. 1977. The recall and verbalization of past experience. In Cole, R. (ed.) *Current Issues in Linguistic Theory*. Bloomington, IN: University of Indiana Press.

Chafe, W. 1980. The deployment of consciousness in the production of a narrative. In Chafe, W. (ed.) *The Pear Stories*. Norwood, NJ: Ablex.

Chafe, W. 1982. Integration and involvement in spoken, written, and oral literature. In Tannen, D. (ed.) *Spoken and Written Language*. Norwood, NJ: Ablex.

Chafe, W. 1985. Linguistic differences produced by differences between speaking and writing. In Olson, D., Torrance, N., and Hildyard, A. (eds) *Literacy, Language, and Learning*. Cambridge: CUP.

Chafe, W. 1987. Cognitive constraints on information flow. In Tomlin, R. (ed.) *Coherence and Grounding in Discourse*. Amsterdam: Johns Benjamin.

Chaudron, C. 1983. Simplification of input: topic reinstatements and their effects on L2 learners' recognition and recall. *TESOL Quarterly*, **17**, 437−58.

Chaudron, C. 1985. A method for examining the input/intake distinction. In Gass, S. and Madden, C. (eds) *Input in Second Language Acquisition*, Rowley, MA.: Newbury House.

Chaudron, C. 1988. *Second Language Classrooms*. Cambridge: CUP.

Chaudron, C. and Parker, K. 1987. Patterns of simplification. Manuscript. University of Hawaii.

Chaudron, C. and Richards, J. 1986. The effect of discourse markers on the comprehension of lectures. *Applied Linguistics*, **7**(2), 113−27.

Chaudron, C., Lubin, J., Sasaki, Y., and Grigg, T. 1986. An investigation of procedures for evaluating lecture listening comprehension. Technical Report No. 5. Center for Second Language Classroom Research, University of Hawaii.

Chaudron, C, Cook, J. and Loschky, L. 1988. Quality of lecture notes and second language listening comprehension. Technical Report No. 7. Center for Second Language Classroom Research, University of Hawaii.

Chen, A. 1982. Diagnosis of a non-native reader of English using miscue analysis and introspection/retrospection. Manuscript. University of California.

Church, K. 1983. Phrase-structure parsing: a method for taking advantage of allophonic constraints. Ph.D. dissertation, MIT.

Church, K. 1987. Phonological parsing and lexical retrieval. In Frauenfelder, U. and Tyler, L. (eds) *Spoken Word Recognition*. Cambridge, MA: MIT Press.

Clancy, P. 1986. Acquiring communicative style in Japanese. In Schieffelin, B. and Ochs, E. (eds) *Language Socialization Across Cultures*. Cambridge: CUP.

Clark, H. and Clark, E. 1977. *Psychology and Language*. New York: HBJ.

Collins, A. and Loftus, E. 1975. A spreading activation theory of semantic processing. *Psychological Review*, **82**, 407–28.

Coulthard, M. and Montgomery, M. 1981. The structure of monologue. In Coulthard, M. and Montgomery, M. (eds) *Studies in Discourse Analysis*. London: RKP.

Couper-Kuhlen, E. 1986. *English Prosody*. London: Arnold.

Crookes, G. 1986. Task classification: a cross-disciplinary review. Technical Report 4. Center for Second Language Classroom Research, University of Hawaii.

Cross, T. 1978. Mothers' speech adjustments: the contribution of selected child listener variables. In Snow, C. and Ferguson, C. (eds) *Talking to Children: Language input and acquisition*. Cambridge: CUP.

Crystal, D. 1969. *Prosodic Systems and Intonation in English*. Cambridge: CUP.

Crystal, D. 1980. The analysis of nuclear tones. In Waugh, L. and van Schoonefeld, C. (eds) *The Melody of Language*. Baltimore MD: University Park Press.

Dance, F. 1967. A helical model of communication. In Dance, F. (ed.) *Human Communication Theory*. New York: Holt.

Davitz, J. 1964. *The Communication of Emotional Meaning*. New York: McGraw-Hill.

deBeaugrande, R. 1980. *Text, Discourse, and Process*. London: Longman.

deBono, E. 1986. *CORT Thinking*. Oxford: Pergamon Press.

Dechert, H. 1983. How a story is done in a second language. In Faerch, C. and Kasper, G. (eds) *Strategies in Interlanguage Communication*. London: Longman.

DeFleur, M. 1966. *Theories of Mass Communication*. New York: McKay.

Demyankov, V.Z. 1983. Understanding as an interpreting activity. *Voprosy yazykoznaniya*, **32**, 58–67.

Dickinson, L. 1987. *Self-instruction in Language Learning*. Cambridge: CUP.

Diehl, R., Kluender, K., Foss, D., Parker, E. and Gernsbacher, M. 1988. Vowels as islands of reliability. *Journal of Memory and Language*, **26**(5), 564–73.

Dirven, R. and Oakeshott-Taylor, J. 1986. Listening comprehension (Part I). *Applied Linguistics*, **7**(3), 326–43.

DiVesta, F. and Gray, S. 1972. Listening and note-taking. *Journal of Educational Psychology*, **63**(1), 8–14.

DiVesta, F. and Gray, S. 1973. Listening and note-taking: immediate and delayed recall as functions of variation in thematic continuity, note-taking, and length of listening-review intervals. *Journal of Educational Psychology*, **64**(3), 274–87.

Dolitsky, M. 1984. *Under the tumtum tree: from nonsense to sense, a study of non-automatic comprehension. Pragmatics and Beyond, V.* Amsterdam: John Benjamins.

Doyle, W. 1983. Academic work. *Review of Educational Research,* **53**(2), 159—99.

Duncan, S. 1972. Some signals and rules for taking turns in conversations. *Journal of Personality and Psychology,* **23**, 283—92.

Dunkel, P. 1985. Listening and note-taking: what is the effect of pre-training in note-taking? *TESOL Newsletter,* **19**, 30—1.

Dunkel, P. 1988. The content of L1 and L2 students' lecture notes and its relation to test performance. *TESOL Quarterly,* **22**, 259—82.

Dunkel, P. and Pialorsi, F. 1982. *Advanced Listening Comprehension.* Rowley, MA: Newbury House.

Duran, R.P., Canale, M., Penfield, J., Stansfield, C.W. and Liskin-Gasparro, J.E. 1987. TOEFL from a communicative viewpoint on language proficiency: a working paper. In Freedle, R. and Duran, R. (eds) *Cognitive and Linguistic Analysis of Test Performance.* Norwood, NJ: Ablex.

Duranti, A. 1986. The audience as co-author. *Text,* **6**(3) 239—48.

Eades, D. 1987. You gotta know how to talk . . . information seeking in Southeast Queensland Aboriginal society. In Pride, J. (ed.) *Cross Cultural Encounters: Communication and miscommunication.* Melbourne: River Seine.

Edmondson, W. 1981. *Spoken Discourse: A model for analysis.* London: Longman.

Ehrlich, S. 1982. Construction of text representation in semantic memory. In Le Ny, J-F. and Kintsch, W. (eds) *Language and Comprehension.* Amsterdam: North-Holland.

Eisenberg, A. 1986. Teasing: verbal play in two Mexican homes. In Schieffelin, B. and Ochs, E. (eds) *Language Socialization Across Cultures.* Cambridge: CUP.

Ellis, A. and Beattie, G. 1986. *The Psychology of Language and Communication.* London: Weidenfeld and Nicolson.

Ellis, R. 1985. *Understanding Second Language Acquisition.* Oxford: OUP.

Ellis, R. and Wells, C. 1980. Enabling factors in adult—child discourse. *First Language,* **1**, 46—62.

Ellman, J. and McClelland, J. 1984. Exploiting the lawful variability of the speech wave. In Perkell, J. and Klatt, D. (eds) *Invariance and Variability in the Speech Wave.* Hillsdale, NJ: Erlbaum.

Ervin-Tripp, S. 1972. On sociolinguistic rule: alternation and co-occurrence. In Gumperz, J. and Hymes, D. (eds) *Directions in Sociolinguistics: The ethnography of communication.* New York: Holt.

Farina, A. 1973. Development of a taxonomy of human performance: a review of descriptive schemes for human task behavior. *JSAS Catalog of Selected Documents in Psychology,* **3**,23, Ms. no. 318.

Fillmore, C. 1968. The case for case. In Bach and Harms (eds) *Universals of Linguistic Theory.* New York: Holt.

Fillmore, C. 1977. Topics in lexical semantics. In Cole, R. (ed.) *Current Issues in Linguistic Theory.* Bloomington, IN: University of Indiana Press.

Findahl, O. and Hoijer, B. 1982. The problem of comprehension and recall of broadcast news. In Le Ny and Kintsch (eds) *Language and Comprehension.* Amsterdam: North-Holland.

Fischhoff, B. 1982. Debiasing. In Kahneman, D., Slovic, P. and Tversky, A. (eds) *Judgment under Uncertainty: Heuristics and biases*. Cambridge: CUP.

Fivush, R. and Fromhoff, F. 1988. Style and structure in mother-child conversations about the past. *Discourse Processes, 11*(3), 337–56.

Fleishman, E. and Quaintance, M. 1984. *Taxonomies of Human Performance: The description of human tasks*. New York: Academic Press.

Flores d'Arcais, G. and Schreuder, R. 1983. The process of language understanding: a few issues in contemporary psycholinguistics. In Flores d'Arcais, G. and Jarvella, R. (eds) *The Process of Language Understanding*. New York: Wiley.

Fløttum, K. 1985. Methodological problems in the analysis of student summaries. *Text, 5*, 291–308.

Frederici, A. and Schoenle, P. 1980. Computational disassociation of two vocabulary types: evidence from aphasia. *Neuropsychologia, 18*, 11–20.

Fredericksen, C. 1972. Effects of task-induced cognitive operations on comprehension and memory processes. In Fine, J. and Freedle, R. (eds) *Developmental Issues in Discourse: I*. Norwood NJ: Ablex.

Freedle, R. and Fellbaum, C. 1987. An exploratory study of the relative difficulty of TOEFL's listening comprehension items. In Freedle, R. and Duran, R. (eds) *Cognitive and Linguistic Analysis of Test Performance*. Norwood, NJ: Ablex.

Fried-Booth, D. 1987. *Project Work*. Oxford: OUP.

Fries, C.C. 1945. *Teaching and Learning English as a Foreign Language*. Ann Arbor: University of Michigan Press.

Fries, C.C. 1961. Preparation of teaching materials, practical grammars, and dictionaries, especially for foreign learners. *Language Learning, 9*(1), 43–50.

Gairnes, R. and Redman, S. 1987. *Working with Words: A guide to teaching and learning vocabulary*. Cambridge: CUP.

Galvin, K. 1972. *An Interpersonal Approach to Speaking*. Lincolnwood, IL: National Textbook Company.

Galvin, K. 1985. *Listening by Doing*. Lincolnwood, IL: National Textbook Company.

Ganong, W. 1980. Phonetic categorization in auditory word recognition. *Journal of Experimental Psychology, 6*, 11–125.

Garnham, A. 1986. *Psycholinguistics: Central topics*. London: Methuen.

Garnes, S. and Bond, Z. 1980. A slip of the ear. In Fromkin, V. (ed.) *Errors in Linguistic Performance*. New York: Prentice-Hall.

Garrod, S. 1986. Language comprehension in context: a psychological perspective. *Applied Linguistics, 7*(3), 226–38.

Garrod, S. and Sanford, A. 1985. On the real-time character of interpretation during reading. *Language and Cognitive Processes, 1*(1), 43–59.

Gass, S. and Varonis, E. 1985. The effect of familiarity on the comprehensibility of non-native speech. *Language Learning, 34*(1), 65–89.

Geist, U. 1987. The three levels of continuity in a text. *Journal of Pragmatics, 6*, 737–50.

Gerot, L. 1987. Integrative work: an exploration in what makes reading comprehension test questions easy or difficult. In Benson, J. and Greaves, W. (eds) *Systemic Perspectives on Discourse*. Norwood, NJ: Ablex.

Ginsberg, D. 1986. Friendship and post-divorce adjustment. In Gottman, J. and

Parker, J. (eds) *Conversations of Friends: Speculations on affective development*. Cambridge: CUP.

Givon, T. 1979. *On Understanding Grammar*. New York: Academic Press.

Glison, E. 1988. A plan for teaching listening comprehension: adaptation of an instructional reading model. *Foreign Language Annals*, **21**, 9–16.

Godard, D. 1984. Same setting, different norms: phone call beginnings in France and the United States. *Language in Society*, **6**, 209–19.

Goethals, G. and Reckman, R. 1982. Recalling previously held attitudes. In Neisser, U. (ed.) *Memory Observed*. San Francisco: Freeman.

Goffman, E. 1974. *Frame Analysis*. New York: Harper and Row.

Goffman, E. 1981. *Forms of Talk*. London: Blackwell.

Goldenberg, N., Tenen, P., and Switzer, R. (eds) 1981. *Casenote Legal Briefs: Contracts*. Beverly Hills, CA: Casenotes Publishing Company.

Goldstein, K. 1984. *Language and Language Disturbances*. New York: Grune and Stratton.

Goldstein, L. 1980. Bias and asymmetry in speech perception. In Fromkin, V. (ed.) *Errors in Linguistic Performance*. New York: Prentice-Hall.

Goodenough, W. 1957. Cultural anthropology and linguistics. In Report of the seventh annual round table meeting on linguistics and language study. In Garvin, P. (ed.) *Georgetown Series on Language and Linguistics*, **9**, 167–73.

Goodwin, C. 1981. *Conversational Organization: Interaction between speakers and hearers*. New York: Academic Press

Goodwin, C. 1986. Audience diversity, participation, and interpretation. *Text*, **6**(3), 283–316.

Greene, J. 1986. *Language Understanding: A cognitive approach*. Milton Keynes: Open University Press.

Greenlee, M. 1981. Learning to tell the forest from the trees: unravelling discourse features of a psychotic child. *First Language*, **2**(5), 83–102.

Grice, H.P. 1969. Utterer's meaning and intentions. *Philosophical Review*, **78**, 147–77.

Grice, H.P. 1975. Logic and conversation. In Cole, P. and Morgan, J. (eds) *Syntax and Semantics: Speech acts*. New York: Academic Press.

Grice, H. P. 1981. Presupposition and conversational implicature. In Cole, P. (ed.) *Radical Pragmatics*. New York: Academic Press, pp. 183–98.

Grosjean, F. and and Gee, J. 1987. Prosodic structure and spoken word recognition. In Frauenfelder, U. and Tyler, L. (eds) *Spoken Word Recognition*. Cambridge, MA: MIT Press.

Gumperz, J. 1983. *Discourse Strategies*. Cambridge: CUP.

Halliday, M. 1976. Theme and information in the English clause. In Halliday, M. (ed.) *System and Function in Language*. Oxford: OUP.

Halliday, M. 1980. *Language as Social Semiotic*. London: Edward Arnold.

Halliday, M. 1986. Spoken and written language. Paper read at Japan Association of Language Teachers convention. November, 1986, Hamamatsu, Japan.

Halliday, M. and Hasan, R. 1983. *Cohesion in English*. London: Longman.

Harri-Augstein, S. and Thomas, L. 1984. Conversational investigations of reading: the self-organized learner and the text. In Alderson, C. and Urquhart, A. (eds) *Reading in a Foreign Language*. London: Longman.

Harrigan, J. 1985. Listeners' body movements and speaking turns. *Communication Research*, **12**(2), 233–50.

Hawaii English Language Institute Academic Listening Test (The Harper

Academic Listening Test). 1984. University of Hawaii at Manoa.

Hatch, E. 1983. *Psycholinguistics: A second language perspective*. Rowley, MA: Newbury House.

Hedley, C. and Barratta, A. (eds) 1985. *Contexts of Reading*. Norwood, NJ: Ablex.

Henning, G. 1987. *A Guide to Language Testing*. Cambridge, MA: Newbury House.

Henzell-Thomas, J. 1985. Learning from informative text: prediction protocols as a means of assessing the interaction between top-down and bottom-up processes. Ph.D. thesis, University of Lancaster.

Heritage, J. 1984. A change of state token and aspects of its sequential placement. In Atkinson, J. and Heritage, J. (eds) *Structures of Social Action*. Cambridge: CUP.

Heritage, J. and Atkinson, J. 1984. Introduction to Atkinson, J. and Heritage, J. (eds) *Structures of Social Action*. Cambridge: CUP.

Heyman, J. 1986. Formulating topic in the classroom. *Discourse Processes*, **9**, 37–55.

Hieke, A. 1984. The resolution of dynamic speech in L2 listening. *Language Learning*, **37**(1), 123–40.

Hinds, J. 1984a. Topic continuity in Japanese. *Typological Studies in Language*, 43–95.

Hinds, J. 1984b. Topic maintenance in Japanese narratives and Japanese conversational interaction. *Discourse Processes*, **7**, 465–82.

Hinds, J. 1985. Misinterpretations and common knowledge in Japanese. *Journal of Pragmatics*, **9**, 7–19.

Hodgson, V. 1984. Learning from lectures. In Martin, F., Hounsell, D. and Entwistle, N. (eds) *The Experience of Learning*. Edinburgh: Scottish Academic Press.

Hoffman, R., Kirsten, L, Stopek, S. and Cicchetti, D. 1982. Apprehending schizophrenic discourse: a structural analysis of the listener's task. *Brain and Language*, **15**, 207–33.

Hogg, R. and McCully, C. 1986. *Metrical Phonology*. Cambridge: CUP.

Holmes, J. 1987. Sex differences and miscommunication: some data from New Zealand. In Pride, J. (ed.) *Cross-Cultural Encounters*. Melbourne: River Seine.

Hornby, A. 1950. The situational approach to language teaching. *English Language Teaching*, **4**, 98–104.

Horowitz, D. 1986. Essay examination prompts and the teaching of academic writing. *English for Special Purposes*, **5**(2), 107–20.

Hosenfeld, C. 1979. Cindy: a learner in today's foreign language classroom. In Born, W. (ed.) *The Foreign Language Learner in Today's Classroom Environment*. Northeast Conference Reports, Northeast Conference on the Teaching of Foreign Languages, Middlebury, VT.

Howatt, A. 1984. *A History of English Language Teaching*. Oxford: OUP.

Hron, A., Kurbjoh, I., Mandler, H., and Schnotz, W. 1985. Structural inferences in reading and listening. In Rickheit, G. and Stroher, H. (eds) *Inferences in Text Processing*. Amsterdam: Elsevier.

Hudson, S. and Tanenhaus, M. 1985. Phonological code activation during listening. *Journal of Psycholinguistic Research*, **14**(6), 557–68.

Humphreys-Jones, C. 1986. Resolving misunderstandings. In McGregor, G. and

White, R.S. (eds) *The Art of Listening*. London: Croom Helm.

Hymes, D. 1967. Models of interaction of language and social setting. *Journal of Social Issues*, **33**(2), 8–28.

Ishii, S. 1984. Enryo-Sasshi communication: a key to understanding Japanese interpersonal relationships. *Cross Currents*, **10**(2), 49–60.

James, W. 1890. The Principles of Psychology. London: Dover Publications. Reprinted edition, 1950.

Janda, 1985. Note-taking English as a simplified register. *Discourse Processes*, **8**(4), 437–54.

Jarvella, R. 1971, Syntactic processing of connected speech. *Journal of Verbal Learning and Verbal Behavior*, **10**, 409–16.

Johnson, A. 1978. *Quantification in Cultural Anthropology*. Stanford, CA: Stanford University Press.

Johnson-Laird, P. 1984. *Mental Models*. Cambridge: CUP.

Johnstone, B. 1985. Arguments with Khomeini: rhetorical situation and persuasive style in cross-cultural perspective. *Text*, **6**(2), 171–88.

Kahneman, D. and Triesman, A. 1984. Changing views of attention and automaticity. In Parasuranan, R. and Davies, R. (eds) *Varieties of Attention*. New York: Academic Press.

Kahneman, P. 1973. *Attention and Effort*. New York: Prentice-Hall.

Kay, P. 1987. Three properties of the ideal reader. In Freedle, R. and Duran, R. (eds) *Cognitive and Linguistic Analysis of Test Performance*. Norwood, NJ: Ablex.

Kelch, K. 1985. Modified input as an aid to comprehension. *Studies in Second Language Acquisition*, **7**, 81–90.

Kellerman, E. and Sharwood Smith, M. 1986. *Cross-linguistic Influence in Second Language Acquisition*. Oxford: Pergamon Press.

Kintsch, W. 1975. *The Representation of Meaning and Memory*. Hillsdale, NJ: Erlbaum.

Klatt, D. 1979. Speech perception: a model of acoustic-phonetic analysis and lexical access. *Journal of Phonetics*, **7**, 279–312.

Klatt, D. 1981. Lexical representations for speech production and perception. In Myers, T., Laver, J, and Anderson, J. (eds) *The Cognitive Representation of Speech*. Amsterdam: North-Holland.

Klein, W. 1987. *Second Language Acquisition*. Cambridge: CUP.

Knowles, G. 1986. *Patterns of Spoken English*. London: Longman.

Krashen, S. 1981. *Second Language Acquisition and Second Language Learning*. Oxford: Pergamon Press.

Krashen, S. 1988. Do we learn to read by reading? In Tannen, D. (ed.) *Linguistics in Context*. Norwood, NJ: Ablex.

Krashen, S. and Terrell, T. 1983. *The Natural Approach: Language acquisition in the classroom*. Oxford: Pergamon Press.

Kraus, R. 1987. The role of the listener: addressee influences on message formulation. *Journal of Language and Social Psychology*, **6**, 81–98.

Kreckel, M. 1981. Tone units as message blocks in natural discourse: segmentation of face-to-face interaction by naive native speakers. *Journal of Pragmatics*, **5**, 459-76.

Kreckel, M. 1982. Communicative acts and shared knowledge: a conceptual framework and its empirical applications. *Semiotica*, **40**, 45–88.

Labov, W. 1972. Rules for ritual insults. In Sudnow, D. (ed.) *Studies in Social Interaction*. London: Free Press.

Labov, W. and Fanshell D. 1977. *Therapeutic Discourse: Psychotherapy as conversation*. New York: Academic Press.

Lackner, J. and Garrett, M. 1972. Resolving ambiguity: effects of biasing context in the unattended ear. *Cognition*, **1**, 359–72.

Ladd, R. 1980. *Intonational Meaning*. Chicago: University of Chicago Press.

Ladefoged, P. 1967. *Three Areas of Experimental Phonetics*. Oxford: Oxford University Press.

Langer, J. 1984. Examining background knowledge and text comprehension. *Reading Research Quarterly*, **19**.

Larsen-Freeman, D. and Long, M. 1990. *Introduction to Second Language Acquisition Research*. London: Longman.

Laver, J. 1972. Voice quality and indexical information. In Laver and Hutchinson (eds) *Communication in Face to Face Interaction*. Harmondsworth: Penguin.

Lea, W. 1980. Prosodic aids to speech recognition. In Lea, W. (ed.) *Trends in Speech Recognition*. Englewood Cliffs, NJ: Prentice-Hall.

Lebauer, R. 1984. Using lecture transcripts in EAP lecture comprehension courses. *TESOL Quarterly*, **18**, 1–19.

Leech, G. 1983. *Principles of Pragmatics*. London: Longman.

Legutke, M. and Thiel, W. 1983. Airport: Ein Projekt für den Englischunterricht in Jahrgangsstufe 6. Frankfurt: Verlag Moritz Diesterweg.

Lehiste, I. 1972. The units of speech perception. In Gilbert, J. (ed.) *Speech and Cortical Functioning*. New York: Academic Press.

Lenneberg, E. 1967. *Biological Foundations of Language*. New York: Wiley.

Leont'ev, A. 1973. Some problems in learning Russian as a foreign language. *Soviet Psychology*, **11**(4), 1–117.

Levine, J., Romashko, T. and Fleishman, E. 1973. Evaluation of an abilities classification system for integrating and generalizing human performance research findings. *Journal of Applied Psychology*, **58**, 149–57.

Levinson, S. 1983. *Pragmatics*. Cambridge: CUP.

Lewis, M. and Anderson, J.R. 1985. Discrimination of operator schemata in problem solving: learning from examples. *Cognitive Psychology*, **17**, 26–65.

Liberman, A. M. 1970. The grammar of speech and language. *Cognitive Psychology*, **1**, 301–23.

Liberman, A. and Mattingly, I. 1985. The motor theory of speech perception revised. *Cognition*, **21**, 1–36.

Liberman, A.M. and Studdert-Kennedy, M. 1978. Phonetic perception. In Held, R. (ed.) *Handbook of Sensory Physiology VII: Perception*. New York: Springer-Verlag.

Liberman, A.M., Delattre, D. and Cooper, F. 1952. The role of selected stimulus variables in the perception of unvoiced stop consonants. *American Journal of Psychology*, **65**, 497–516.

Liberman, A., Cooper, F., Shankweiler, D. and Studdert-Kennedy, M. 1967. Perception of the speech code. *Psychological Review*, **74**, 431–61.

Lindsay, D. and Norman, D. 1977. *Human Information Processing*, 2nd edn. New York: Academic Press.

Locke, John. 1689. An essay concerning human understanding. Oxford: OUP (1975).

LoCastro, V. 1987. Aizuchi: A Japanese conversational routine. In Smith, L. (ed.) *Discourse Across Cultures*. New York: Prentice-Hall International.

Lockman, A. and Klappholz, A. 1980. Toward a procedural model of contextual reference resolution. *Discourse Processes*, **3**, 25–71.

Loftus, E. 1975. Leading questions and the eye-witness report. *Cognitive Psychology*, **7**, 560−72.

Long, M. 1980. Input, interaction, and second language acquisition. Ph.D. dissertation, University of California, Los Angeles.

Long, M. 1981. Questions in foreigner talk discourse. *Language Learning*, **31**(1), 135−58.

Long, M. 1983. Native speaker/non-native speaker conversation and the negotiation of comprehensible input. *Applied Linguistics*, **4**, 126−41.

Long, M. 1985. A role for instruction in second language learning. In Hyltenstam, N. and Pienemann, M. (eds) *Modeling and Assessing Second Language Acquisition*. London: Multilingual Matters.

Long, M. and Crookes, G. 1987. Intervention points in second language classroom research. In Das (ed.) *Patterns of Classroom Interaction in Southeast Asia*. Singapore: RELC.

Long, M. and Porter, P. 1985. Group work, interlanguage talk, and second language acquisition. *TESOL Quarterly*, **19**(2), 207−228.

Long, M. and Sato, C. 1983. Classroom foreigner talk discourse: forms and functions of teachers' questions. In Seliger, H. and Long, M. (eds) *Classroom-oriented Research*. Rowley, MA: Newbury House.

Lorch, R., Lorch, E. and Matthews, P. 1981. On-line processing of the topic structure of a text. *Journal of Verbal Learning and Verbal Behavior*, **19**, 350−69.

Lynch, A. 1983. *Study Listening*. Cambridge: CUP.

McClelland, J. 1987. A case for interactionism in language processing. In Coltheart, M. (ed.) *Psychology of Reading*. Hillsdale, NJ: Erlbaum.

McClelland, J. and Rumelhart, D. 1981. An interactive activation model of context effects in letter perception: I. An account of basic findings. *Psychological Review*, **88**, 375−407.

McGregor, G. 1986. Listening outside the participation framework. In McGregor, G. and White, R.S. (eds) *The Art of Listening*. London: Croom Helm.

McGregor, G. 1987. *Language for Hearers*. Oxford: Pergamon Press.

McTear, M. 1985. *Conversations with Children*. London: Blackwell.

Mandelbaum, J. 1987. Couples sharing stories. *Communication Quarterly*, **35**(2), 144−70.

Mandler, J. and Johnson, N.S. 1977. Remembrance of things parsed: story structure and recall. *Cognitive Psychology*, **9**, 111−51.

Mann, S. 1983. Problems in reading and listening and how they may be solved by the reader/hearer. Paper presented at TESOL convention, Toronto.

Marslen-Wilson, W. and Tyler, L. 1980. The temporal structure of spoken language comprehension. *Cognition*, **8**, 1−72.

Marslen-Wilson, W. and Tyler, L. 1981. Central processes in speech understanding. In Higgins, Lyons and Broadbent (eds) *The Psychological Mechanisms of Language*. London: Royal Society and British Academy.

Maseide, P. 1987. The permanent context construction: a neglected aspect of therapeutic discourse. *Text*, **7**(1), 67−87.

Mason, A. 1982. *Understanding Academic Lectures*. New York: Prentice-Hall.

Maturana, H. 1980. Biology of cognition. In Maturana, H. and Verela, F. (eds) *Autopoesis and Cognition*. Dordrecht: Reidl.

Mehler, J., Segui, J. and Carey, P. 1981. Monitoring ambiguity as a listening process. *Journal of Memory and Language*, **78**(17), 29−35

Meyer, B. 1975. *The Organization of Prose and its Effects on Memory*. Amsterdam: North-Holland.

Miller, G. 1962. Decision units in the perception of speech. *IRE Transactions on Information Theory*, **8**, 81—3.

Miller, G. and Johnson-Laird, P. 1976. *Language and Perception*. Cambridge, MA: Harvard University Press.

Milroy, L. 1986. Comprehension and context: successful communication and communication breakdown. In McGregor, G. and White, R.S. (eds) *The Art of Listening*. London: Croom Helm.

Mohan, B. 1986. *Language and Content*. Reading, MA: Addison-Wesley.

Morley, D. D. 1987. Subjective message constructs: a theory of persuasion. *Communication Monographs*, **54**, 183—92.

Morrow, K. 1985. The evaluation of tests of communicative performance. *Prospect*, **1**(2)

Morton, J. 1969. Interaction of information in word recognition. *Psychological Review*, **76**, 165—78.

Morton, J. 1970. A functional model for memory. In Norman, D. (ed.) *Models of Human Memory*. New York: Academic Press.

Morton, J. 1979. Word recognition. In Morton, J. and Marshall, J. (eds) *Psycholinguistics Series 2: Structures and processes*. London: Elek.

Morton, J., Hammersley, R., and Bekerian, D. 1985. Headed records: a model for memory and its failures. *Cognition*, **20**, 1—23.

Morton, K. and Saljo, R. 1976. On qualitative differences in learning, I: outcomes and processes. *British Journal of Education Psychology*, **46**, 4—11.

Munby, J. 1978. *Communicative Syllabus Design*. Cambridge: CUP.

Murphy, J. 1985. Exploring listening comprehension in an interactive context. *TESOL Newsletter*, December, 1—2.

Neisser, U. 1982. Memory: what are the important questions? In Neisser, U. (ed.) *Memory Observed: Remembering in natural contexts*. San Francisco: Freeman.

Nemser, W. 1974. Approximative systems of foreign language learners. *IRAL*, **9**, 115—23.

Newman, J. 1985. Processing spoken discourse: effects of position and emphasis on judgements of textual coherence. *Discourse Processes*, **8**, 205—27.

Nisbett, R.F. and Wilson, D.T. 1977. Telling more than we can know: verbal reports on mental processes. *Psychological Review*, **84**(3), 231—59.

Nix, D. 1983. Links: A teaching approach to developmental progress in children's reading comprehension and meta-comprehension. In Fine, J. and Freedle, R. (eds) *Developmental Issues in Discourse, Volume X*. Norwood, NJ: Ablex.

Noller, P. 1984. *Nonverbal Communication and Marital Interaction*. Oxford: Pergamon.

Nord, J. 1975. A case for listening comprehension. *Philologia*, **7**, 1—25.

North Western Regional (UK) Advisory Council for Further Education. 1983. Listening with understanding. Test paper in English as a Second Language.

Nunan, D. 1988. *The Learner-centred Curriculum*. Cambridge: CUP.

Nunan, D. 1989. *Designing Tasks for the Communicative Classroom*. Cambridge: Cambridge University Press.

Ochs, E. 1986. Introduction. In Schieffelin and Ochs (eds) *Language Socialization Across Cultures*. Cambridge: CUP.

O'Keefe, B. and Shepherd, G. 1987. The pursuit of multiple goals in face to face persuasion interactions. *Communication Monographs*, **54**, 396–419.

Oller, J. 1983. Evidence for a general language proficiency factor: an expectancy grammar. In Oller, J. (ed.) *Issues in Language Testing Research*. Rowley, MA: Newbury House.

Oller, J. 1987. Testing in a communicative curriculum. *Forum*, **25**(4), 42–6.

Oring, E. 1986. Jokes and the discourse on disaster. *American Anthropologist*, **88**, 276–90.

Paivio, A. 1971. *Imagery and Verbal Processes*. New York: Holt.

Palincsar, A. and Brown, A. 1984. Reciprocal teaching of comprehension-fostering and comprehension-monitoring activities. *Cognition and Instruction*, **7**(4), 117–45.

Palmer, H.E. 1921. *The Oral Method of Teaching Languages*. Cambridge: Heffer.

Pask, G. and Scott, B. 1972. Learning strategies and individual competence. *International Journal of Man–Machine Studies*, **7**, 217–25.

Pellowe, J. 1986. Hearer's intentions. In McGregor, G. and White, R.S. (eds) *The Art of Listening*. London: Croom Helm.

Perdue, C. 1984. Understanding, misunderstanding, and breakdown. In Perdue, C.(ed.) *SLA by Adult Immigrants*. Rowley, MA: Newbury House.

Perkins, K. and Jones, B. 1985. Measuring passage contribution to ESL reading comprehension. *TESOL Quarterly*, **19**, 137–53.

Perrig, W. and Kintsch, W. 1985. Propositional and situational representations of text. *Journal of Memory and Language*, **4**, 503–18.

Peters, A. and Boggs, S. 1986. Interaction routines as cultural influences upon language learning. In Schieffelin, B. and Ochs, E. (eds) *Language Socialization Across Cultures*. Cambridge: CUP.

Pica, T., Young, R. and Doughty, C. 1987. The impact of interaction on comprehension. *TESOL Quarterly*, **21**(4), 737–58.

Pisoni, P. and Luce, P. 1987. Acoustic-phonetic representations of speech. In Frauenfelder, U. and Tyler. L. (eds) *Spoken Word Recognition*. Cambridge, MA: MIT Press.

Pittman, J. and Gallois, C. 1986. Predicting impressions of speakers from voice quality: acoustic and perceptual measures. *Journal of Language and Social Psychology*, **5**, 237–46.

Porter, D. and Roberts, J. 1981. Authentic listening activities. *ELT Journal*, **36**(1), 37–47.

Postovsky, L. 1974. Effects of delay in oral practice at the beginning of second language learning. *Modern Language Journal*, **58**, 229–39.

Prabhu, N.S. 1987. *Second Language Pedagogy: A perspective*. Oxford: OUP.

Pride, J. 1987. Introduction. In Pride, J. (ed.) *Cross-cultural Encounters*. Melbourne: River Seine.

Prince, E. 1981. Toward a taxonomy of given-new information. In Cole, P. (ed.) *Radical Pragmatics*. New York: Academic Press.

Resnick, L. 1984. Comprehending and learning: implications for a cognitive theory of instruction. In Mandl, H., Stein, N. and Trabasso, T. (eds) *Learning and Comprehension of Text*. Hillsdale, NJ: Erlbaum.

Ricento, T. 1987. Ellipsis in conversation. *Journal of Pragmatics*, **11**(6), 751–76.

Richards, J. 1983. Listening comprehension: approach, design, procedure. *TESOL Quarterly*, **17**(2), 219–39.

Richards, J. and Schmidt, R. 1983. Conversational analysis. In Richards, J. and Schmidt, R. (eds) *Language and Communication*. London: Longman.

Riesbeck, C. 1982. Realistic language comprehension. In Lenhert, W. and Ringle, M. (eds) *Strategies for Natural Language Processing*. Hillsdale, NJ: Erlbaum.

Riley, P. 1981. Viewing comprehension: L'oeil ecoute. In *The Teaching of Listening Comprehension*. London: The British Council.

Riley, P. and Zoppis, C. 1985. The sound and video library. In Riley, P. (ed.) *Discourse and Learning*. London: Longman.

Rivers, W. and Temperley, E. 1984. *Teaching Foreign Language Skills*. Chicago: University of Chicago Press.

Rixon, S. 1981. The design of materials to foster particular listening strategies. In *The Teaching of Listening Comprehension*. London: The British Council.

Robinson, G. 1985. *Cross-cultural Communication*. Oxford: Pergamon Press.

Rost, M. 1986. *Strategies in Listening*. London: Lingual House.

Rost, M. 1987. Interaction of listener, speaker text, and task. Ph.D. thesis. University of Lancaster.

Rulon, K. and McCreary, J. 1986. Negotiation of content: teacher-fronted and small-group interaction. In Day, R. (ed.) *Talking to Learn*. Rowley, MA: Newbury House.

Rutherford, W. 1987. *Second Language Grammar: Learning and Teaching*. London: Longman.

Sacks, H., Schegloff, E., and Jefferson, G. 1974. A simplest systematics for the organization of turn-taking in conversation. *Language*, **50**, 696−735.

Samnda, G. 1989. *Task Design*. Oxford: OUP.

Samuels, S. 1984. Factors influencing listening: inside and outside the head. *Theory into Practice*, **23**(3), 183−9.

Sanders, R. 1985. The interpretation of nonverbals. *Semiotica*, **55**(3/4), 195−216.

Sanjek, R. 1971. Brazilian racial terms. Some aspects of meaning and learning. *American Anthropologist*, **73**(1), 1126−43.

Savignon, S. 1987. What's what in communicative language teaching. *Forum*, **25**(4), 16−21.

Saville-Troike, M. 1982. *The Ethnography of Communication*. London: Blackwell.

Schank, R. 1972. Conceptual dependency: a theory of natural language understanding. *Cognitive Psychology*, **3**, 552−631.

Schank, R. 1982. Reminding and memory organization. In Lenhert, W. and Ringle, M. (eds) *Strategies for Natural Language Processing*. Hillsdale, NJ: Erlbaum.

Schank, R. and Abelson, R. 1977. Scripts, plans, and knowledge. In Johnson-Laird, P. and Wason, P. (eds) *Thinking: Readings in cognitive science*. Cambridge: CUP.

Schank, R. and Riesbeck, C. 1981. *Inside Computer Understanding*. Hillsdale, NJ: Erlbaum.

Scherer, K., Feldstein, S, Bond, R. and Rosenthal, R. 1985. Vocal cues to deception: a comparative channel approach. *Journal of Psycholinguistic Research*, **14**(4), 409−25.

Schieffelin, B. and Ochs, E. (eds) 1986. *Language Socialization Across Cultures*. Cambridge: CUP.

Schlesinger, I. 1977. *Production and Comprehension of Utterances*. Hillsdale, NJ: Erlbaum.

Schmalhofer, F. and Glavanov, D. 1986. Three components of understanding a programmer's manual: verbatim, propositional, and situational representations. *Journal of Memory and Language*, **25**, 279−94.

Schramm, W. 1954. How communication works. In Schramm, W. (ed.) *The Process and Effects of Mass Communication*. Urbana, IL: University of Illinois Press.

Schwartz, J. 1980. The negotiation for meaning: repair in conversations between second language learners of English. In Larsen-Freeman, D.(ed.) *Discourse Analysis in Second Language Research*. Rowley, MA: Newbury House.

Schwartz, M.1984. What the classical aphasia categories don't tell us and why. *Brain and Language,* **21**, 3–8.

Schwartz, M. and Flammer, A. 1981. Text structure and title – effects on comprehension and recall. *Journal of Verbal Learning and Verbal Behavior,* **20**, 61–6.

Scollon, R. and Scollon, S.B. 1981. Cooking it up and boiling it down: children's story retellings. In Freedle, R. (ed.) *Advances in Discourse Processes*. Norwood, NJ: Ablex.

Scott, M., Carioni, L, Zannatta, M., Bayer, E. and Quintanilh, T. 1984. Using a 'standard exercise' in teaching reading comprehension. *ELT Journal,* **38**, 114–20.

Searle, J.R. 1975. A taxonomy of illocutionary acts. *Language in Society,* **5**, 1–23.

Seidenberg, M., Tanenhaus, M., Leiman, J., Benkowski, M. 1982. Automatic access of meaning of ambiguous words in context. *Cognitive Psychology,* **14**, 489–537.

Selkirk, E. 1984. *Phonology and Syntax: The relation between sound and structure*. Cambridge, MA: MIT Press.

Sexton, M. 1976. Acceptance, defiance, and evasion in a psychiatric meeting. Manuscript. University of Lancaster

Shannon, C. and Weaver, W. 1949. *The Mathematical Theory of Communication*. Urbana, IL: University of Illinois Press.

Sheerin, S. 1987. Listening comprehension: teaching or testing? *ELT Journal,* **41**, 126–31.

Sinclair, J. and Coulthard, M. 1975. *Towards an Analysis of Discourse*. Oxford: Oxford University Press.

Small, S. and Rieger, C. 1982. Parsing and comprehending with word experts. In Lenhert, W. and Ringle, M. (eds) *Strategies for Natural Language Processing*. Hillsdale, NJ: Erlbaum.

Smith, F. 1981. *Reading*. Cambridge: CUP.

Snow, C. and Hoefnagel-Hohle, M. 1982. School-age second language learners' access to simplified linguistic input. *Language Learning,* **32**, 411–30.

Sperber, D. and Wilson, D. 1982. Mutual knowledge and relevance in theories of comprehension. In Smith, N. (ed.) *Mutual Knowledge*. London: Academic Press.

Sperber, D. and Wilson, D. 1986. *Relevance*. London: Blackwell.

Strevens, P. 1987. Cultural barriers to language learning. In Smith, L. (ed.) *Discourse Across Cultures*. New York: Prentice-Hall International.

Studdert-Kennedy, M. 1981. Perceiving phonetic segments. In Myers, T., Laver, J, and Anderson, J. (eds) *The Cognitive Representation of Speech*. Amsterdam: North-Holland.

Swinney, D. 1982. The structure and time-course of information interaction during speech comprehension. In Mehler, J., Walker, E. and Garrett, M. (eds) *Perspectives on Mental Representation*. Hillsdale, NJ: Erlbaum.

Szatrowski, P. 1987. Vividness and narrative events in Japanese conversational narratives. In Tomlin, R. (ed.) *Coherence and Grounding in Discourse*. Amsterdam: Johns Benjamin.

Tadros, A. 1982. The notion of predictive structure and its pedagogical applications. Manuscript. University of Birmingham.

Tannen, D. 1982. The oral/literate continuum in discourse. In Tannen, D. (ed.) *Spoken and Written Language: Exploring orality and literacy*. Norwood, NJ: Ablex.

Tannen, D. 1984. *Conversational Style: Analyzing talk among friends*. Norwood, NJ: Ablex.

Tannen, D. 1985. Relative focus on involvement in oral and written discourse. In Olson, D., Torrance, N., and Hildyard, A. *Literacy, Language, and Learning*. Cambridge: CUP.

Taylor, T. and Cameron, D. 1987. *Analysing Conversation*. Oxford: Pergamon Press.

Thomas, H. 1982. Survey review of materials for the development of listening skills. *ELT Journal*, **36**, 192–9.

Thomas, J. 1983. Cross-cultural pragmatic failure. *Applied Linguistics*, **4**(2), 91–111.

Thomas, J. 1985. The dynamics of discourse: a pragmatic approach to the analysis of confrontational interaction. Ph.D. thesis. University of Lancaster.

Thorndyke, P. and Yekovich, F. 1980. A critique of schema-based theories of human story memory. *Poetics*, **9**, 23–49.

TOEFL (The Test of English as a Foreign Language). 1983. Princeton, NJ: Educational Testing Service.

Tomlin, R. 1985. Foreground–background information and the syntax of subordination. *Text*, **5**, 85–122.

Toulmin, S., Rieke, R., and Janik, A. 1983. *An Introduction to Reasoning*, 2nd edn. New York: Macmillan.

Tracy, K. 1984a. The effect of multiple goals on conversational relevance and topic shift. *Communication Monographs*, **51**(3), 274–87.

Tracy, K. 1984b. Staying on topic: an explication of conversational relevance. *Discourse Processes*, **7**, 447–64.

Traeger, G. and Smith, H.L. 1957. *An Outline of English Structure: Studies in linguistics, 3*. Washington DC: American Council of Learned Societies.

Treisman, A. 1969. Strategies and models of selective attention. *Psychological Review*, **84**, 1–66.

Trevarthan, C. 1977. Descriptive analysis of infant communicative behavior. In Schaffer, H. (ed.) *Studies in Mother–infant Interaction*. New York: Academic Press.

Tyler, L. and Marslen-Wilson, W. 1977. The on-line effect of semantic context on syntactic processing. *Journal of Memory and Language*, **16**, 683–92.

Tyler, L. and Marslen-Wilson, W. 1986. The effects of context on the recognition of multimorphemic words. *Journal of Memory and Language*, **25**, 741–52.

Tyler, L. and Frauenfelder, U. 1987. The process of spoken word recognition: an introduction. In Frauenfelder and Tyler (eds) *Spoken Word Recognition*. Cambridge, MA: MIT Press.

Tyler, S. 1978. *The Said and the Unsaid*. New York: Academic Press.

Underwood, M. 1989. *Teaching Listening*. London: Longman.

Ur, P. 1984. *Teaching Listening Comprehension*. Cambridge: CUP.

van Ek, J. and Alexander, L.G. 1980. *Threshold Level in English*. Oxford: Pergamon.

van Lier, L. 1988. *The Classroom and the Language Learner*. London: Longman.

van Peer, H. 1987. *Stylistics and Psychology: Investigations of foregrounding*. London: Croom Helm.

Varadi, T. 1983. Strategies of target language learner communication: message adjustment. In Faerch, C. and Kasper, G. (eds) *Strategies in Interlanguage Communication*. London: Longman.

Wagner-Gough, J. 1975. Comparative studies in second language learning. MA thesis, University of California, Los Angeles.

Watson-Gegeo, K. 1989. Ethnography in ESL: defining the essentials. Manuscript. University of Hawaii.

Weizenbaum, J. 1966. ELIZA — a computer program for the study of natural language. *Communication of the Association for Computing Machinery, 9*, 36–45.

Welford, A. 1968. *Fundamentals of Skill*. London: Methuen.

Wells, G. 1982. *Learning through Interaction: The study of language development*. Cambridge: CUP.

Wells, J. 1970. Local accents of England and Wales. *Journal of Linguistics, 6*, 231–52.

Wells, J. 1982. *Accents of English*. Cambridge: CUP.

Wenden, A. and Rubin, J. 1987. *Learner Strategies in Language Learning*. New York: Prentice-Hall International.

Werth, P. 1984. *Focus, Emphasis, and Coherence*. London: Croom Helm.

Wheaton, G., Eisner, E., Mirabella, G. and Fleishman, E. 1976. Ability requirements as a function of changes in the characteristics of an auditory signal identification task. *Journal of Applied Psychology, 61*, 663–76.

Widdowson, H. 1979. *Language Purpose and Language Use*. Oxford: OUP.

Wilkins, D. 1976. *Notional Syllabuses*. Oxford: OUP.

Williams, D. 1984. Listening and note-taking. In *Zhongyiug Yaivei Jiaoxie* (Language Learning and Communication). Peking.

Williams, T. 1987. The nature of miscommunication in the cross-cultural employment interview. In Pride, J. (ed.) *Cross Cultural Encounters: Communication and miscommunication*. Melbourne: River Seine.

Willis, J. 1983. 101 ways to use video. In McGreen, J. (ed.) *Video Applications in English Language Teaching*. Oxford: Pergamon.

Winitz, H. and Reeds, J. 1975. *Comprehension and Problem Solving as Strategies for Language Training*. The Hague: Mouton.

Winograd, T. and Flores, F. 1987. *Understanding Computers and Cognition*. Reading, MA: Addison-Wesley.

Wright, T. 1987. *Roles of Teachers and Learners*. Oxford: OUP.

Yalden, J. 1987. *Principles of Course Design in Language Teaching*. Cambridge: CUP.

Zabrucky, K. 1986. The role of factual coherence in discourse comprehension. *Discourse Processes, 9*, 197–220.

Glossary and transcription conventions

allophonic variation − an alternative realization of a phoneme in a particular phonological environment, often resulting from co-articulation with another phoneme, is called an **allophone** of the phoneme (e.g. the flapped /t/ in the American English pronunciation of 'butter' is an allophone of /t/).

Allophonic variations are interpretable by hearers of a language as equivalent, even though they may be perceived as quite different by speakers/hearers of other languages.

anaphoric and exophoric reference

 anaphoric − the use of a word or phrase to refer back to another word or phrase used earlier in the discourse or assumed to be recoverable by the listener is called **anaphora**; anaphoric expressions are those in which the speaker utilizes anaphora, or **anaphoric reference** (e.g. in *He doesn't like it, 'it'* is an anaphoric reference to a thing or action that has been explicitly mentioned before or is assumed to be understood by the listener.)

 exophoric − the use of a word of phrase to refer to something that is observable by the speaker and listener is called **exophora**; exophoric expressions are those in which the speaker utilizes **exophoric reference** (e.g. in *Look at that, 'that'* is an exophoric reference to an observable thing or action.)

back-channelling (or back channel behaviour) − feedback that a listener gives to a speaker that indicates how the listener is responding to the speaker's message (e.g. nodding, saying 'I see' or 'Hmm.')

clitics and stressed syllables

 clitics − unstressed syllables in lexical words (e.g. in the word *im**pos**sible*, the first, third, and fourth syllables are clitics) and unstressed grammatical words in phonological phrases (e.g. in the phrase in the **park**, the words *in* and *the* are clitic syllables). A leading clitic is **proclitic**, a trailing clitic is **enclitic**.

 Problems of intelligibility may arise when unstressed **grammatical words** (words belonging to classes with closed membership: articles, prepositions, pronouns, conjunctions, modals, auxiliary verbs, and copula verbs) in the clitic segments are perceived as part of the **lexical words** (words belonging to classes with open membership: verbs, nouns, adjectives, and most adverbs).

cloze entropy (or clozentropy) − a method of determining **acceptable responses** in a cloze passage by giving the test passage to a mastery group (e.g. native speakers of a language) to determine a range of possible and probable responses. (e.g. in the following cloze passage: ... *This is a method of _____ acceptable* *responses* ..., a mastery group might produce the following responses: *determining, deciding, finding, estimating, getting.* All of these could be considered acceptable responses.)

exchange structure — an organization of a conversation in terms of turn-taking features, emphasing information control (speaker and listener roles) and adherence to norms of interaction.

paratactic and hypotactic organization
  paratactic — The placing of utterances in sequence without connectors or with temporal connectors (e.g. *and, then*) is called **parataxis**; a **paratactic expression** is one in which the speaker uses parataxis.
  hypotactic — the subordination of one syntactic structure to another is called **hypotaxis**: a **hypotactic expression** is one in which the speaker uses hypotaxis.
    Although the following expressions refer to same events and sequence
      (i)   *After I ate dinner, I went home.*
      (ii) *I ate dinner, I went home.*
  understanding *(i)* involves processing a hypotactic organization of information (which is said to be more comprehensive or **synoptic**); understanding *(ii)* involves processing a paratactic organization (which is said to be more sequential or **dyamic**)

phonotactic knowledge — the arrangement of distinctive segmental and prosodic sequences in a language is called **phonotactics**; the knowledge of the conventions of possible and probable sound combinations in words, stress sequences, and intonation contours for a specific language is called phonotactic knowledge.

propositional and base meaning
  propositional meaning — a representation of an utterance (or of a longer discourse) which consists of references for lexical expressions and case-relational links (e.g. agent-object-location) between these references.
  base meaning — categories of cultural concepts, orientations, experiences, and conflicts that are required to interpret a discourse appropriately. Base meanings can be formulated in terms of possible dimensions of interpretation, rather than as statements or propositions.

representation — a cognitive mapping of an utterance or of a larger discourse which allows the listener to recall the utterance. A listener may have representations of an utterance at different levels of processing (e.g. **phonological, propositional**, or **schematic**.)

rhotic — dialects in which a consonantal /r/ remains after a vowel are referred to as **rhotic dialects** or rhotic accents (e.g. most North American dialects, some dialects in Scotland and southern Ireland).

speech processing
  top-down speech processing — use of concepts at the next higher level of language representation to provide consistencies, eliminate implausible interpretations, and assemble received data into a congruent structure (e.g. using knowledge of **word formation rules** to interpret a *phonological*

sequence; using knowledge of **phrase structure rules** to interpret a sequence of words).

bottom-up speech processing — analyzing (**parsing**) incoming speech in order to represent the speech signal as lexical items with syntactic organization. Through bottom-up speech processing, the listener builds a **composite meaning** for an utterance; however, use of concepts at higher levels of discourse organization is necessary in order to interpret the relevance of the utterance.

task — a unit of analysis for action in a social context

real-world task — a unit of work that involves a means of achieving an objective and which may or may not entail language use.

pedagogic task — any structured learning activity which has a specified objective, input appropriate to the objective, a specified working procedure, and a range of possible outcomes for those who participate.

testing task — a structured activity which has a specified outcome (or range of outcomes) and a set of criteria for evaluation of performance.

TRANSCRIPTION CONVENTIONS

Transcribed conversations include the following conventions. Note that different authors utilize different conventions to denote the same occurrence; hence, the repetition in the table below.

transcription convention	use of the convention
:	a lengthening of a sound
+	a short pause
...	a short pause
(.)	a measured pause of less than a second
(.5)	a measured pause of .5 seconds, etc.
=	absence of a pause between the end of one speaker's turn and the beginning of the next speaker's turn
[	simultaneous speech by two or more speakers
T	start of a new speaker's turn (T1, T2, etc.)

Index